A WEST COUNTRY ANTHOLOGY

Companion Volume compiled by Maurice Lindsay
Scotland: An Anthology

Also by S. H. Burton
The North Devon Coast
The South Devon Coast
The Coasts of Cornwall
Great Men of Devon
Devon Villages
The West Country
Exmoor

A WEST COUNTRY ANTHOLOGY

Compiled by
S. H. BURTON

ROBERT HALE · LONDON

ISBN 0 7091 4899 2

Robert Hale & Company
63 Old Brompton Road
London SW 7

Printed in Great Britain by
Ebenezer Baylis and Son Limited
The Trinity Press, Worcester, and London

Contents

Illustrations

PICTURE CREDITS

Mary Evans Picture Library, 1 and 2; From *A Walk Through Some of the Western Counties of England* by Richard Warner (1800), 3; Exeter Cathedral Library and Exeter University, 6; the remainder from *Views in Devonshire and Cornwall*, published by Henry Besley, Exeter 1761. (Courtesy the Exeter City Library).

Introduction

"A man," said Dr. Johnson, "will turn over half a library to make one book." He was not referring specifically to the anthology-maker, but his remark stirred in my mind as I sat down to write the 'Foresay' to this work.

Nearly thirty years of reading—and collecting—West Country books have stored my memory with the raw material from which this compilation has been assembled. My problem, therefore, was not so much what to put in as what to leave out. (And if that sounds like a description of the two sides of the same coin, I cannot help it: obverse and reverse *are* different, and calling 'heads' or 'tails' can be a vital choice.)

Again, I had to give the book a shape. Admirable 'county' anthologies have been made in which the chosen extracts are grouped under such headings as 'Characters' or 'Fishing' or 'Wild Life' and so on. But this book was not planned as a 'county' book: it had to range over the whole of the region that we call the West Country. To achieve such coverage made the 'county' approach inappropriate—though the individual counties are frequently and necessarily named—and I was reluctant to adopt a conventional grouping of the material, since—with so large a field to survey—the various sections would either have been very thin or too few in number to provide the lineaments of the detailed and truthful portrait that I hoped to paint.

It was a very old friend of mine who gave me the idea for which I was long in looking: the idea that, I am bold enough to claim, provides this book with a meaningful shape. In 1800 the Rev. Richard Warner published a book called *A Walk Through Some of the Western Counties of England*. I bought it in Exeter in those blissful days when that city had a varied range of second-hand bookshops and stalls, and it has been my good companion ever since.

Deliberately, Richard Warner stands first in this anthology for—and I use *his* words—like him

> I may at least promise you some variety, and perchance some novelty also; since it is my intention to carry you through the labouring orchards of Somersetshire; to sink you full many a fathom deep into the mines of Cornwall; to lead you along the crags of the Danmonian shore . . . to ferry you over the Belerian sea, bewilder you amongst the Cassiterides, and at length conduct you safely home through the rich vales of Devonshire.

I do not follow his route closely, for this journey does not begin where his did; and it ends where all western travels must terminate—at Land's End. But, like him, I try to take my reader a-journeying: westwards from Arthur's old frontier—westwards always—to the narrowing of the land and the thunder of the sea—westwards to where the granite cliffs confront the ocean —westwards to where the sun sets and England ends.

It seemed good to me then—when this book took shape—to arrange the extracts so that (though topography sometimes imposed zig-zags) we might travel together through the western counties; and I believed that this long journey, ranging through time and space, might teach both compiler and reader to recognize the character of the West Country: to salute its splendid past—and in so doing to aspire for its re-birth—before finally standing on 'Pedn an Laaz' and there glimpsing 'with magic in our eyes' the submerged cities, towers and churches of fabled Lyonnesse.

'Foresay' was the word that I used some minutes ago. An affectation, you may think, for *Introduction* or *Preface*; and it must be confessed that William Barnes's 'Wessex words' have not caught on. But since he and Thomas Hardy gave me—as they have given thousands—my first insight into West Country speech and ways, it seemed natural enough to employ the term early on in this book: just as it was natural that those two great writers should be dominant where the westward journey began. But I have tried throughout to open up byways and I have avoided those pieces and those writers most often laid under tribute by earlier anthologists. It has been my pleasure to collect much from works long out of print; to flavour my book with hitherto unpublished material both in prose and verse; to use current newspapers and periodicals of the West Country; and thus, in Thomas Westcote's words, to intermix a pleasant tale with serious discourse; and think it no harm occasionally to beguile the road with tales told in taverns and ballads sung by the way.

Mere novelty, however, has not been a criterion. Each passage had to pass two tests to merit inclusion: intrinsic literary quality or historical interest; and the capacity *in the context in which it was placed* to illuminate a facet of West Country life. To the arrangement of context much thought has been given, for—though the idea of a westward journey dictated the overall plan— the juxtaposing of the extracts within that plan was a challenging, exacting and necessary task. With what success the work has been done the reader must decide.

I have refrained from burdening the text with footnotes, being unwilling to come between the reader and the great variety of authors with whom he may here renew old friendship or form new acquaintance. Where explanation seemed essential I have supplied it briefly in square brackets within the extracts.

So, too, in the body of the work, I have left the passages unattributed. The authors and the works are identified at the beginning and the end of the book and may, thus, be readily discovered. (Dates of publication or, where more informative, of composition are also supplied.) I find it pleasant to guess at authorship and date—particularly when perplexity may be speedily resolved —and I like to think that my readers will be gratified to recognize, many miles west of their starting-point, an author in whose company they set out, or one whose cheerful presence, having earlier made light walking of steep roads, later accompanies them over moorland tracks, through city streets or down leafy lanes.

My debts for help received are acknowledged in the 'Author's Index' which also indicates the copyright passages which I have been given permission to use. I must add that the Dedication expresses my thanks to one whose scholarship has often directed my reading and whose friendship has smoothed my path in my West Country journeys.

As these, the final words, are written, I search for a quotation from the many passages assembled here that can stand as a text for the whole of this work; and I believe that the spirit of the book is alive in lines taken from Frederic Smith's poem, "Routes" (Extract Number 4).

> One is at first the stranger
> And the place is a stranger
> Until one surrenders to it.

S. H. BURTON

Dulverton.
     August 1972–December 1973

1 Setting Out

Should fortune be propitious, and after the long series of inclement weather which we have experienced, indulge us with a few weeks of cloudless skies, I may at least promise you some variety, and perchance some novelty also; since it is my intention to carry you through the 'labouring orchards' of Somersetshire; to sink you full many a fathom deep into the mines of Cornwall; to lead you along the crags of the Danmonian shore,

> Where the great vision of the guarded mount
> Looks towards Namancos and Bayona's hold

to ferry you over the Belerian Sea, bewilder you amongst the Cassiterides, and at length conduct you safely home through the rich vales of Devonshire.

Such is my plan; but as its execution must depend on things so uncertain as wind and weather, the art of controlling or regulating which we moderns are not in possession of, you will not, I hope, accuse me either of idleness or caprice, should it be of necessity somewhat circumscribed: for I candidly confess, that halcyon days alone will induce me to cross in solitude and silence the naked hills of Cornwall, or tempt the dangers of that strait which proved fatal to Sir Cloudesley Shovel.

2 Pleasant Tales and Serious Discourse

I hope I may intermix a pleasant tale with a serious discourse, and an unwritten tradition with a chronicled history, old ancient armories and epitaphs, well near buried in oblivion (matters not supervacual nor unworthy to be received and kept living, unless we could be content to have our own name and remembrance to perish with our bodies), ancient families now extinct, or rather transanimated into others; some etymologies seeming and perchance strange and far-fetched; old, new, serious, jovial, curious, trivial; for these and matters of such nature may, without peradventure, give recreation to a wearied body and mind (that reads for recreation), with more delight and content for variety, than dislike the severe critic for simplicity, vulgarity, or doubt of verity.

Some few things will occur in reading, and to be collected out of divers authors; but much more is to be sought for variety, in dark and obscure places, by industrious labour; wherein, aiming conjectures, if they err, are to be pardoned (for he that divineth in things of this quality, upon bare supposals, may as well shoot short, as overshoot, the mark he aimeth at), for they be not seriously alledged, but only to furnish and beautify the edifice, as pictures and maps in a gallery.

3 Prospects

There is in us an unquenchable expectation, which at the gloomiest time persists in inferring that because we are *ourselves*, there must be a special future in store for us, though our nature and antecedents to the remotest particular have been common to thousands.

4 Routes

Away from the built-up areas
Is the direction to take,
Staying longest
In isolated places,
Avoiding the tourists,
Making a note to return
In the off-season.

Going back a different way
Finding small places
Not on the original plan
(Complete and satisfying worlds
Created to a personal formula),
The circular route always
More satisfying.

The road is not known,
Part of the adventure
The wheel under one's hands,
Flexible, firm;
(In another age a different speed
And a view over the hedge).

There are signposts,
The names ancient,
In another language,
Meaningful if one has the code;
And directions given by those who live there.

One is at first the stranger,
And the place is a stranger

Until one surrenders to it.
Places are older than persons,
Possessed of enormous patience,
Having seen countless visitors,
Shocked sometimes
By thoughtless additions,
But accepting change
Absorbing what can be absorbed.

This is one route.
There are others.

5 Foot-Loose and Fancy-Free

You, who in these days of vehement bustle, business, and competition, can still find time to travel for pleasure alone—you, who have yet to become emancipated from the thraldom of railways, carriages, and saddle-horses—patronize, I exhort you, that first and oldest established of all conveyances, your own legs! Think on your tender partings nipped in the bud by the railway bell; think of crabbed cross-roads, and broken carriage-springs; think of luggage confided to extortionate porters, of horses casting shoes and catching colds, of cramped legs and numbed feet, of vain longings to get down for a moment here, and to delay for a pleasant half-hour there—think of all these manifold hardships of riding at your ease; and the next time you leave home, strap your luggage on your shoulders, take your stick in your hand, set forth delivered from a perfect paraphernalia of incumbrances, to go where you will, how you will—the free citizen of the whole travelling world! Thus independent, what may you not accomplish?—what pleasure is there that you cannot enjoy? Are you an artist?—you can stop to sketch every point of view that strikes your eye. Are you a philanthropist? —you can go into every cottage and talk to every human being you pass. Are you a botanist, or geologist?—you may pick up leaves and chip rocks wherever you please, the live-long day. Are you a valetudinarian?—you may physic yourself by Nature's own simple prescription, walking in fresh air. Are you dilatory and irresolute?—you may dawdle to your heart's content; you may change all your plans a dozen times in a dozen hours; you may tell 'Boots' at the inn to call you at six o'clock, may fall asleep again (ecstatic sensation!) five minutes after he has knocked at the door, and may get up two hours later, to pursue your journey, with perfect impunity and satisfaction. For, to you, what is a timetable but waste paper?—and a 'booked place' but a relic of the dark ages? You dread, perhaps, blisters on your feet —sponge your feet with cold vinegar and water, change your socks every ten miles, and show me blisters after that, if you can!

6   *The Nature of Little Towns*

Little towns are like little children in this respect, that they interest most when they are enacting native peculiarities unconscious of beholders. Discovering themselves to be watched they attempt to be entertaining by putting on an antic, and produce disagreeable caricatures which spoil them.

7   *The Lost Lands of the West*

The two provinces [of Devon and Cornwall] in their union is, by some, supposed to be much larger in former times than both are now; extending it half in length from the farthest point of the island Scilly in the west, unto the eastmost confines of the Durotriges and Belgians, containing both Dorset and Somerset shires. And some affirm that in former ages (long since, I think), Scilly was continent land with Cornwall, and separated by the violent irresistible force of raging storms of Neptune in his fury; for which they allege not only an ancient tradition from father to son, but a reason, that it is now with Denshire under one bishop (though in some times they have been several sees under several bishops); and also this instance, that in a fair sunshine day, sea-faring men see and discern plainly sundry ruins, as monuments of houses and churches under the waters: but I will leave it for them to make it good; I will give no security for it.

8   *Presidential Days*

Yet here I cannot but confess that I have been informed (and have seen some reason to persuade me to believe it), that this county [of Devon] together with Cornwall, Somerset, and Dorset, was some time governed by a president, as Wales, and some parts in the north; but surely the continuance was not long; for I think the inhabitants had rather be at the cost to fetch judgments and decrees from the pure spring head at Westminster, than to have them given at home: so the lawyers have a longer journey to travel, yet the profession holds good and in request, though they go far to work.

9   *The Wessex Shires*

Under the year 837 in the Chronicle there is a reference to an engagement between the Danes and the ealdorman Æthelhelm leading the men of Dorset—*mid Dornsae tum*. The first element of this name is related to the first element of the name 'Dorchester' and the second element means 'inhabitants', 'dwellers'. This second element in the nominative plural forms *sæ te* or *sæ tan* is commonly found as part of a compound name referring originally to the people inhabiting a particular area and being subsequently transferred to the area inhabited by them. It is found in the Midlands also in the Old English names *Tomsæ tan*, *Wreocensæ tan* and *Pecsæ tan* referring respectively to those who dwelt by the Tame, the Wrekin and the Peak, but it now survives only in the two southern English names Dorset and Somerset. The first element of Somerset is to be associated with the first element of Somerton and there is a reference to the *Sumursæ te* and their ealdorman under the year 845 in the Chronicle. The element 'shire', from O.E. scir, is first recorded in association with Dorset in the tenth century. In the case of Somerset it is not recorded before the twelfth century, but the term is used of Wiltshire at a much earlier date. The death of one AE*oe*lm, called ealdorman of Wiltshire, is recorded under 898 in the Chronicle—*Æoelm Wiltunscire ealdormon*, but here too the territorial name has displaced an earlier name which referred to the people who lived there rather than to the area in which they lived. As early as 800 the Chronicle refers to an engagement in which an ealdorman of the *Hwicce* was defeated by an ealdorman leading the *Wilsæ tan*, a name which derives its first element from the river-name Wylye. There is a reference to Hampshire, in the form *Hamtunscire*, under the year 755 in the Chronicle, but this particular passage cannot safely be used as evidence for the currency of the term 'shire' in the territorial sense at this date.

Evidence of this kind, and similar evidence relating to Berkshire and Surrey, indicates that in the first half of the ninth century there were in Wessex recognizable groups of people who were called by names corresponding with those of the modern counties and who were led in time of war by an official called an ealdorman. By this date the Viking attacks had begun, but they had not yet become so grave a menace as to have had any great effect upon the existing methods of defence and administration. We may therefore regard it as probable that by about the year 800 the kingdom of Wessex was already divided into what we may loosely call shires, even though there may be some anachronism in applying the term to that date, and that such shires were administered by an ealdorman, one of whose functions was to lead his men in battle. A passage in the laws issued *c*.690 by Ine, king of Wessex, states that as penalty for certain offences an ealdorman is to lose his *scir*. This passage might be used as evidence that the West Saxon shires are as old as the seventh century, but the term *scir* in Old English is also used in the abstract sense of 'office'. For example the office of bishop, abbot or bailiff could be called *scir* and it would be unwise to assume that the word *scir* in Ine's code necessarily has the meaning 'shire' which it bore in later times. It is, of course, impossible to define precisely the areas occupied by the *Wilsæ tan* or the *Sumursæ tan* in the ninth century, but it is reasonable to suppose that the requirements of defence, amongst other things, had led to a fairly exact definition of boundaries before the end of Alfred's reign.

10 Strong and Mighty Men

The air in these parts (although much subject unto rain and showery dews, as is the whole island (far more than were in the continent), and therefore called by some Matulam Planetarum), is very healthy, temperate, sweet, and pure (I mean not that purity which an ancient father believed, or rather supposed, is upon the mount of Olympus, where the air, he saith, is so thin and pure that it can neither support the birds that offer to fly therein, nor useful for the breathing of men used to a grosser air); but healthy, clear from damps, breathing long life to the Inhabitants: for our forefathers, who accustomed themselves to measure the delicacy of food and rest by the yard of hunger and weariness, lived temperately and frugally; content with what the earth afforded for satisfying of nature's want; yea, in the most ancient times, as Diodorus Siculus affirmeth, with bark and roots, and especially a certain confection, whereof the quantity of a bean would satisfy nature in such sort, that after the taking thereof they neither hungered nor thirsted (as Dio Nicæus saith), in a long time after.

They were then strong and mighty men of renown, able to endure much labour and travel in all weathers, lived to a great age (as we read in Plutarch, who reporteth to 120 years), in health and ability of body: the longer (as it is thought) for not being weakened with delicacies: for when they neglected their strong and manly exercises and temperate diet, delighting in the sweetness of foreign dainties, and in the excess of their own, it weakened the strength of the one, and shortened the length of the other.

11 Nature's Gifts

Of grain we want no sort that the kingdom yields. We are also furnished with great variety of fruits, and of most of them sundry choice of species. Of herbs and plants, such diversity in colour, fashion, taste, smell, and nature, as Gerrard's best aid will hardly be able to describe them. And for variety of flowers (for those are not unsought for neither of our ladies and gentry) Lady Flora herself (though canonized by the Romans for a goddess) will be to seek, to find out, or coin names severally to distinguish them. Some quantity of timber we have yet left of the great store we had in elder times: for as trade and traffic began and increased, that commodity was lessened to build ships: and as the inhabitants multiplied, so fields were grubbed for enlarging of tillage, as far more necessary and needful: and as wealth augmented, the like vastation was made thereof for building of towns, and in fine, fair and large houses, both in city and country.

For fish, because you shall judge and believe me in the rest, I will give your caterer a bill (such as was once given me by Mr. Mayor's officer) what our market yields, for our better remembrance: but our unskilfulness to marshall them in their due place hath caused me to follow the alphabet:

A	Dory	Haddock	O	Sharpe
Anchovies	Dabb	Housewife	Oysters	Sturgeon
B	Dogfish	K	P	Stockfish
Bass	E	Kites	Porpoise	Sole
Bream	Eels	L	Pingers	Smelt
Buckles	F	Ling	Plaice	Sprat
Bulheads	Flookes	Limpets	Pipers	Sparklings
Buckhorn	Flounders	Lumpe (or sea	Peel	Scallops
		owl)	Penecot	Shrimps
C	G	Lobsters	Perch	
Carp	Gurnard	Lampreys	Pollock	T
Conger	Graveling	Loaches	Pilchard	Turbot
Colfish	Guilthead	M	R	Trout
Cod	Gofion	Mackrell	Roach	Tench
Chubb	Gudgeon	Milwill	Ray	Tubdure
Cockles	H	Muscells	Rochet	Tunny
Crab	Herring	Mullet	S	Thornback
Crevice	Hake	Millers	Scad	W
Cree	Haberdine	Minows	Salmon	Whiting
D	Hound	N	Shott	Whelks
Dace	Holibut	Newlandfish	Seal	Wrinkles

12 The Manly Sports

Their ancient exercises have been archery, hurling, wrestling, football, dancing, and such like forcible exercises of strength and activity; recreating and hardening, and enabling their bodies and minds for more noble (though more uneasy and dangerous) martial employment; for which they are apt and in readiness with the foremost at all times. But these exercises have been of late (by a strong and potent zeal, and a severe execution of laws) forced out of the country, neglected and out of use; and hunting, hawking, and bowling crept in, and somewhat in request with the better sort; and with the inferior, actions of far worse quality.

13 A Curious Temper

To those musing weather-beaten Westcountry folk who pass the greater part of their days and nights out of doors, Nature seems to have moods in other than a poetical sense: predilections for certain deeds at certain times, without any apparent law to govern or season to account for them. She is read as a person with a curious temper; as one who does not scatter kindnesses and cruelties alternately, impartially, and in order, but heartless severities or overwhelming generosities in lawless caprice. Man's case is always that of the prodigal's favourite or the miser's pensioner. In her unfriendly moments there seems a feline fun in her tricks, begotten by a foretaste of her pleasure in swallowing the victim.

14   Old Moore Got It Right

On the morning of the 9th of March, 1891, when inhabitants of the three westernmost counties in England set about preparing for the routine duties of daily life, nothing seemed to indicate that, with the approach of nightfall, the gravest atmospheric disturbance of the century—in that part of the country, at all events—would come to spread terror and destruction throughout town and country. The month, so far, had not been a gentle one. Following in the footsteps of a memorably genial February, March had been somewhat harsh and cold, without yielding the rain that was by this time greatly needed. There were rumours of 'a change of some sort', of an approaching 'fall of something', and other vaticinations of the same familiar character floating about, but in the West Country these wise sayings fall so thick and fast and frequently as to possess little more significance than the most oft-repeated household words. When the day drew on, and signs of a rising gale were uncomfortably apparent on every hand, recollections of a promised storm from the Observatories of the United States began to be awakened, but it was found on sifting the matter, that if this were the disturbance indicated, it had come about a fortnight too soon. Students of *Old Moore's Almanack* were better informed, and it is probable that if this ill wind blew good to anybody, it was in the shape of discovery that by virtue of the truth of his forecast, a favourite and venerable prophet was deserving of honour at the hands of the people of his own country. Unhappily, however, there is nothing to show that advantage had been taken of this warning, in any practical sense. On the contrary, the blast came down swiftly upon a community that was almost wholly unprepared to receive it, and one of the saddest parts of the story of its fury will be the account of the devastation wrought among the unprotected flocks and herds.

15   The Witty Bishop

Aldhelm, who was born c.640, was educated partly at Malmesbury, an Irish foundation whose abbot he later became, and partly at Canterbury. In 705 he became the first Bishop of Sherborne and he died in office four years later. Like Bede he drank deeply from the streams of Irish and Mediterranean scholarship, but their waters produced in him a state of intellectual intoxication which delighted its beholders, but which left little to posterity. His most popular works were a poem on virginity and a prose treatise on the same subject. His poem began with an elaborate double acrostic in which the initial and final letters of the lines formed one and the same hexameter verse, reading the initial letters downwards and the final letters upwards. In such mental gymnastics lay his chief delight and we may be sure that in this present world he would have enjoyed both *Finnegan's Wake* and the more elaborate forms of crossword puzzle. There is more of interest and value to be found in his letters. In one of these, addressed to Geraint of Cornwall on the errors of the British Church in the south-west, he showed that he could write straightforward Latin prose, but in another, in which he sought to demonstrate the excellence of English teaching, he used such a wealth of vocabulary and such an overwhelming weight of metaphor, simile and alliteration that the letter itself is scarcely intelligible.

16   Sir Walter's Dark Days

Meanwhile Lady Raleigh resided from time to time at Sherborne, her husband a close prisoner in the Tower. She was there twice in 1605, the year of the Gunpowder Plot. And it was noted, for everything the Raleighs did was suspect, that in September of that year 'she did cause all the armour to be scoured'. All sorts of dark reasons were alleged, but one person who was examined and who seems to have had a sense of humour, gave it to be, 'as he thinketh, because it was rusty'. Again, on another occasion, it was reported that 'she caused the house to be dressed up, where before all things lay in disorder'. The truth was that poor Lady Raleigh lived in hopes of her husband's liberation; hopes which were never fulfilled till too late, when Sir Walter, an old man, was driven on his last, most hopeless and fatal venture, the second voyage to Guiana.

Then, at last, the courts in their own good time and in their own way, pronounced: the flaw in the drafting of the deed was held to invalidate Raleigh's claim on behalf of his son. The King had put up with a long delay, and he was now free to give it [Raleigh's estate] to his favourite Carr. Ordinary folk in London, who had never liked Raleigh, commented like the assiduous letter-writer Chamberlain: 'So he may say with Job: Naked came I into the world, etc'. Raleigh wrote a despairing appeal to the favourite: 'I beseech you not to begin your first building upon the ruins of the innocent'. It was all in vain; Carr knew very well that Raleigh had had no compunction in building upon the ruins of others. The curious thing was that when, after changing hands twice, the King had it in his hands again and pressed it upon Villiers, the succeeding favourite, Villiers, who was a better man than Carr, protested to James, almost as if the echo of Raleigh's words were in his ears: 'Do not build my fortune upon another man's ruins.'

So it was granted to Lord Digby, along with the earldom of Bristol, for the strenuous service of having gone twice on embassy to Spain. And in their family it remains.

17 Pack Monday Fair

Sherborne is also famous for its Pack Monday Fair held in October. It has been claimed that the fair got its name because the workmen had a spree when they 'packed up' in preparation for leaving the town after finishing the abbey church. More probably the name refers to the packmen who attended all the old fairs in the countryside. During my lifetime the pleasure fair lasted for a week but the cattle, sheep and horse sale was on Monday. The proceedings opened at midnight on Sunday when a noisy procession paraded through the town making 'rough music'. In the reign of King Henry VIII it was complained that labourers and artificers used their 'riotous expenses and unlawful games to the great trouble and inquieting of the inhabitants next thereto adjoining'. It sounds like an accurate description of the midnight opening of the fair. Unfortunately in 1962 and 1963 hooliganism and silly damage added to the noise, and in 1964 the Chief Constable of Dorset turned up with one hundred policemen and suppressed the traditional procession.

18 Sophocles in the West Country

At length could be discerned in the dusk, about half a mile to one side, gardens and orchards sunk in a concave, and, as it were, snipped out of the woodland. From this self-contained place [Little Hintock—Hermitage, 5 miles south of Sherborne] rose in stealthy silence tall stems of smoke, which the eye of imagination could trace downward to their root on quiet hearthstones, festooned overhead with hams and flitches. It was one of those sequestered spots outside the gates of the world where may usually be found more meditation than action, and more listlessness than meditation; where reasoning proceeds on narrow premises, and results in inferences wildly imaginative; yet where, from time to time, dramas of a grandeur and unity truly Sophoclean are enacted in the real, by virtue of the concentrated passions and closely-knit interdependence of the lives therein.

19 A Lonely Road

At one place, on the skirts of Blackmoor Vale, where the bold brow of High-Stoy Hill is seen a mile or two ahead, the leaves lie so thick in autumn as to completely bury the track. The spot is lonely, and when the days are darkening the many gay charioteers now perished who have rolled along the way, the blistered soles that have trodden it, and the tears that have wetted it, return upon the mind of the loiterer.

The physiognomy of a deserted highway expresses solitude to a degree that is not reached by mere dales or downs, and bespeaks a tomb-like stillness more emphatic than that of glades and pools. The contrast of what is with what might be, probably accounts for this. To step, for instance, at the place under notice, from the edge of the plantation into the adjoining thoroughfare, and pause amid its emptiness for a moment, was to exchange by the act of a single stride the simple absence of human companionship for an incubus of the forlorn.

20 A Haunted Land

Superstitions linger longest on these heavy soils [the clay of Blackmoor Vale]. Having once been forest, at this shadowy time it seemed to assert something of its old character, the far and the near being blended, and every tree and tall hedge making the most of its presence. The harts that had been hunted here, the witches that had been pricked and ducked, the green-spangled fairies that 'whickered' at you as you passed—the place teemed with beliefs in them still, and they formed an impish multitude now.

21 The Valley of Little Dairies

This fertile and sheltered tract of country, in which the fields are never brown and the springs never dry, is bounded on the south by the bold chalk ridge that embraces the prominences of Hambledon Hill, Bulbarrow, Nettlecombe-Tout, Dogbury, High Stoy, and Bubb Down. The traveller from the coast, who, after plodding northward for a score of miles over calcareous downs and cornlands, suddenly reaches the verge of one of these escarpments, is surprised and delighted to behold, extended like a map beneath him, a country differing absolutely from that which he has passed through. Behind him, the hills are open, the sun blazes down upon fields so large as to give an unenclosed character to the landscape, the lanes are white, the hedges low and plashed, the atmosphere colourless. Here, in the valley, the world seems to be constructed upon a smaller and more delicate scale; the fields are mere paddocks, so reduced that from this height their hedge-rows appear a network of dark green threads overspreading the paler green of the grass. The atmosphere beneath is languorous, and is so tinged with azure that what artists call the middle distance partakes also of that hue, while the horizon beyond is of the deepest ultramarine. Arable lands are

few and limited; with but slight exceptions the prospect is a broad rich mass
of grass and trees, mantling minor hills and dales within the major. Such is
the Vale of Blackmoor.

22   *Evening in Casterbridge*

To birds of the more soaring kind Casterbridge [Dorchester] must have
appeared on this fine evening as a mosiac-work of subdued reds, browns,
greys, and crystals, held together by a rectangular frame of deep green.
To the level eye of humanity it stood as an indistinct mass behind a dense
stockade of limes and chestnuts, set in the midst of miles of rotund down and
concave field. The mass became gradually dissected by the vision into
towers, gables, chimneys, and casements, the highest glazings shining
bleared and bloodshot with the coppery fire they caught from the belt of
sunlit cloud in the west. From the centre of each side of this tree-bound
square ran avenues east, west, and south into the wide expanse of corn-land
and combe to the distance of a mile or so . . .

The lamplights now glimmered through the engirdling trees, conveying a
sense of great snugness and comfort inside, and rendering at the same time
the unlighted country without strangely solitary and vacant in aspect,
considering its nearness to life. The difference between burgh and champaign
was increased, too, by sounds which now reached them above others—the
notes of a brass band. The travellers returned into the High Street, where
there were timber houses with overhanging stories, whose small-paned
lattices were screened by dimity curtains on a drawing-string, and under
whose barge-boards old cobwebs waved in the breeze. There were slate
roofs patched with tiles, and tile roofs patched with slate, with occasionally
a roof of thatch.

The agricultural and pastoral character of the people upon whom the town
depended for its existence was shown by the class of objects displayed in the
shop windows. Scythes, reap-hooks, sheep-shears, bill-hooks, spades,
mattocks, and hoes at the ironmonger's; bee-hives, butter-firkins, churns,
milking-stools and pails, hay-rakes, field-flagons, and seed-lips at the
cooper's; cart-ropes and plough-harness at the sadler's; carts, wheel-barrows,
and mill-gear at the wheelwright's and machinist's; horse-embrocations at
the chemist's; at the glover's and leather-cutters, hedging-gloves, thatcher's
knee-caps, ploughman's leggings, villager's pattens and clogs.

They came to a grizzled church, whose massive square tower rose un-
broken into the darkening sky, the lower parts being illuminated by the
nearest lamps sufficiently to show how completely the mortar from the joints
of the stonework had been nibbled out by time and weather, which had
planted in the crevices thus made little tufts of stone-crop and grass almost
as far up as the very battlements. From this tower the clock struck eight, and
thereupon a bell began to toll with a peremptory clang. The curfew was still

High-Street, Dorchester

The Dorchester Station, from the Roman Amphitheatre

rung in Casterbridge, and it was utilized by the inhabitants as a signal for shutting their shops. No sooner did the deep notes of the bell throb between the house-fronts than a clatter of shutters arose through the whole length of the High Street. In a few minutes business at Casterbridge was ended for the day.

23 Leave Be

The solitude of Maiden Castle has never been disturbed since the Romans left. There are forty-six acres of easily ploughable land inside the ramparts, but it was not ploughed even in the desperate food shortage of the last war. There was a Government directive forbidding local Agricultural Executive Committees from ploughing barrows and ancient dykes, but there was only one long barrow which would have seemed obvious to a committee member. I was on the staff of the committee and cannot remember any serious suggestion of ploughing. It may seem a little strange to outsiders but there is a long tradition against disturbing this very ancient place. At least one of the Saxon invaders is buried there with his arms, so the Saxons certainly had a look at it, but there is no record of a settlement. There would be no luck in ploughing Maiden Castle. After dark it is not pleasant to be alone there, at least it was not pleasant during the war when there were no friendly lights from Dorchester.

24 A Country Town

The yeomen, farmers, dairymen, and townsfolk, who came to transact business in these ancient streets, spoke in other ways than by articulation. Not to hear the words of your interlocutor in metropolitan centres is to know nothing of his meaning. Here the face, the arms, the hat, the stick, the body throughout, spoke equally with the tongue. To express satisfaction the Casterbridge [Dorchester] market-man added to his utterance a broadening of the cheeks, a crevicing of the eyes, a throwing back of the shoulders, which was intelligible from the other end of the street. . . .

Thus Casterbridge was in most respects but the pole, focus, or nerve-knot of the surrounding country life; differing from the many manufacturing towns which are as foreign bodies set down, like boulders on a plain, in a green world with which they have nothing in common. Casterbridge lived by agriculture at one remove further from the fountain-head than the adjoining villages—no more. The townsfolk understood every fluctuation in the rustic's condition, for it affected their receipts as much as the labourer's; they entered into the troubles and joys which moved the aristocratic families ten miles round—for the same reason. And even at dinner-parties of the professional families the subjects of discussion were corn, cattle-disease, sowing and reaping, fencing and planting; while politics were viewed by them less from their own stand-point of burgesses with rights and privileges than from the standpoint of their county neighbours.

25   *Roman Remains*

Casterbridge [Dorchester] announced old Rome in every street, alley, and precinct. It looked Roman, bespoke the art of Rome, concealed dead men of Rome. It was impossible to dig more than a foot or two deep about the town fields and gardens without coming upon some tall soldier or other of the Empire, who had lain there in his silent unobtrusive rest for a space of fifteen hundred years. He was mostly found lying on his side, in an oval scoop in the chalk, like a chicken in its shell; his knees drawn up to his chest; sometimes with the remains of his spear against his arm; a fibula or brooch of bronze on his breast or forehead; an urn at his knees, a jar at his throat, a bottle at his mouth ; and mystified conjecture pouring down upon him from the eyes of Casterbridge street-boys and men, who had turned a moment to gaze at the familiar spectacle as they passed by.

Imaginative inhabitants, who would have felt an unpleasantness at the discovery of a comparatively modern skeleton in their gardens, were quite unmoved by these hoary shapes. They had lived so long ago, their time was so unlike the present, their hopes and motives were so widely removed from ours, that between them and the living there seemed to stretch a gulf too wide for even a spirit to pass.

26   *Time Stands Still*

In comparison with cities, Weatherbury [Puddletown] was immutable. The citizen's *Then* is the rustic's *Now*. In London, twenty or thirty years ago are old times; in Paris ten years, or five; in Weatherbury three or four score years were included in the mere present and nothing less than a century set a mark on its face or tone. Five decades hardly modified the cut of a gaiter, the embroidery of a smock-frock, by the breadth of a hair. Ten generations failed to alter the turn of a single phrase. In these Wessex nooks the busy outsider's ancient times are only old; his old times are still new; his present is futurity.

27 Inviolate Egdon

A Saturday afternoon in November was approaching the time of twilight, and the vast tract of unenclosed wild known as Egdon Heath [between Dorchester and Wareham] embrowned itself moment by moment. Overhead the hollow stretch of whitish cloud shutting out the sky was as a tent which had the whole heath for its floor.

The heaven being spread with this pallid screen and the earth with the darkest vegetation, their meeting-line at the horizon was clearly marked. In such contrast the heath wore the appearance of an instalment of night which had taken up its place before its astronomical hour was come: darkness had to a great extent arrived hereon, while day stood distinct in the sky. . . .

The place became full of a watchful intentness now; for when other things sank brooding to sleep the heath appeared slowly to awake and listen Every night its Titanic form seemed to await something; but it had waited thus, unmoved, during so many centuries, through the crises of so many things, that it could only be imagined to await one last crisis—the final overthrow. . . .

Only in summer days of highest feather did its mood touch the level of gaiety. Intensity was more usually reached by way of the solemn than by way of the brilliant, and such a sort of intensity was often arrived at during winter darkness, tempests, and mists. Then Egdon was aroused to reciprocity; for the storm was its lover and the wind its friend. Then it became the home of strange phantoms; and it was found to be the hitherto unrecognized original of those wild regions of obscurity which are vaguely felt to be compassing us about in midnight dreams of flight and disaster, and are never thought of after the dream till revived by scenes like this. . . .

To recline on a stump of thorn in the central valley of Egdon, between afternoon and night, where the eye could reach nothing of the world outside the summits and shoulders of heathland which filled the whole circumference of its glance, and to know that everything around and underneath had been from prehistoric times as unaltered as the stars overhead, gave ballast to the mind adrift on change and harassed by the irrepressible New. The great inviolate place had an ancient permanence which the sea cannot claim. Who can say of a particular sea that it is old? Distilled by the sun, kneaded by the moon, it is renewed in a year, in a day, or in an hour. The sea changed, the fields changed, the rivers, the villages, and the people changed, yet Egdon remained.

28 The Valley of the Great Dairies

The ripe hue of the red and dun kine absorbed the evening sunlight, which the white-coated animals returned to the eye in rays almost dazzling, even at the distant elevation on which she [Tess] stood.

The bird's-eye perspective before her was not so luxuriantly beautiful, perhaps, as that other one which she knew so well; yet it was more cheering. It lacked the intensely blue atmosphere of the rival vale, and its heavy soils and scents; the new air was clear, bracing, ethereal. The river itself, which nourished the grass and cows of these renowned dairies, flowered not like the streams in Blackmoor. Those were slow, silent, often turbid; flowing over beds of mud into which the incautious wader might sink and vanish unawares. The Var [Frome] waters were as clear as the pure River of Life shown to the Evangelist, rapid as the shadow of a cloud, with pebbly shallows that prattled to the sky all day long. There the water-flower was the lily; the crow-foot here ... Her hopes mingled with the sunshine in an ideal photosphere which surrounded her as she bounded along against the soft south wind.

29　*Where We Did Keep Our Flagon*

When we in mornèn had a-drow'd
The grass or russlèn haÿ abrode.
The lit'some maïdens an' the chaps,
Wi' bits o'nunchèns in their laps,
Did all zit down upon the knaps
　　Up there, in under hedge, below
　　The highest elem o' the row,
　　　Where we did keep our flagon.

There we could zee green vields at hand,
Avore a hundred on beyand,
An' rows o' trees in hedges roun'
Green meäds, an' zummerleäzes brown,
An' thorns upon the zunny down,
　　While aïer, vrom the rockèn zedge
　　In brook, did come along the hedge,
　　　Where we did keep our flagon.

There laughèn chaps did try in plaÿ
To bury maïdens up in haÿ,
As gigglèn maïdens tried to roll
The chaps down into zome deep hole,
Or sting wi' nettles woone o'm's poll;
　　While John did hele out each his drap
　　O' eäle or cider, in his lap
　　　Where he did keep the flagon.

Woone day there spun a whirlwind by
Where Jenny's clothes wer out to dry;
An' off vled frocks, a'most a-catch'd
By smock-frocks wi' their sleeves outstratch'd,
An' caps a-frill'd an' eäperns patch'd;
  An' she a-steärèn in a fright,
  Wer glad enough to zee em light
    Where we did keep our flagon.

30 *William Barnes*

Until the last year or two there were few figures more familiar to the eye in the county town of Dorset on a market day than an aged clergyman, quaintly attired in caped cloak, knee breeches and buckled shoes with a leather satchel strung over his shoulders and a stout staff in his hand. He seemed usually to prefer the middle of the street to the pavement, and to be thinking of matters which had nothing to do with the scene before him. He plodded along with a broad firm tread, notwithstanding the slight stoop occasioned by the years. Every Saturday morning he might have been seen thus trudging up the narrow South Street, his shoes coated with mud or dust according to the state of the roads between his rural home and Dorchester, and a little grey dog at his heels, till he reached the four cross ways in the centre of the town. Halting here opposite the public clock, he would pull his old-fashioned watch from its deep fob and set it with great precision to London time. This the invariable first act of his market visit, having been completed to his satisfaction, he turned round and methodically proceeded about his other business.

To those who knew Mr. Barnes in his prime, it may have been a matter for conjecture why a man of his energies should not at some point or other in his career have branched off from the quiet byways of his early manhood into the turmoils of the outer world. The explanation seems to be that the poetic side of his nature, though not always dominant, was but faintly ruled by the practical at any time, that his place-attachment was strong almost to a fault, and thus his cosmopolitan interests, though lively, were always subordinate to those local hobbies and solicitudes whence came alike his special powers and his limitations. Few young people who have seen him in later years can realize the robust, upright form of his middle life, the ruddy cheek and the bright quick eye. Those who knew him well and long, entertained for him a warm affection, while casual visitors from afar were speedily won to kindly regard by the simplicity of his character, his forbearance, and the charming spurts of youthful ardour which would burst out as rays even in his latest hours.

31   My Orcha'd in Linden Lea

'Ithin the woodlands, flow'ry gleäded,
  By the woak tree's mossy moot,
The sheenèn grass-bleädes, timber-sheäded,
  Now do quiver under voot;
An' birds do whissle auver head,
An' water's bubblèn in its bed,
An' there vor me the apple tree
Do leän down low in Linden Lea.

When leaves that leätely wer a-springèn
  Now do feäde 'ithin the copse,
An' painted birds do hush their zingèn
  Up upon the timber's tops;
An' brown-leav'd fruit's a-turnèn red,
In cloudless zunsheen, auver head,
Wi' fruit vor me, the apple tree
Do leän down low in Linden Lea.

Let other vo'k meäke money vaster
  In the aïr o' dark-room'd towns,
I don't dread a peevish meäster;
  Though noo man do heed my frowns,
I be free to goo abrode,
Or teäke my hwomeward road
To where, vor me, the apple tree
Do leän down low in Linden Lea.

32   The Geäte A-Vallèn To

In the zunsheen of our zummers
  Wi' the häytime now a-come,
How busy wer we out a-vield
  Wi' vew a-left at hwome,
When waggons rumbled out ov yard
  Red wheeled, wi' body blue,
And back behind 'em loudly slamm'd
  The geäte a-vallèn to.

Drough day sheen ov how many years
  The geäte ha' now a-swung,
Behind the veet o' vull-grown men
  And vootsteps of the young.

Drough years o' days it swung to us
   Behind each little shoe,
As we tripped lightly on avore
   The geäte a-vallèn to.

In evenèn time o' starry night
   How mother zot at hwome
And kept her bläzing vire bright
   Till father should ha' come,
And how she quicken'd up and smiled
   And stirred her vire anew,
To hear the trampèn ho'ses' steps
   And geäte a-vallèn to.

There's moon-sheen now in nights o' Fall
   When leaves be brown vrom green,
When to the slammèn o' the geäte
   Our Jenny's ears be keen,
When the wold dog do wag his tail,
   And Jeän could tell to who,
As he do come in drough the geäte,
   The geäte a-vallèn to.

And oft do come a saddened hour
   When there must goo away
One well-beloved to our heart's core,
   Vor long, perhaps for aye:
And oh! it is a touchèn thing
   The lovèn heart must rue
To hear behind his last farewell
   The geäte a-vallèn to.

33   The Song of Freedom

God is our Guide! From field, from wave,
   From plough, from anvil, and from loom,
We come, our country's rights to save,
   And speak the tyrant faction's doom;
We raise the watchword 'Liberty'
We will, we will, we will be free!

God is our Guide! No swords we draw,
   We kindle not war's battle fires,

By reason, union, justice, law,
　We claim the birthright of our sires;
We raise the watchword 'Liberty'
We will, we will, we will be free!

34   A Respite for Wessex

The situation for Wessex was a grave one, the more so as no help could now
be expected from other parts of the country, but five years had passed since
the first attack and there is an indication of at least one way in which the
interval had been profitably spent in the record that in the summer of 875
Alfred's own ships had been able to engage and rout a small force of Vikings
at sea. Leaving Cambridge in the autumn of 875 the Danes made straight
for Wareham, at the inner end of Poole harbour, apparently expecting to
make contact with reinforcements which, according to one authority, were
making their way up Channel from the west, perhaps from Ireland. If this
was the plan, its later stages miscarried owing to a storm which destroyed a
large number of Viking ships off Swanage. The land force found itself in no
position to risk an open battle and was compelled to submit to terms whereby
hostages were given in guarantee of a pledge to leave Wessex, but the pledge
was broken and the Danes slipped away to Exeter by night, eluding the
pursuit of Alfred's army which was unable to overtake them before they
reached the security of Exeter's defences. It is evident from the willingness
with which the Danes gave further hostages that Alfred remained in command of the situation and in the summer of 877 the invaders left Wessex and
crossed to Gloucester in Mercian territory.

35   Knollsea and the Dorset Coast

Knollsea [Swanage] was a seaside village lying snug within two headlands
as between a finger and thumb. Everybody in the parish who was not a
boatman was a quarrier, unless he were the gentleman who owned half the
property and had been a quarryman, or the other gentleman who owned the
other half, and had been to sea.
　The knowledge of the inhabitants was of the same special sort as their
pursuits. The quarrymen in white fustian understood practical geology, the
laws and accidents of dips, faults, and cleavage, far better than the ways of
the world and mammon; the seafaring men in Guernsey frocks had a clearer
notion of Alexandria, Constantinople, the Cape, and the Indies than of any
inland town in their own country. This, for them, consisted of a busy portion,
the Channel, where they lived and laboured, and a dull portion, the vague

unexplored miles of interior at the back of the ports, which they seldom thought of. . . .

Upon the irregular slope between the house and the quay was an orchard of aged trees wherein every apple ripening on the boughs presented its rubicund side towards the cottage, because that building chanced to lie upwards in the same direction as the sun. Under the trees were a few Cape sheep, and over them the stone chimneys of the village below; outside these lay the tanned sails of a ketch or smack, and the violet waters of the bay, seamed and creased by breezes sufficient to raise waves; beyond all a curved wall of cliff, terminating in a promontory, which was flanked by tall and shining obelisks of chalk rising sheer from the trembling blue race beneath. . . .

On one of the spires of chalk into which the hill here had been split was perched a cormorant, silent and motionless, with wings spread out to dry in the sun after his morning's fishing, their white surface shining like mail. . . . Far below on the right hand it was a fine day, and the silver sunbeams lighted up a many-armed inland sea which stretched round an island with fir-trees and gorse, and amid brilliant crimson heaths wherein white paths and roads occasionally met the eye in dashes and zigzags like flashes of lightning. Outside, where the broad Channel appeared, a berylline and opalized variegation of ripples, currents, deeps, and shallows, lay as fair under the sun as a New Jerusalem, the shores being of gleaming sand.

36 The Isle of Slingers

Portland hath bene of auncient tyme be al likelihood environid with the se, and yet berith the name of an isle. It is eminent and hilly ground on the shore of it, and a great plain yn the midle of it. The cumpace of it is countid to be about a 7. miles. But if a man should cumpace it by the very rootes and depe shore the cumpace wold mount to a x miles.

The soile is sumwhat stony: and the shore very rokky. The isle is fruteful of corn and gresse: and hath plenty of sheepe.

There be at this present tyme about a 80. housis in the isle. Ther hath beene al most as many mo as it apperith by ruines.

There is but one streat of houses in the isle, the residew be sparkelid [scattered].

There is a castlet or pile not far from [the] streate: and is set on a high rokke hard by the se cliffes a little above the est end of the chirch. The paroche chirch that is but one at this tyme in the isle, is longe and sumwhat low, buildid in the hangging rootes of an hille by the shore. This chirch and paroche is about a mile dim. to go to it from the kinges new castelle in the isle: and to go to it by cumpace of the shore it is 3. miles or more. Sum say that in tymes past ther was a nother paroch chirch in the isle: but I there lernid no certente of it.

There be very few or utterly no trees in the isle, saving the elmes about the chirch. Ther would grow more if they were ther plantid: yet is the isle very bleke.

The people bring wood thither out of Wight and other places. They brenne [burn] also cowe dung dryed with the hete of the sunne.

The people of the isle lyve most now by tillage, and sumwhat faulle from fishing.

The people be good there in slynging of stonys, and use it for defence of the isle.

The people ther be politique inough in selling theyr commoditiees and sumwhat avaritiose.

The personage sette in the high streat is the best building in the isle.

The Bisshop of Winchester is patrone of the chirch.

The isle is the kinges: and much of the land there is holden of hym.

37   Limestone Land

A person who differed from the local wayfarers was climbing the steep road which leads through the sea-skirted townlet definable as the Street of Wells, [Fortune's Well—Portland] and forms a pass into that Gibraltar of Wessex, the singular peninsula once an island, and still called such, that stretches out like the head of a bird into the English Channel. It is connected with the mainland by a long thin neck of pebbles 'cast up by rages of the se', and unparalleled in its kind in Europe. . . . What had seemed usual in the isle when he lived there always looked quaint and odd after his later impressions. More than ever the spot seemed what it was said once to have been, the ancient Vindilia Island [Portland], and the Home of the Slingers. The towering rock, the houses above houses, one man's doorstep rising behind his neighbour's chimney, the gardens hung up by one edge to the sky, the vegetables growing on apparently almost vertical planes, the unity of the whole island as a solid and single block of limestone four miles long, were no longer familiar and common-place ideas. All now stood dazzlingly unique and white against the tinted sea, and the sun flashed on infinitely stratified walls of oolite,

> The melancholy ruins
> Of cancelled cycles. . . .

with a distinctiveness that called the eyes to it as strongly as any spectacle he had beheld afar.

38 God Save King Henn'

God save Kinge Henn' the VIII of that name and Prins Edward, begotten of Quene Jane, my Ladi Mari that goodli virgin, and the Ladi Elizabeth so towardli, with the Kinges honorable counselers.

39 Chamber-Lye

The shortage of manure on the Island led to a curious practice, which Stevenson describes as 'Chamber-lye', and of which he gives the following details: 'In the Isle of Portland they have a practice of long standing, of preserving all the urine that is made in winter, carrying it out in casks, and distributing it over the wheat crops, in a manner somewhat similar to that used in watering the streets of large towns. This kind of manure has been found to answer well, as may be believed, from the average produce of the Isle being 18 bushels of wheat per acre, while that for the rest of the country is not 17¾ bushels, and the Isle of Portland is remarkably poor land. The urine is generally put on the land between September and March: it will be serviceable if spread on the land intended for wheat, but not so much if put on the young plants; and care is needed not to put it on the wheat near the approach of hot weather, for this would entirely destroy the crop.'

40 Hewers of Stone

I went to the hewers of stone [in July 1635], which was carried for the reparation of St Paules church in London. There were about 200 workemen, some hewing out of the cliffe alofte, some squareinge, some carryeing down, others ladeinge. Some stones there were ready squared and formed, of 9, 10 and 11 tonnes weight, as they said; some of them ready squared aloft and sent downe in Carts made of purpose.

41 The Opening of Portland's Bridge

Portland Ferry Bridge was opened in grand style, not, however, by any particular personage, but by a great procession, principal items in which was a detachment of the 6th Dragoon Guards and Weymouth Town Band. They marched up to Wyke from the King's Statue and thence across the Bridge, followed by tenants, landowners and the responsible Committee. Cheers and music greeted the first passing of this spot, toll free. Then, joined by a party from Portland, on to the Portland Arms for a 'sumptuous event'. After the ceremony the troops went through a great variety of military evolutions and displayed great adroitness in performing the sword exercises, much to the gratification of the numerous collection of individuals congregated together.

42   A Coach Goes into Portland

The great novelty of the day was the circumstance of a Stage Coach and four horses going into Portland. . . . Mr Gaulton, the landlord of the Antelope Inn at Dorchester, being determined to surprise the Portlanders, sent the 'Victoria' coach into the Island with the procession. Now persons need not feel the least timidity, as the island can be safely reached by land, without the necessity of crossing by boat.

43   Education in the Nick

The whole number of prisoners [at Portland] is divided into twelve classes, each class consisting of seventy men, with the exception of one class coming on the Saturday afternoon, of which the number is forty-six. These classes are again sub-divided into two divisions, each of which one master superin-tends. Each whole class is opened by singing a hymn of two verses, after which a collect is repeated by one of the masters, and then a chapter of the Bible is read verse by verse by the prisoners. This occupies about fifteen or twenty minutes, and then the system is pursued as described in the plan as follows:

Time	First Division	Second Division
First Hour	Writing	Reading, History or Geography
Second Hour	Reading, History or Geography	Writing
Remainder, Third Hour	Viva Voce questions on Arithmetic, etc.	Viva Voce questions on Arithmetic, etc.
	Issuing Library Books	Issuing Library Books

After which the whole concludes with singing a verse, and a blessing.

44   The Zwellen Downs

The zwellen downs, wi' chalky tracks
A-climmen up their zunny backs,

Do hide green meads an' zedgy brooks,
An' clumps o' trees wi' glossy rooks,
An' hearty vo'k to laugh an' zing,
An' parish-churches in a string,
Wi' tow'rs o' merry bells to ring,
An' white roads up athirt the hills.

45 *Night on Norcombe*

Norcombe Hill—not far from lonely Toller Down—was one of those spots
which suggest to a passer-by that he is in the presence of a shape approaching
the indestructible as nearly as any to be found on earth. It was a featureless
convexity of chalk and soil—an ordinary specimen of those smoothly
outlined protuberances of the globe which may remain undisturbed on some
great day of confusion, when far grander heights and dizzy granite precipices
topple down.

The hill was covered on its northern side by an ancient and decaying
plantation of beeches, whose upper verge formed a line over the crest,
fringing its arched curve against the sky, like a mane. Tonight these trees
sheltered the southern slope from the keenest blasts, which smote the wood
and floundered through it with a sound as of grumbling, or gushed over its
crowning boughs in a weakened moan. . . .

Between this half-wooded, half-naked hill, and the vague, still horizon
that its summit indistinctly commanded, was a mysterious sheet of fathom-
less shade—the sounds from which suggested that what it concealed bore
some humble resemblance to features here. The thin grasses, more or
less coating the hill, were touched by the wind in breezes of differing powers,
and almost of differing natures—one rubbing the blades heavily, another
raking them piercingly, another brushing them like a soft broom. The
instinctive act of human-kind was to stand and listen, and learn how the
trees on the right and the trees on the left wailed or chaunted to each other
in the regular antiphonies of a cathedral choir; how hedges and other shapes
to leeward then caught the note, lowering it to the tenderest sob; and how
the hurrying gust then plunged into the south, to be heard no more.

The sky was clear—remarkably clear—and the twinkling of all the stars
seemed to be but throbs of one body, timed by a common pulse. The
North Star was directly in the wind's eye, and since evening the Bear had
swung round it outwardly to the east, till he was now at a right angle with
the meridian. A difference of colour in the stars—oftener read of than seen
in England—was really perceptible here. The kingly brilliance of Sirius
pierced the eye with a steely glitter, the star called Capella was yellow,
Aldebaran and Betelgueux shone with a fiery red.

To persons standing alone on a hill during a clear midnight such as
this, the roll of the world eastward is almost a palpable movement. The

sensation may be caused by the panoramic glide of the stars past earthly objects, which is perceptible in a few minutes of stillness, or by the better outlook upon space that a hill affords, or by the wind, or by the solitude; but whatever be its origin, the impression of riding along is vivid and abiding. The poetry of motion is a phrase much in use, and to enjoy the epic form of that gratification it is necessary to stand on a hill at a small hour of the night and ... long and quietly watch your stately progress through the stars. After such a nocturnal reconnoitre it is hard to get back to earth, and to believe that the consciousness of such majestic speeding is derived from a tiny human frame.

46 Sweet Be'mi'ster

Sweet Be'mi'ster, that bist a-bound
By green an' woody hills all round,
Wi' hedges, reachen up between
A thousan' vields o' zummer green.

47 The Parret Roars

I ferried over the river Parret, at that time quite at ebb, and not more than a quarter of a mile across. This stream, one of the most considerable in Somersetshire, rises at a town (called, after itself, South-Parret) in Dorsetshire, lends a name to another place on the border of Somersetshire, passes South-Petherton, sweeps by Langport, gives trade and commercial animation to Bridgwater, and discharges itself into the Bristol Channel at the Start-Point. As I had been informed that it was remarkable for the impetuosity with which the tide enters its mouth, I waited about an hour and a half, till the commencement of the flood, in order to observe the phenomenon. Its approach is announced by a distant roaring sound, which gradually increases upon the ear, until the cause itself appears; a volume of water, like one vast wave, sometimes rising to the height of four feet (though when I saw it, not more than two) rushing on with irresistible violence, and covering instantaneously the steep banks, which had been left dry by the recess of the tide. It is called a Boar, in allusion, I presume, to the formidable sounds which this indomitable animal emits; and affords no bad idea of his violence and noise, when roused to fury by the spear of the hunter, or the attack of his dogs.

48 Total Immersion

The font [at South-Brent] also lays claim to a considerable antiquity, being deep and capacious, intended for the total immersion of the infant to be baptized. This, you know, was the ancient mode of performing the ceremony, and only disused within these two centuries, when good sense getting the better of prejudice, the custom almost universally disappeared, to the great benefit of population since the chances must have been very considerably against any infant which was thus, within the month, unmercifully plunged over head and ears into a bath of cold water. Little accidents, indeed, frequently occurred, whilst the practice continued, to the poor half-drowned children; one of which has been thought of sufficient importance to be incorporated into the page of metrical history. It relates to King Ethelred, the miserable ideot whose inglorious reign saw the Danish power established in this country. Archbishop Dunstan had the honour of baptising the royal babe; but the shock or the fright, occasioned by the immersion, produced in the infant the most unseemly and offensive effects. The prelate, whose olfactory nerves were probably somewhat distressed by the circumstance, returned the child to its nurse in a passion, exclaiming at the same time, 'Per Deum et matrem ejus, ignavus homo erit!' [By GOD and his mother, this will be a most scurvy scoundrel!] a prophecy which subsequent events completely accomplished.

49 Scurrilous Bench-Ends

The only curiosity of South-Brent is its little church, which has many vestiges of antiquity both within and without. Its seating is particularly curious, being certainly anterior to the reformation. Instead of pews, it has (like the Russian churches) a regular series of plain oaken benches, with a back to each, running from either side towards the middle of the church, at right angles with the wall. The flat boards, which form the terminations of these seats, are curiously and variously carved with subjects most grotesque and ludicrous; such as a fox or an ass in a mitre; a pig roasting, and a monkey acting the part of turnspit; a party of geese hanging a pig; a monkey at prayers; a pig preaching, etc. These caricature carvings I should consider as instances of practical satire by the parochial clergy against the mendicant orders; for it is well known that the most inveterate antipathy subsisted between the parish-priests and the friars, in consequence of that considerable influence which the latter had obtained by their absurd vows and itinerant preaching.

50   The Laugh of the Coxcomb

Leaving Axbridge, a short mile brought me to Cross, through which runs the turnpike-road from Exeter to Bristol. This publick way it was necessary for me to pursue for nearly six miles, almost every step affording an opportunity for the exercise of philosophy, and the triumphs of temper. You know what walking in Wales is, what its pleasures, and what its inconveniences are; and will, I believe, allow, that the former out-weigh and out-number the latter considerably. But in England it is a very different thing. The pedestrian here has to encounter many little slights and many petty affronts, much inattention and much inpertinence; so that if he have not thrown into the bundle of requisites for his journey, an ounce of coolness and a packet of good-humour, the odds are, that he pursues his ramble in irritability and peevishness, and returns home in disgust and disappointment. He must have courage enough to meet with indifference, what an excellent observer of human life emphatically calls, 'the scornful reproof of the wealthy, and the despitefulness of the proud'; the grin, the sneer, and the laugh of the coxcomb or the blockhead, whom Fortune, in her blindness, has perched up in a phaeton, or mounted upon a gelding. Such a fiery ordeal as this I was obliged to undergo for two hours, and then turned, right joyfully, towards East Brent, a pleasing little village, with its spire-crowned church, planted at the north-eastern extremity of Brent Knoll, one of those conoidal hills which rise suddenly out of the flats of Somersetshire. A Roman entrenchment, on the summit of this eminence, was an irresistible inducement to climb its steep sides; though distinct from this curious remain of ancient castrametation, the prospect from this lofty station amply recompensed the trouble of reaching it.

51   The Somerset Levels

From the appearance of the country many miles to the westward and southward of Glastonbury, there can be no doubt of the tradition being founded in fact, that the sea in distant ages flowed up considerably to the east of that town. One extensive uniform flat presents itself, varied here and there with insular protuberances, swelling out into bold hills, for the most part of a conoidal form. On this tract, in many places, various marine substances have been found, confirming the tradition of the dominion which Old Ocean is said formerly to have maintained over it. Indeed, till within these few years past, he continued to exercise his claim here; and, during high tides, frequently flooded this ancient territory of his waves. And even now, though by well-constructed drains the lands are converted from a marsh to meadow grounds, a marine inundation would certainly take place, were the embankments at Huntspill, raised to check the ocean tide, by any accident to be destroyed. A farmer at work in his fields was highly apprehensive of

Culbone Church, Somersetshire

Lynmouth

this event, having heard the dykes had been damaged by the late rains, and assured me, that were they to give way, the country must be inundated, as the ground on which we stood, lay considerably below high-water mark. Along the margin of the drains by which I proceeded towards Wookey, the rich perfume of the Calamus Aromaticus, or sweet-scented flag, occasionally 'stole upon the air,' and filled it with fragrance. . . . The myrica or sweet-gale, also, with its serrated leaves and dry berry, the ancient substitute for hops, presented itself in almost every part of the uncultivated moor. A most agreeable character of landscape marks the country, through the whole distance between this moor and the village of Wookey; beautiful and well-wooded knolls swell out on all sides; the flat grounds are rich and verdent; the magnificent cathedral of Wells, with its fret-work towers and elegant chapter-house, disclose themselves at intervals; and the lofty tor of Glastonbury towers above everything to the eastward.

52 Arthur's Company

At Llongborth [Langport] saw I, hewing with steel,
The brave men of Arthur,
Emperor and director of toil.

53 Where Sleeps the King?

Anoeth bid bet y arthur [Mysterious is the grave of Arthur]

54 The Celtic West

Christ, son of Mary, my cauldron of pure descent.

55 A Good Match

If the Abbot of Glastonbury married the Abbess of Shrewsbury, they would have more land than the King of England.

4

56   *The Thorns Bloom at Christmas*

The hawthorns also that groweth in Werall [Wearyall Hill]
Do burge and bear green leaves at Christmas,
As fresh as other in May when the nightingale
Wrests out her notes musical as pure as glass.

57   *A Sceptical Traveller*

You will probably tax me with the want of curiosity, when I confess to you,
that I left Glastonbury yesterday without visiting the spot which has been
immortalized by the miraculous conversion of a dry walking-staff into a
flourishing hawthorn-tree; but understanding from a sagacious cobbler,
that the original sacred plant had long since fallen a prey to the mis-directed
zeal of certain sacrilegious Puritans, who discredited the account of its
preternatural origin; and collecting also, that the hawthorn-trees now
existing in the neighbourhood, and said to be legitimate descendants of
Joseph's staff, were only bastard slips, on which no dependence was to be
placed for the exhibition of the miracle; I did not think it worth while to
ascend Weary-all hill, the former scene of this wonder.

58   *Faith Affirmed*

I knowe that England do keep the right day that Christ was born on, above
all the Nations of Christendome, because we have a miracle hath often
been seene in England upon that day, for we have a tree in England, called
the Holy Thorne, by Glassenbury Abbey, nigh the Bathe, which on the 25
day of December, which is our Christmasse day, hath constantly blossomed;
which the people of that place have received from antiquitie, that it was that
kind of thorne, wherewith Christ was crowned.

59   *The Moors Adventurous*

The Latin from whence this history was drawn into Romance was taken in
the Isle of Avalon, in a holy house of religion that standeth at the head of
the Moors Adventurous, there where King Arthur and Queen Guenievre
lie.

60 King Arthur's Vision

The Graal appeared at the sacring of the Mass, in five several manners that none ought not to tell, for the secret things of the sacrament ought none to tell openly but he unto whom God hath given it. King Arthur beheld the changes, the last whereof was the change into a chalice.

61 The Good King Fisherman

The good King Fisherman is dead that made every day our service be done in the most holy chapel there where the most Holy Graal every day appeared, and where the Mother of God abode from the Saturday until the Monday that the service was finished.

62 Cadbury-Camelot

The French poets were vague—perhaps deliberately vague—about the topography of Camelot. Malory in the *Morte d'Arthur* always identifies it with Winchester. But when Caxton came to print the *Morte d'Arthur* he referred in his preface to "the toune of Camelot, which dyvers now lyvyng hath seen" in Wales, meaning perhaps by this the Roman walls of either Caerleon or Caerwent. Leland rejected both these attributions and identified Cadbury Castle as "Camallate, sumtyme a famose toun or Castelle". It is not clear whether he did this because he found some genuine folk memory of Arthur preserved locally, or because having just passed through the villages of Queen Camel and West Camel he saw the massive defences of Cadbury towering before him, and the derivation Camelot>Camel leapt to his mind. This is indeed quite likely, because he then corrupted the local place-names to suit his identification, referring to Queen and West Camallat. However that may be, his identification was a happy one. Repeated by generations of antiquaries, it formed one of the inspirations of the recent excavations which revealed at Cadbury Castle a major fortification of the Arthurian period.

63 Christian Soldier

The Battle of Badon in which Arthur carried the cross of Our Lord Jesus Christ on his shoulders for three days and nights and the Britons were victors.

64   A Tudor Monarch Seeks his King

'Tis thine, O Henry! [Henry VII] to renew.
Thither, when conquest has restor'd
Yon recreant Isle, and sheath'd the sword,
When Peace with palm has crown'd thy brows,
Haste thee to pay thy Pilgrim vows.
There, observant of my lore,
The pavement's hallow'd depth explore;
And thrice a fathom underneath
Dive into the vaults of death;
There shall thine eye, with wild amaze,
On his gigantick stature gaze;
There shalt thou find the monarch laid,
All in warrior weeds array'd;
Wearing in death his helmet-crown
And weapons huge of old renown.
Martial Prince! 'tis thine to save
From dark oblivion ARTHUR'S grave.

65   Local Emotion

To me, who contemplate with particular pleasure the ancient ecclesiastical
architecture of this kingdom, and admire the pageantry of the Romish ritual,
though I lament the purposes to which it is applied, scenes like the ruins of
Glastonbury Abbey afford considerable gratification. My imagination
readily enters into "the deeds of the days of other years"; and while I tread
the hallowed spot, reverts with ease to, and interests itself in the transactions
which it has witnessed, the grandeur it has exhibited, the vicissitudes it has
suffered. Nor am I at pains to check this mental delusion, since I hold it to be
an incontrovertible axiom, that man is ever the better for seriousness and
contemplation. Were an authority required for a truth so self-evident, I
could not offer a better than a passage from [Dr Johnson] the first of English
moralists, a passage that deserves to be written in letters of gold, and is
worthy to be inscribed on every heart. "To abstract the mind from all local
emotion would be impossible, if it were endeavoured, and would be foolish
if it were possible. Whatever withdraws us from the power of our senses;
whatever makes the past, the distant, or the future predominate over the
present, advances us in the dignity of thinking beings. Far from me and
from my friends be such frigid philosophy, as may conduct us indifferent
and unmoved over any ground which has been dignified by wisdom, bravery,
or virtue. That man is little to be envied, whose patriotism would not gain
force upon the plain of Marathon; or whose piety would not grow warmer
among the ruins of Iona."

66 A Bishop's Feasting Hall

The external appearance of the Bishop's palace at Wells, with its battlements and moats, its gates and redoubts, conveys the idea of the sullen retreat of an ancient feudal chieftain, rather than what it really is, the elegant mansion of modern courtesy and literary taste. When one contemplates the site of its ancient hall, which formerly stretched on the south side of the court or area, in length 120 feet, and in breadth 70, the scene of old hospitality, where, on the frequently recurring festival, "the beards wagged all", where each chin shone with the lard of the buttery, and each nose reddened with the strong ale of the cellar, we are almost tempted to scold the all-grasping Henry VIII for putting a period to such merriment; but feel still more indignant with the hypocritical or fanatical republicans of the last century, who wantonly reduced to ruins what the royal cormorant had spared—the walls which had in times of yore been consecrated to good-living.

67 The Great Forest

The western edge of Salisbury Plain was formerly marked by a wide belt of forest-land running north and south approximately along the present boundary between Wiltshire and Somerset. This belt of woodland which still formed part of the royal forests in the thirteenth century, played an important role in the history of Wessex. The Welsh knew it as the Great Forest (*Coit Maur*—Asser, ch. 55) and the English as Selwood (*Sealwudu*). In the eighth century it marked the boundary between the two West Saxon bishoprics, Winchester and Sherborne, and in the ninth it gave protection to Alfred while he reorganized his forces against the Danes. At the end of Ceawlin's reign, late in the sixth century, it marked the western limit of the English advance and it continued so to do for upwards of half a century.

68 Fen and Forest

Woodland was much valued not only for its game, but also as swine pasture and as the source of building materials and fuel. The metaphor of wood-cutting was adopted by Alfred in the preface of his translation of Augustine's *Soliloquies* and here perhaps better than anywhere else in the records of the time the Anglo-Saxon woodlands come vividly to life.

> Then I gathered for myself staves and props and bars, and handles for all the tools I knew how to use, and crossbars and beams for all the structures which I knew how to build, the fairest pieces of timber, as many as I could carry. I neither came home with a single load, nor did it suit me to bring home all the

wood, even if I could have carried it. In each tree I saw something that I required at home. For I advise each of those who is strong and has many wagons, to plan to go to the same wood where I cut these props, and fetch for himself more there, and load his wagons with fair rods, so that he can plait many a fine wall, and put up many a peerless building, and build a fair enclosure with them.

Fen, no less than forest, was a dominant feature in parts of the Anglo-Saxon landscape. The fens of Somerset played a decisive part in the history of England late in the ninth century because, with the additional protection given by Selwood, they provided Alfred with a secure stronghold during the third Danish attack against the kingdom of Wessex.

69   A Scholar King

To my venerable and most pious lord, ruler of all the Christians of the Island of Britain, Alfred, king of the Anglo-Saxons, Asser, lowest of all the servants of God, wishes thousandfold prosperity in both the present and future life, according to his prayers and desires.

Now, Alfred was loved by his father and mother, and indeed by everybody with a united and immense love, more than all his brothers, and was always brought up in the royal court, and as he passed through his childhood and boyhood he appeared fairer in form than all his brothers, and more pleasing in his looks, his words and his ways. And from his cradle a longing for wisdom before all things and among all the pursuits of this present life, combined with his noble birth, filled the noble temper of his mind. . . . He listened attentively to Saxon poems day and night, and hearing them often recited by others committed them to his retentive memory. A keen huntsman, he toiled unceasingly in every branch of hunting. . . . He was without equal in his skill and good fortune in that art. . . .

When his mother one day was showing him and his brothers a certain book of Saxon poetry which she held in her hand, she said, "I will give this book to whichever of you can learn it most quickly." And moved by these words, or rather by divine inspiration, and attracted by the beauty of the initial letter of the book, Alfred said in reply to his mother, forestalling his brothers, his elders in years though not in grace, "Will you really give this book to one of us, to the one who can soonest understand and repeat it to you ?" And, smiling and rejoicing, she confirmed it, saying, "To him will I give it". Then taking the book from her hand he went immediately to his master, who read it to him. And when it was read, he went back to his mother and repeated it. . . .

Nor, indeed, were King Alfred's children allowed to live idly and carelessly without a liberal education among the other occupations of this present life which are fitting for nobles; for they have learnt carefully psalms and Saxon books, especially Saxon poems, and they frequently make use of books.

Meanwhile the king, in the midst of wars and frequent hindrances of this present life, and also of the raids of the pagans and daily infirmities of body, did not cease, single-handed, assiduously and eagerly with all his might, to govern the kingdom, to practice every branch of hunting, to instruct his goldsmiths and all his craftsmen, and his falconers, hawkers and dog-keepers, to erect buildings to his own new design more stately than had been the custom of his ancestors, to recite Saxon books, and especially to learn by heart Saxon poems, and command others to do so. . . . He showed zeal for almsgiving, and generosity both to his countrymen and to strangers from all nations, and very great and matchless kindness and pleasantness towards all men, and skill in searching into things unknown. And many Franks, Frisians, men of Gaul, pagans, Welsh, Scots and Bretons willingly submitted to his lordship, both noblemen and men of humble rank; and he ruled them all in accordance with his own honourable nature just like his own people, and loved and honoured them, and enriched them with money and rights. . . .

Forthwith, like the prudent bee, which arises in the summer-time at dawn from its beloved cells and, directing its course in swift flight through the unknown ways of the air, alights upon many and various blossoms of herbs, plants and fruits, and finds and carries home what pleases it most, he turned afar the gaze of his mind, seeking abroad what he had not at home.

70   Crisis in the West

Æthelred died in April 871 and was immediately succeeded by his brother Alfred who was hard pressed for the remainder of the year. Summarizing the year's fighting, a West Saxon annalist wrote "in the course of the year nine general engagements were fought against the host in the kingdom to the south of the Thames, besides those innumerable forays which Alfred, the king's brother, and a single ealdorman and king's thegns rode on, which were never counted. And in the course of this year were slain nine jarls and one king; and this year the West Saxons made peace with the host." With his forces exhausted by the year's fighting there was little else that Alfred could do except pay the price which he might hope would bring a respite to his kingdom. His hope was justified. The Danes left Reading for London and did not come back to Wessex for five years.

71   Athelney and Triumph

Early in January 878 that part of the Danish army which had remained at

Gloucester under Guthrum turned south again to make a third and last attempt to conquer Wessex. Guthrum's forces must have been considerably smaller than those which had assaulted Wessex on the two previous occasions, yet something like panic was caused among the West Saxons by this third visitation. Some of them fled overseas and others submitted to the Danes, but Alfred himself, accompanied by a small force, fell back to the inner fastnesses of his kingdom west of Selwood. Early in the year his position, which had already seemed hopeless to many, was yet more gravely threatened by the descent of another Danish force upon the coast of Devonshire, but the new invaders suffered a sharp defeat while attempting to besiege an English force on Countisbury Hill.

At Easter of 878 Alfred built a small fortification at Athelney in the Somerset marshes and with this as his base he organized a series of harassing raids against the enemy in preparation for warfare on a large scale when the time was ripe. Early in May he was strong enough to leave the security of the marshes and to cross back to the eastern side of Selwood where the men of Somerset joined forces with those of Wiltshire and the nearer part of Hampshire. The combined levies advanced north-eastwards along the western scarp of Salisbury Plain towards Guthrum's camp at Chippenham. At Edington, fifteen miles south of Chippenham, Alfred won a decisive victory. A fortnight later the Danes again undertook to leave Wessex and after another week Guthrum and thirty of his army leaders were received by Alfred at Aller, close by Alfred's stronghold at Athelney. Guthrum was baptized at Aller and then led his army back to Chippenham whence it moved to Gloucester and finally, in 879, to East Anglia whose lands it proceeded to occupy.

72 *Wedmore and Peace*

In this year (878) in midwinter after Twelfth Night the enemy army came stealthily to Chippenham and occupied the land of the West Saxons and settled there. They drove a great part of the people across the sea, and conquered most of the others; and the people submitted to them, except King Alfred. He journeyed in difficulties through the woods and fen-fastnesses with a small force.

And the same winter the brother of Ivar and Healfdene was in the Kingdom of the West Saxons, in Devon, with 23 ships. And he was killed there and 840 men of his army with him. And there was captured the banner which they called 'Raven'.

And afterwards at Easter, King Alfred with a small force made a stronghold at Athelney, and he and the section of the people of Somerset which was nearest to it proceeded to fight from that stronghold against the enemy. Then in the seventh week after Easter he rode to 'Egbert's Stone' east of Selwood, and there came to meet him all the people of Somerset and of

Wiltshire and of that part of Hampshire which was on the side of the sea, and they rejoiced to see him. And then after one night he went from that encampment to Uey, and after another night to Edington, and there fought against the whole army and put it to flight, and pursued it as far as the fortress, and stayed there a fortnight. And then the enemy gave him preliminary hostages and great oaths that they would leave his kingdom, and promised also that their king should receive baptism, and they kept their promise. Three weeks later King Guthrum with 30 of the men who were most important in the army came to Alfred at Aller, which is near Athelney, and the king stood sponsor to him at his baptism there; and the unbinding of the chrism took place at Wedmore. And Guthrum was twelve days with the king who honoured him and his companions greatly with gifts.

73 Eels and Grapes among the Rhines

Bishop Ralph visited Muchelney in 1335 and censured the monks for making their beds too comfortable. Had he ever slept within those stone walls on endless winter nights, listening to the banshee wind screaming over those flat unscreened lands then deep-flooded for many months of the year? Muchelney has always been a watery place. Domesday Book records that it had two fisheries producing six thousand eels. But Muchelney must have got plenty of sunshine, for Domesday Book states that it possessed a vineyard also. And indeed on a summer day it is a warm and tranquil place sequestered from the noisy highways, drowsing amid its fresh moorland pastures, its cottage gardens full of flowers, including the garden of the fifteenth-century Priest's House, a low-built cottage—originally only one storey—with stone mullioned windows, once perhaps the home of the steward of the abbey lands.

74 King's Sedgemoor

As I passed over the hills to the northward of Somerton this morning, a favourable sky allowed my eye to range along the immense flat called King's Sedgemoor, formerly covered with the waters of the ocean, and even now exhibiting marks of this derivation in several marine plants which are scattered over its face. These circumstances render it interesting, indeed, to the naturalist; but the patriot and philanthropist also will not be unmoved, when he adverts to the events of its more modern history; when he recollects that this is the spot where the brave, mild, benevolent, but unfortunate Monmouth wept over the lost fortunes of a generous though hopeless cause; the dreadful scene where those ruthless instruments of a tyrant and bigot, Feversham, Kirke, and Jefferies, acted their horrid tragedies.

75 *Gildas Lived Here*

Apart from pirates various people have attempted to live on Flat Holm and Steep Holm, but with a few exceptions have had to abandon their enterprise. These two islands are difficult of access, for Steep Holm lies three miles offshore and Flat Holm is over two miles from Steep Holm. Currents are dangerous and more than one islander has smashed a good boat on the rocks when landing. Impossible to be self-supporting on such islands—unless one were like the sixth-century hermit Gildas who seems to have subsisted largely on shellfish while living on Steep Holm and writing his peevish chronicles. 'Enough to make anyone peevish, living in such a place,' as someone aptly remarked when mentioning St Gildas' writings, for who would want to live long on an island without streams or trees and with only the grey waters of the Bristol Channel to look upon? Fragments of a stone wall show that fourteenth-century monks occupied a small priory on Steep Holm while a ruined inn proves that some born optimist once tried to earn his living there.

Thomas Clark, a member of the well-known Quaker family at Street, wrote in his diary, in August 1831, a most interesting account of a visit to Steep Holm from Weston-super-Mare, a rowing-boat taking three hours over the journey. He landed on a pebble-strewn beach at the eastern end, and saw men cutting the road that now winds around the island. He ate his sandwiches in the ruined inn where the workmen had installed beds and frying-pans, and afterwards wandered about delightedly finding the many rare plants for which Steep Holm has always been noted; they flourish there still, for many of them grow on the rocky and inaccessible ridge of the island and cannot be uprooted by looting visitors (although Mr Clark was guilty of taking home what specimens he could to plant in his garden). Round-headed garlic grew there, the tree mallow, the caper-spurge, the henbane, spleenwort and pellitory, as well as coral-berried cuckoo-pint, ivy on the boulders, brilliant golden ragwort and samphire in the fissures of rocks.

'One that gathers samphire, dreadful trade!' wrote Shakespeare, as if this plant must always favour a site dangerous for humans. In Shakespeare's day they put it in salads. Mr Clark found too the single pink peony (or 'piony' as he calls it, like Shakespeare) that draws botanists to the island to this very day. But in 1831 the island cannot have been the home of birds that it is nowadays, for Mr Clark mentions rabbits, snails, butterflies, as the only form of animal life, whereas I heard a recent visitor to the island say that you had difficulty in walking without stepping upon a bird and indeed that on the greater part of its craggy steeps only a bird could find a foothold.

76 Egg Shackling

Today we met a friend who is headmaster at the school of the Sedgemoor village called Stoke St Gregory. Tomorrow will be Shrove Tuesday, so he asked if we would like to see the Egg Shackling ceremony that the children celebrate every Shrove Tuesday, keeping it up even after the institution of egg-rationing. I should like to watch the Egg Shackling, for so far I have only seen the photographs of it that appear in local newspapers. It isn't performed anywhere else, as far as I know, and nobody knows how it began. Every Shrove Tuesday morning each child brings to school an egg on which he has pencilled his name, and gives it to his schoolmaster who shakes or 'shackles' the eggs in a sieve over his head, removing every egg as it cracks. The owner of the last uncracked egg wins a prize of money and a victor's cap, and before the war the cracked eggs used to be made into pancakes.

77 A Ken Contest

A candidate for election to a School Board of Managers writes to his tailor in 1873:
Deer Sir,
We are in the midst of a ken contest for the election of a school board And I have 2 requests to ask from you 1st that you atend and give me your suport 2d that you allow me my new sute on that day.
I remain yours truly
P.S. Be sure and atend as I am afried I am to be beet.

78 Withies on the Levels

The longest life of a withy-bed is thirty years, the crop, which declines after the twelfth year, touching its peak round about the seventh when it may reach the figure of 250 bundles of withies per acre. When a new bed is to be made a summer fallowing after ploughing is generally regarded as an essential preparation of the ground, although seasons for ploughing, planting, and weeding, vary very much in different localities, according to land conditions, flooding and so on. Willow stocks selected for planting are called 'sets' and you need nearly 20,000 of them to plant one acre. The planting, the care of the withy-beds and their crop of slim swift-growing osiers, are skilled and specialized operations.

The beds need cleaning at least twice a year, for such intruders as gindweed —commonly called 'withywind'—are hostile to the growing shoots and must be weeded out, either by the hoe or a special weeding hook. In one district, where the withies are spaced more widely, the horse-hoe is employed. Weeding takes place in April or May, and in July, but many growers avoid one weeding by stocking their withy-beds in spring with sheep or bullocks. Remember it takes a man about a week to hoe one acre. Bullocks and sheep perform a two-fold task. As well as keeping down weeds they eat back the sappy young willow-shoots, so that a stronger growth is encouraged and the damage of a late May frost to the tender shoot is avoided. Frost is a major enemy of the young withy, for if its terminal bud dies the stock sends out lateral branches, and then the withy will not do for basket-making because it will be scarred and brittle at the rough spots where the lateral shoots sprang out.

Different varieties of withy possess fascinating and picturesque names— Black Mole, Champion Rod, Black Spaniard, Long Skein, Blue Violet, Red Bud or Dicky Meadows. Black Mole is easily the favourite of Somerset withy-growers, regarded as the best cropper and the willow least susceptible to rust.

Cutting of the withies takes place any time after the willow leaves fall, from November onwards, and should be finished by early March lest the withies use sap needed for nourishing the new shoots. The cutter uses a sickle-shaped hook and a skilled man cuts from thirty to forty bundles a day. Withies cut in autumn or winter are generally 'pitted' (and those that will go to the basket-maker classed as 'whites' must be)—that is, they are placed in pits that have a bed of stone or branches and contain several inches of water. If not removed from the pit before springtime, the vital young willow-rod is found valiantly putting out its buds and silver-furred catkins. The pit, which may hold hundreds of bundles, needs an annual cleaning. The rhines that drain the moorland withy-beds require dredging and banking. Do you begin to see the amount of labour represented by a wicker basket quite apart from the expert craftsmanship of the basket-maker himself?

On removal from the pits the withies go to a grower's yard for sorting, and on moors that get heavily flooded they are transported to the road by boat. They are sorted according to length and I have seen them placed in a tub sunken in the earth beside a measuring-stick. The sorter throws out rough and cankered rods. The rest he makes into bundles three foot two inches in girth, knocking the lower ends of the rods neatly into position with a kind of bat, tying each bundle with two bands, each made by skilfully twirling a slim green withy and looping the end. He can sort and tie about eighty bundles a day.

Imagine a huge horizontal boiler or tank, built out of doors on a brick pedestal, a red furnace glowing beneath, a strong cloyingly sweet smell issuing from the bubbling steaming liquid inside the boiler. Climb the steps and peer down to see dozens of withy bundles steeped in brown and boiling water, cooking energetically until organic substances in the bark dye the willow-rod a deep buff colour and the bark loosens for stripping. This process is called buffing, and can take place any time in the year. After several hours' boiling the buffed withies pass into a shed where, amid loud clangour and rattle, they are stripped in machines, a half-bundle at a time, by ruddy-cheeked and strong-armed country-women whose hands, holding the newly boiled rods, are dyed the colour of walnut-stain. They need to be strong, for the stripping machine almost drags the withy-bundle from one's grasp. The skin of the withy tightens again on cooling. Rods that cannot be stripped immediately after buffing—and the majority cannot be—must, on removal from the storage barn, soak a while, before stripping, in what the Somerset growers call 'lew water', using the real old Anglo-Saxon word for 'lukewarm'. Stripping the withies seems always to have been carried out by women, often at home, for machine-stripping is an innovation. By a hedge close to a great Dutch barn stacked with withy-bundles both green and buffed, where men measured rods and knelt to tie them up with pliant bands of willow, we saw the old-fashioned 'breaks', double pieces of steel in wooden frames through one of which a girl expertly dragged a withy-rod and peeled it of its wet brown bark. Till recently this was the only method in general use; indeed, for the unboiled withies called 'whites' that are liked for linen-baskets and food-baskets, it is still the favoured method for removing the brownish-grey skin that adheres tightly to the white body of the rod. Stripped withies are laid to dry in the sun'; they must not mildew.

79   Pocock of the Poldens

Between Cossington and Chilton Polden runs a stream with a Holy Well where pilgrims used to dip water for bathing sore eyes. At rural celebrations, like harvest suppers, old men of Chilton Polden used to sing a kind of 'Shiny Night' ditty, commemorating not a poacher but one of those rustic Robin Hoods who seem to have been fairly common in the eighteenth century. It went like this:

> Run, boys, run, the moon is shining bright.
> Pocock's in his cave and his purse is light.
> But when the night is murk and dark
> He's off with his steed, blithe as a lark.

Pocock was the local bandit who lived in a cave divided into three compartments, one for his horse from whom he never parted. Like Turpin's mount, this horse was shod with shoes that turned on a pivot so that its hoof-prints deceived the pursuers. (I have never discovered whether the making or wearing of such horseshoes was really feasible!) Pocock had a long and hair-raising career, robbing rich travellers along the Polden roads and giving generously to the poor. But after an informer betrayed his hiding-place he was dragged to the gallows.

80   The Sorrows of Nathan Porter

Much sympathy had been expressed with Nathan Porter of Spaxton, who had lost two cows. They died from 'fardebound', or retention of too much food. Funds were being raised to meet the owner's loss.

81   Admiral Blake

By 1652 the Somerset merchant found himself in supreme command and ready for a grand show-down with the Dutch whose effrontery at sea had culminated in a refusal to strike the Dutch flag to an English captain in English waters. A series of actions against the great Tromp ended in near disaster for Blake when Tromp, with eighty-seven ships to Blake's forty-five and employing every art of his grand seamanship, drove Blake in *Triumph* and his mauled fleet into the Thames for shelter. Overwhelmed by "the sense of my own insufficiency" Blake wrote to Cromwell asking to be relieved of command, a request not granted. A year later the Dutch fleet had been temporarily vanquished, Tromp killed, and the English navy armed itself with new vigour to meet the challenge of Spain.

    Then followed four years of battle and blockade, of enduring hardship and unrelenting pursuit until, one April morning, an English privateer reported that the galleons of the Spanish Plate fleet were anchored at Santa Cruz de Teneriffe. Joyfully twenty-three men-of-war, heeling under a freshening gale, swept westward out of Cadiz Bay, among them ships named after West Country towns, Plymouth, Bristol, Lyme, Langport, Bridgwater, Taunton. They found the galleons lying in the huge crescent-shaped roadstead protected by the guns of the castle and of forts built along the curving palm-green shore, lying broadside to the sea and secure in their refuge because the caprices of the wind might leave an enemy fleet becalmed. They masked the guns of the fort, though, and after calling his crews to prayer the Puritan seaman sent in his frigates under Stainer's command to lay themselves alongside the galleons, while he himself followed to engage the shore defences. During the first stage of the battle the galleons' position made the guns of the forts ineffective. One by one the Spanish ships blew up, sank, or were boarded in hand-to-hand combat, fired, or scuttled. Superb seamanship got the English ships out of the roadstead into the open sea, not a ship lost although Stainer's was riddled and had rigging shot away, sixty men killed, and a victory won that "startled the world more than any since Gustavus Adolphus". But it took all Blake's qualities of leadership to make his seamen leave their prizes behind them in the bay.

    England celebrated with a day of thanksgiving, but Blake did not live to receive her thanks, for the strain of warfare had broken his health and before the voyage he had made his will. His last desire was to die in his own West Country so the flagship *George* detached herself and bore up for

Plymouth, but Blake lived only long enough to sight the Lizard and on an August night summoned his captains for a farewell, reminding them that certain men must be promoted to the rank of midshipmen and that the crews blockading Cadiz must not be forgotten.

Newbolt wrote these lines about his last hours; Newbolt who lived a while at Aisholt, tiny Quantock village with reddest of ploughed fields, not far from the home of Blake's mother.

Only to look once more on the land of the memories of childhood,
Forgetting weary winds and barren foam,
Only to bid farewell to the combe and the orchard and the moorland,
And sleep at last among the fields of home.
Here lay the Sound and the Island with green leaves down beside the water,
The town, the Hoe, the masts with sunset fired,
Dreams! Ay, dreams of the dead! For the great heart faltered on the threshold,
And darkness took the land his soul desired.

They brought his embalmed body in full panoply by barge up the Thames for burial at Westminster. Charles II later had the bones flung into a common pit.

Blake shunned all publicity when alive and has been largely forgotten since his death. In his native town he got no memorial for about 250 years, but today his statue stands in the middle of Bridgwater, a massive figure in the dress of an officer of the New Model Army, stretching an arm seawards. The town he knew is changing rapidly. Its woollen-weaving industry perished with the advent of machinery, but the dark hand of the Industrial Revolution was not laid on the town. It drowsed for well over another 150 years in the midst of Somerset farmlands and sold their fat cattle in its market. But the twentieth century is industrializing it with amazing rapidity, and the market-town produces cellophane, bricks and tiles, carpets and electrical equipment.

Little boats still tie up in the docks. Dutch boats with names like *Vesta* and *Filja*, Scandinavian boats with wooden figure-heads, *Susie Oliver* bringing timber from Hull, Welsh boats bringing coals as in Defoe's day, *Somerset Crowpill* and *Sandholm* carrying sand dredged up off the coast at Brean, Irish boats like *James Postlethwaite* and *Agnes Craig*. Overlooking it all is a gilded cockerel, perched on one of the tallest spires in England, the spire crowning the red sandstone tower—both old when Blake was born—of St Mary's Church where Blake was baptized 350 years ago this autumn.

His naval career occupied only nine years.

82 The Properties of Bells

And here, though it may seem to some a trivial subject, to speak of the invention and first deviser of bells, yet considering the musical sound, and necessary use we have of them for clocks and convocating people to divine service, (which God commanded Moses should be done with silver trumpets,) I cannot think but they were first invented by Divine Inspiration: for when Christians began to multiply and disperse abroad in remote places, they could not easily be called together by the voice of man (as is now in use among the Turks), nor by sound of trumpet, but by a louder and fuller sound. And it is worthy observation that no law sect, or any professed religion, have any use of bells for service in their temples, but only Christians.

These are said to be first invented at Nola, by Paulinus, an excellent bishop there, of equal standing with St Augustine and St Jerome, between whom passed several letters yet extant: he was the first that used them in his church and bishoprick; and hence it may well be thought that bells in the Latin word are called Nola. Other properties ascribed to bells are somewhat strange, as resisting tempests, dividing thunders, extinguishing sudden fires, expelling devils and making them quake and tremble; which though by reasons and arguments strongly maintained, yet in regard it will require a large belief, I will speak no further.

83   Bells at Work

Before passing away from these ancients it may be interesting to note some of the work they did in years long gone by.

The Curfew was introduced by William the Conqueror from Normandy in 1068, and was abolished by Henry I in 1100. It sounded every night at 8 p.m., and then all fires and lights had to be extinguished. This may seem now to be a very hard law, but it was enacted with a view to preventing a conflagration at a time when houses were chiefly built of wood and other light material. It is curious how in many places the custom of ringing the Curfew has lingered on into our own day.

The Sanctus Bell was hung usually in a bell-cote between the chancel and the nave, and during the celebration of the mass three strokes were struck upon it by the priest or his server as the Sanctus (Holy, Holy, Holy) was sung. At the lesser altars of the church handbells would be used for this purpose. The Sanctus Bell is to be distinguished from the Sacring Bell which was sounded at the elevation of the Host.

The Passing Bell. Canon 67 ordered: 'When anyone is passing out of this life a bell shall be tolled, and the minister shall not then slack to do his duty. And after the party's death if it so fall out, then there shall be rung no more than one short peal, and one other before the burial, and one other after the burial.'

This explains the inscription so often found on old tenors:

> I to the Church the living call,
> And to the grave I summon all.

or—

> I sound to bid the sick repent,
> In hope of life when breath is spent.

At the present day the Passing Bell has sadly fallen from its high estate, and instead of rousing the parishioners to prayer for the passing soul and to thoughts of their own mortality, it is often not rung until hours after the death and calls forth no particular emotion from those who hear it.

The Passing Bell was also sometimes called the Soul Bell.

> Toll the bell a solemn toll,
> Slow and solemn let it be.
> Cry for the departing soul
> Miserere Domine.

The Angelus was a bell rung morning, noon and evening, every day, as a bidding to the people, to the sick in bed, and to the healthy, to those at home, and to those abroad, that they should, as the sound floated through the villages, the maiden in her cottage, and the labourer in the field, reverently kneel and recite the allotted prayers, in remembrance of Christ's incarnation for us, *viz*: 'Angelus Domini,' etc. (hence it was called the Angelus Bell), and 'Ave Maria,' etc (hence called also the Ave Bell).

The ringing of this bell morning and evening was ordered by the constitutions of 1347. The bell rung for the Angelus was usually dedicated to the archangel Gabriel; hence it was also sometimes called the Gabriel Bell; original Gabriel bells are still to be seen at Martock, Brompton Ralph, and (recast) at Preston near Yeovil.

The Pardon Bell. The Angelus was also sometimes called the Pardon Bell on account of the indulgences attached to the recitation of the allotted prayers.

The Sermon Bell. It was customary in old times, and the custom still obtains in some country places, to toll the tenor bell for a few minutes before service on Sunday when there was to be a sermon preached; hence the name.

The Induction Bell. When a new incumbent is inducted to a benefice by the archdeacon it is customary for him to toll a few strokes on one of the bells. Thus at once asserting his authority over the belfry, and at the same time announcing the fact of his induction to the parishioners. There is an old superstition that he will remain in the parish as many years as he strikes the bell.

Such are some of the religious purposes served by the bells of old; but they also entered in a hundred ways into the secular and business life of the people. Thus there was—

The Tocsin Bell. The expression is said to be derived from two old French words 'tocque—sing,' from 'toquer—to strike', and 'sing'—a little bell. It was usually a bell which was rung only in cases of danger or alarm, such as fire, the approach of an enemy, or the outbreak of a revolution. It was rung in a wild and hurried manner.

The Market Bell. This bell gave the signal for the commencement of the business of the market. Before it sounded no buying, selling or even bargaining might be done under heavy penalties. And very stern was the law against 'forestalling', i.e. buying or selling before the whole world was awake and ready.

The Mote Bell summoned the people to the popular assembly.

The Vestry Bell called the parishioners to the discharge of the parish business.

The Harvest Bell and Seedsowing Bell called the labourers to their various works.

The Gleaning Bell fixed the hours for beginning and leaving off gleaning in the harvest fields, ensuring a fair start and a fair chance to all alike.

The Pancake Bell, still rung at Ilminster on Shrove Tuesday, was originally a call to confession before the beginning of Lent.

The confession has been discontinued, and where the bell still rings it is associated with the pancake, which is the only thing which particularly distinguishes Shrove Tuesday now.

The following extract from Hone's *Everyday Book*, 1827, gives a graphic picture of the part bells played in the daily life of Sherborne, *c*. 1820:

At Sherborne they have an almost endless 'ding-dong', 'twing-twang', or 'bim-bone', throughout the day. Happening to be lately there on a market-day I was awakened in the morning, at four o'clock, by the ringing of the 'Church Treble Bell'; and at six o'clock the church 'chimes' were in play; at a quarter before seven the 'Almhouse Bell' began and continued until seven; which is said to be for the purpose of calling King Edward VI Grammar School to their studies, who were no sooner assembled than the 'School Bell' announced the master's approach. At half past eight the 'Almshouse Bell' summoned the almshouse and women to prayers; at nine 'the chimes'. At eleven the 'Wholesale Market Bell'; at twelve the 'Chimes'; at one the 'School Bell' for dinner; at half past one the 'Retail Market Bell'; at three the 'Chimes'; and the church 'Great Bell' tolled twice at a short interval; when, what is appositely called 'the tanging bell', rang until the minister and religiously inclined had assembled for prayer; at four the 'Almshouse Bell'; at six the 'Chimes'; at seven the 'School Bell' for supper; at eight the 'Church Bell' which rang a quarter of an hour, and concluded by giving eight strokes; at nine the 'Chimes', and the 'School Bell' for bed.

Sic transit. Almost every one of these old uses of the bells is passed away, and some are even forgotten, but still the bells, and in some cases the identical bells, remain, and in changed and changing circumstances they do their duty by us as they did by our forefathers.

84 Bisgay and All That

I knew it. I knew it. Never, it seems, can I use the word *bisgay* without a 'what is it?' letter arriving for me the following week. A London correspondent is flummoxed after seeing 'bisgay' in last week's Will Widden tale. Did the clumsy Taum Trimble break the handle of his father's basket? I am asked. No. He broke the handle of the bisgay—just as I said. This puzzlement over bisgay was known to my predecessor in *Notes By the Way*, and it surprised him, as it does me. For the bisgay, a rooting tool, has surely been one of our common garden implements for generations. When the teddies are well up, down between the rows you go with your bisgay to give the teddies a little embankment. Jennings, in his glossary of Somerset dialect, gives bisgay as 'bisgee', a rooting axe, but I would have thought the name was 'proper' enough to stand outside any dialect context—as plain as spade or hoe. I am not aware that it was a name we had coined in the West Country, though I remember seeing a reference somewhere to bisgay having derived from a French word. In any event it always attracts an inquiry. Again to my surprise, there are two other words— linhay (linney) and tallet, which always bring enquiries after they have been used. Yet both have been as common as bisgay.

85 Sermons in Stones

In a pleasing sequestered situation, on the eastern side of these eminences [the Quantocks] lies the ancient village of Stoke-Courcy, called by a barbarous corruption Stogursy. The first of these names is a Saxon appellative, signifying a village; but the agnomen was imposed by the noble Norman family of De Courcy, which in Stephen's reign became possessed of this place, and made it the head of their barony.

That this distinction conferred some consideration on Stoke-Courcy in the feudal times, there is no doubt; it being denominated in ancient records Burgum; and having once, in the reign of Edward III returned members to the national senate: but its importance is now extinguished— one long straggling street, with some intersecting lanes, mark the outline of its ancient population; and an old cross evinces that it formerly possessed, what it has long since lost, a regular market. From what multiplied sources, my friend, is instruction offered to us, if we will not proudly contemn it! Every object in nature affords to the thinking mind some moral hint;

> On every thorn delightful wisdom grows,
> In every rill a sweet instruction flows;

and all the works of art, whether flourishing, or sinking into ruin, appeal to the thoughtfulness of the soul, and rouse the slumbering powers of reflection. The revolutions and decay even of the little town now before us give energy to the moral principle, by teaching to pride a lesson of humility; by whispering to human conceit, that all the glory of man and his works "is but vanity and a lie."

86   The Broom-Squire

At the bottom of the wild and tangled combe called Five Lords [on the Quantocks] there runs a stony lane between hedges of hawthorn and bramble, and on one side of the lane a treble-voiced stream slips between ferns and rushes, flowing over the road after heavy rainfall. A home-made bridge of planks spans the stream at a bend in the lane, and two paces from the bridge a gate opens into the little domain of a broom-squire who is the last of his tribe in this part of England.

At the loud barking of his watch-dog, kennelled under a fuchsia that, like the hydrangeas, flowered profusely in this warm damp garden sheltered by the hills, the broom-squire came from the shed where he was still working at seven in the evening, jacket off, sleeves rolled up, wide straw hat pushed back on his head, a tall old man with the transparent skin of age, a native dignity in his bearing and unhurried speech. Yes, he made brooms, and had made them all his life, learning from his father and grandfather, although he himself had never found a pupil. In his younger days he had supplied the gardeners of several great houses and the ironmongers in half a dozen market-towns—his trade extending as far as Tiverton in Devon—loading his brooms in dozens on his pony-cart. Now he makes brooms, it seems, simply because he enjoys making brooms, and seeks no more customers than stray callers who, walking in the hills, come across the solitary yellow cottage dumped in haphazard fashion at the bottom of a combe.

I thought I would like to buy a broom for the garden. "I'll show 'ee some", said he, "but they'm dear nowadays, two shillings each." He went to his shed to get them and we sat down on a bench by the round, protruding bread-oven that seemed to buttress up the weather-stained wall of the cottage. When he returned he carried three brooms like those the witches ride on in children's fairy-books, and laid them on the uneven paving-stones of the garden path.

"I cuts all my stuff up in the hills,"—he jerked his head towards the steeply mounting wooded combe. " 'Tis all commons up there, always has been. I makes the broom handles of ash or oak—it don't really matter so long as I gets it smooth. In spring I cuts my birch twigs, You don't have to wait for the buds, you must cut before the sap rises. The heather I get just after it's flowered or just before. The heather broom is soft, it's for sweeping garden paths. The birch broom's for brushing leaves off the lawn. They'm two shillings each. I've made hundreds for sixpence."

"Sixpence!" We exclaimed in horror at such poor pay, but he replied that " 'twasn't such poor pay as all that when you could buy bacon at fourpence a pound and now a pound of bacon, if you could buy it, would still cost the price of a broom."

87 A Brendon Hill Story

About the turn of the century, two Brendon Hill workmen were returning home in the dusk after a long day's work on a barn that they were repairing.

With one horse between them, they were 'riding and tying' and they decided to take a short cut across the fields.

Will, who was then walking, reached a field gate where he found Tom dismounted and staring in dismay at the padlock on the gate.

"Us'll 'ave to turn back," said Tom. "Us can climb awver, but the 'orse can't get dru. Geät's locked."

"Zo 'tis," said Will, opening his knapsack and producing an axe. "Zo 'tis. But I've got a kay as'll fit 'un."

88 A Short Way with Prime Ministers

John Bellingham was a Britisher with a grievance. So he shot the Prime Minister dead. He was acting on the word of a civil servant, who had told him to take "whatever measures he thought fit"! History has not repeated itself since Bellingham's assassination of Premier Spencer Perceval in the lobby of the House of Commons in 1812. Grievances can normally be sorted out through the ballot box. In the House itself P.M.s must expect to be verbally assassinated many times—but they can always trust to their nine lives!

It was in an issue of the magazine *Weekend* some time ago that I saw a recap of this singular business of shooting a Prime Minister, and I pick it up for its thread of local interest. The Percevals, an ancient and landed family, became linked with Old Cleeve in the 19th century when Captain Ernest Perceval, youngest son among the eleven children of the murdered Prime Minister, rented Chapel Cleeve House and lived there until the 1860s. He presented Old Cleeve church with its pulpit. Only once, during my reporting years, had I to attend the funeral of a centenarian, and the occasion was rather significant, for the deceased was Miss Frederica Perceval, daughter of Captain Perceval. She had reached her 100th birthday while living in Clevedon, and had expressed a wish to be buried at Old Cleeve. That was in 1937. She was born at Chapel Cleeve and became a skilled artist and sculptress, deriving many of her inspirations from the local countryside.

As to the assassination of Miss Perceval's grandfather, the Rt. Hon. Spencer Perceval, the case was notable chiefly for the trial of John Bellingham —a trial described as an outrage upon justice. Bellingham was a Liverpool businessman who had gone bankrupt, and he had served a prison sentence for it. On a business trip to Russia he had been badly treated in St Petersburg, and it was said that the British Ambassador, Lord Leveson-Gower, had refused to help. In England, Bellingham found himself being passed from one Government department to another in his attempt to get redress; he became disillusioned and then demented, and when a civil servant finally told him to "take whatever measures he thought fit", he took a gun and waited for the Prime Minister. He also waited calmly for his captors, told them he knew what he had done, and that he had done it because the Government had denied him justice.

The law can move quickly when it chooses. Within a week of killing the Prime Minister, Bellingham had been committed, tried, condemned and executed—and his body taken in a cart from Newgate Prison to St Bartholomew's Hospital, where medical students dissected it. Lord Brougham, attacking the manner and speed of Bellingham's trial, declared it an outrage upon justice, and pointed out that an application to delay the trial until evidence of Bellingham's insanity could be brought from Liverpool was refused. British justice, rightly vaunted, is not normally seen in such a poor light, though one or two famous 20th century trials on the capital charge have left people with grave misgivings. Sir Roger Casement's is one; 19-year-old Derek William Bentley's another.

89   A Tiler in the Hills

What a pity Chaucer did not give us a Tiler and his apprentice, riding with a sack full of wooden stamps, another full of white clay and another of powdered glaze! Just such a medieval artisan came one day over the stone bridge spanning the Roadwater stream outside Cleeve Abbey. He travelled in summer and autumn until he found a monastery or church that needed tiles. In winter he dug his clay, weathered it, built a kiln and cut new stamps. In the spring, the frosts over, production started. The tile-maker stood at a trestle table which was sprinkled with sand. At his side he had a bowl of water in which a small stick floated. He rolled wet clay on the table and slapped it into a square mould, removing surplus clay with a bowstring and smoothing the surface with the wet stick. The soft slabs were stacked and dried in the wind. Later the design was 'impressed' by means of a wooden stamp. He filled the impressions with white clay, then glazed and fired the tiles. There were no varieties of colour, the design was white on a red ground, but chemical impurities in the glaze sometimes produced colour changes. As a rule the red turned a rich brown, the white became cream. In 1350 the tiles sold at about 5s. per thousand (£5 or so in modern money).

When the Tiler had satisfied the needs of a monastery he sold off his surplus tiles to anyone in the district. Churches in the neighbourhood of Cleeve Abbey seem to have snatched up job lots. Work finished, the Tiler went whistling on his way, leaving the pavement-layer or Paviour (whose name remains as a West Country surname) puzzling over his big jigsaw puzzle, for some tiles shrank and were hard to fit in.

Up in the Brendon Hills, a few stones show that at Leighland Chapel, a solitary monk from Cleeve used to say Mass every day for any passing wayfarer, or for himself, in the silence of the hills.

90 Sheep Tale

Some years ago, a visitor in Brendon land encountered a farmer who was docking his sheeps' tails.

"I don't think," she said, "that I have ever seen such woolly sheep."

"Aye, aye, missie," was the reply, "they'm 'ool from 'arn t'oof."

Fleeing from the encounter, she asked the next person she met who the 'foreigner' was at the farm up the road.

91 Crook, Crock, Handy-Maid and Brandis

Brendon farmhouses suggest permanence and almost primitive simplicity and they look as if they grew from Brendon soil. They are all built of grey stone—the old quarries are still visible in the hillsides, roots of trees embedded in their stones—and roofed with slate quarried near Treborough where a waterfall pours over black slatey rocks.

I know the kitchen in one of these farmhouses. Cool as a well on a hot day, with flagstoned floor and thick walls, and of such size you could drop a suburban semi-detached house comfortably inside, without counting the long scullery and adjoining brewhouse, now used only on wash-days, and ice-cold except when the copper-fire is going. High-backed oak settles keep back the draughts from the fireside, and to the unaccustomed eye the immense fireplace is the most compelling feature of the room. Graceful iron firedogs, made by a Wiveliscombe smith, support the logs of beech, for no coal is used in this house, and from a bar across the cavernous chimney hang the two serrated iron rods, hooked at the end, that are called crooks. A cauldron swings from one, the kettle from the other, and the second crook is called the 'handy-maid'. At one side of the hearth stands the three-legged witch's cauldron that they call a crock, and older Brendon women tell you how they used to bake cake or loaf in it by setting it over hot coals and piling smouldering coals on the lid. There are two huge iron trivets, also made by the smith, one oval, one triangular, and such a trivet is called a 'brandie' or 'brandis', the name presumably being derived from the word *brand* that means a burning piece of wood.

92   A Stogumber Bride

You will have read Jefferies' *A Manor House in Red Deer Land*? The Manor House at Stogumber, called Combe Sydenham, is the house Jefferies writes about, the house that had a knight's head carved over the door and its rooms full of the sound of summer woods. Here he saw the round stone object called 'Drake's cannon-ball', a meteorite that dropped at the feet of young Elizabeth Sydenham, wakening within her a terrified penitence for her fickleness so that she rushed home to Combe Sydenham, took off her bridal array, said farewell to the lover whom she was on her way to marry, and waited meekly for Drake the buccaneer to sail home and marry her—his second wife—in Stogumber church. George Sydenham, the Cavalier buried in this church, still rides down the combe after midnight, ghostly spurs jingling, the glint of moonlight on his breastplate.

93   Wireless Wonders

The British Broadcasting Company on Tuesday night opened a broadcast station at Cardiff with a range that will render its messages audible over a very wide area. The evening's programme was most clearly heard by Mr Willie Mace, who has installed a receiving set in the garden adjoining his father's residence at Sea View, Causeway Head, Watchet.

94   Free Trade

Towards the end of the seventeenth century smuggling had assumed such serious proportions on the shores of the Bristol Channel that Charles II sent his Surveyor-General of Customs, Culliforde, to make a tour of inquiry of the district in the year 1682. His report makes both amusing and interesting reading, and it seems that one of the chief 'industries' at this time was the 'running of goods', in which almost everyone, from the lord of the manor downwards, was involved. Culliforde stated that the results of 'free trading' in Watchet were such that "from being beggars within this ten years the whole town has grown exceeding rich and now have as great an overseas trade as Minehead". He also wrote, "At Watchet it was found that several small vessels had no other business but that of running goods, and that the collector of customs there usually sat drinking with the masters of ships while gangs of men were unloading them."

95   Watchet in Decline

My road ran immediately through Watchet, otherwise I would have avoided a miserable stinking place, which, like a withered beauty, has only now to boast that it once was handsome.

Commodiously situated on the shore of the Bristol Channel, Watchet formerly enjoyed an extensive trade and a large herring-fishery; but the former (for you know she is a capricious lady) has flown to other ports, and the fish (equally whimsical) have left the shore. Its population is in consequence decreased, and its riches are melted away. A few small ships are indeed still employed in freighting kelp and limestone; but they do injustice to its pier which is large and convenient, and capable of sheltering a great number of vessels. This was first constructed in the reign of Elizabeth, but has been added to at different times, and is at present supported by a duty payed on the importation of all goods at its wharfs. The coast in the neighbourhood affords excellent limestone, which burns into a lime of the most tenacious and adamantine texture. The cement made use of in constructing the Eddystone Lighthouse, that wonder of modern masonry, was composed of the Watchet limestone; and its resisting hardness has been hitherto found unconquerable by the fury of the elements, the convulsions of the tempest, and the madness of the ocean.

96   Woodwall and Unswitch

As promised last week, I have, thanks to readers' interest, a little more to say on the hornet and beetle poem. We can now definitely identify the gobbler. See a green woodpecker, see a 'yuckel'. Had we gone in the first place, as did Mr M. J. Williams, of Wellington, to F. T. Elworthy's *West Somerset Word Book*, we should have found the green woodpecker, or 'woodwall', named as 'yuckel'. And who would argue with the man who earned the title of 'The Somerset Word-Master'? We can now leave the yuckel to his meal, save that Mr Williams asks if this ant-loving bird would really polish off a hornet. That's one for the ornithologists. Another reader 'on' to the yuckel was Miss J. K. Crocker, of Alcombe, who further states that 'yuckel' is the sound the bird makes. In this, Miss Crocker is supported by Mr Williams.

We shall now suppose that the hornet in the hollow tree is still singing 'nation fine', and that the yuckel has not yet arrived. I raised an eyebrow rather needlessly over 'nation', and several readers have been through to me. The hornet, of course, was singing 'damnation fine', as Mr J. Diston, of Elgin Tower, Minehead, points out, remarking on 'nation' as the short euphemism for damnation or 'tarnation' (which itself stands for eternal damnation). And Mr S. Vaulter, of Milverton, recalls an old character, George Bowden, known from Raleigh's Cross to the Barle Valley, who was fond of saying 'nation seized'.

Having got 'nation' and 'yuckel' out of the way, what should crop up (in Mr Diston's letter) but an 'unswitch'. An old Cornishman told him that in his youth he had once fired a gun (blunderbuss was the word he used) through his mother's cottage door at "a girt ol' unswitch" in a tree opposite. He missed, but took the lintel off the doorway, and the shock of the discharge brought down his mother's china cabinet! When Mr Diston asked the man what an unswitch was, he said, not very helpfully: "I'll tell ee. He's a bird and he's not very big and he's not very small. Thass wot he is." Mr Diston discovered later that it was a misselthrush.

97   The Pretty Old Fellow

At Carhampton a fortnight ago (on Old Twelfth Night), they celebrated one of the most ancient country rituals, the wassailing of the apple-trees. Lights twinkled from the dark and leafless orchards, the wind that stirred the creaking branches carried the sound of the men's voices to the village street as the wassailers trooped over the wet grass and disturbed the cropping sheep. In every orchard they surrounded the most ancient tree and fired their sporting guns into the old bare branches so that evil spirits might be scared away. They sent the youngest of their party up into the fork of the tree where he fixed a piece of cake that had been dipped in cider, then they emptied a bucketful of cider around the roots, a libation poured for the tree-spirit so that he may be pleased to grant a liberal crop of fruit next autumn. Afterwards the wassailers joined hands about the tree and sang the traditional Apple-wassail song:

> Old Apple Tree, Old Apple Tree,
> We be come to wassail thee,
> To bear and to bow
> Apples enow.
> Hats full! Caps full! Three bushel bags full!
> Barns full!
> Apples and pears—
> And a little heap, under the stairs,
> Hurray!

Here is another song sometimes sung at the wassailing:

> Wassail, wassail, in our town,
> The cup is white but the ale is brown,
> The jug is made of the best of clay.
> Come pretty old fellow and I will drink to thee.

Whichever song they choose as their serenade to the "pretty old fellow", they conclude with ringing cheers and a tossing-up of hats before going back to the village to drink cider. If the night is very cold, they put ginger in their drink.

98   Casks and Cider

Casks take up much more space upon a floor, when they are lying on their sides than when standing up on end. If a cask is full, both ends will be wet, when it is lying down; but, when a cask is standing up, the top end will be dry, and then will shrink and let the air in. (The ends are not as air-tight as the sides, as the cooper takes an end out when he scrapes a cask inside.) A little air soon spoils a cask of cider; and some of the big cider-growers have thought it worth their while to reconstruct their cellars and provide the extra space for casks to lie down on their sides instead of standing up. They might have saved all this by doing a very simple thing that I do here. When a cask is standing up, there is a shallow pan on top formed by the top end of the cask and the surrounding chine. Keep this pan filled with water, and that will keep the top end wet, so that it does not shrink and let the air in.

99   Arnie Knows the Way

"Can you tell me," said the motorist to Arnie Bladderwick, "if this is the right way to get to Blackworthy Barton farmhouse?" "Ees, zur," says Arnie. "Jis' kip gwain straight vore the way thee'rt gwain, an' whan thees git to a plaace where thee cass'n git no vurder, thaas the plaace thee'rt lookin' vur."

100   Dunster Castle

The recess of the tide allowed me to keep the sands from hence to Minehead, a distance of six miles; the Channel spreading to the right, and an undulating line of hills rising to the left. On the brow of one of these eminences, the proud turrets of Dunster Castle, the seat of John Fownes Luttrell, esq., shoot up from a venerable wood, and produce a beautiful variety in the majestick gloom of the deep mass of shade which surrounds them. From the point where it first became an object in the picture, the castle appeared to stand on the side of a hill, with a large proportion of its wooded declivity rising behind the building. I soon found, however, that this was but a *deceptio visus*; for on approaching the place, the higher ground receded from its neighbour, and I perceived that the castle had chosen a spot worthy of its dignity, the broad summit of an isolated hill. The sheltered situation, indeed, which, from afar, it appeared to have assumed, though every way congenial to modern ideas of comfort as well as beauty, would have been but ill-calculated for the unsettled period of the Saxon heptarchy, when it was originally constructed; or for the rude times of feudal insolence, when its walls were to ensure impunity to rapine and violence. The Baron of old, knowing that he was surrounded with robbers like himself, would not, unwarily, plant his retreat in a spot commanded by adjoining eminences: the bold brow of the precipitous cliff, or the lofty summit of the solitary hill, could alone afford him security in that state of desultory warfare, in which his own inordinances, sanctioned by the practices of the feudal ages, perpetually kept him; and these were the fastnesses which he pitched upon for his residence. Dunster Castle, in conformity to this principle, is situated on a spot favourable to resistence—a steep eminence at the southern extremity of the town, overlooking a great extent of country, and commanding an uninterrupted view of the Bristol Channel and the coast of Wales.

101   Alas, Poor Minehead!

But like Watchet, Minehead can now only refer to its quondam importance; for though the pride of extinguished greatness be sufficiently visible here, yet the extensive commerce and proportionate affluence, which, in times of yore, inspired this inflation, and gave it some sort of consistency, have long since become the 'mere shadows of a shade'.

The Middle Town, in which my comfortable caravanserai stands, the Plume of Feathers, kept by the worthy Mr Mansfield, runs along the declivity of an hill, somewhat more than a quarter of a mile from the Quay-Town, and has the conveniences of a post-office, shops, and lodging-houses. The Upper-Town drops down the eastern slope of a lofty eminence, called Greenaleigh, and has nothing to recommend its shabby irregular lanes, but the extensive prospect necessarily given to it by its elevation.

But though Minehead has long since deplored the loss of its extensive trade, some appearance of cheerfulness and animation has been given it, till within these few years, by the company which resorted thither in the summer season for the purpose of bathing. What should have occasioned the desertion of those who sought health or pleasure on its shores, is not easily to be accounted for; since it seems to unite all the advantages, without the usual concomitant inconveniences of a bathing-place. The shore is hard and fine; the machines commodious; the lodgings reasonable; provisions cheap and plenty; and though its access be rendered easy by an excellent turnpike-road, which runs to Bristol, yet its distance from the metropolis, and the populous parts of England, is sufficiently great to prevent those felicity hunters, the teasing insects of fashion, from disturbing with their impertinent buzzings the pensive or rational pleasures of them who choose to enjoy Nature at Minehead, during the summer season. To these inducements may be added the salubrity of its climate, which, like that of Cythera, is so soft and serene, that the myrtle-tree will live in the neighbourhood of this place, uninjured through all the roughness of an English winter.

102 A Murex from the Severn Sea

A species of *patellæ*, too, is very common on the rocks of Minehead, a good substitute for the famous murex of antiquity, that produced the invaluable Tyrian dye, with which the ancients stained their wool.

A small vein running over the head of the fish contains this precious liquor, with which if linen be stained, and the characters exposed to different degrees of the light of the sun, they will change their hue, and become successively (from a dull white) pea-green, deep green, blue and purple; the linen being then washed in scalding water, the marks upon it will blaze out into a splendid crimson colour, which no future washing can obliterate.

103 Finding the Way

To unravel the intricacies of the West Somerset and North Devon cross-roads required more sagacity, as well as patient research, than fall to the lot of most men; the traveller, therefore, who is not gifted with a large share of these qualities, will probably, in attempting to thread their mazes, at least double the actual distance between his stages. This, at least, has been my case; and notwithstanding the particular directions which the good people of this country, civil even to servility, afforded me, I have formed such a zig-zag line of march for these three days past, as, if measured, would certainly extend to sixty miles instead of forty, the real distance.

I will not deny, however, that I have been amply repaid for all these deviations from the right road, since many scenes of grandeur and beauty have discovered themselves to me in consequence, which I should otherwise have lost. The country, more varied and majestick every step, has regaled me with hills lofty and bold, vales deep and rich; whilst the coast has been equally entertaining in another way, disclosing, ever and anon, a tremendous scene of dark romantick rocks, fretted below into caverns by an unruly ocean, and their proud heads torn and scarred by the tempests of heaven.

104 *Porlock-Fashion*

A long descent introduced me into the little sea-port town of Porlock, situated about six miles to the westward of Minehead, shut out from the surrounding country by lofty hills, but open towards the sea, on which it safely looks, from the bottom of a recess or bay, about one league from one extremity to another. Of these points the eastern one rises with prodigious magnificence from the ocean, whose maddened waves have torn its front into misshapen crags, and scooped its sides into stupendous caverns; the western extremity is of a softer character, and slopes gradually to the shore, sheltering, from the prevalent south-westerly storms, the quay and a small pier (one mile and a half from Porlock), where the little commerce of the place is transacted, and its fleet (consisting of two sloops, which trade to Bristol and Wales) is freighted and unladen. An odd effect is produced by the very unusual style of architecture, in which the houses are, for the most part, built; for here, as in other small country places distant from the seat of the arts, one model is generally followed in constructing the dwellings of their inhabitants. At Porlock they rise to the height of two stories, and are mostly thatched; but the fashion of that place has determined, that the chimneys, instead of preserving their usual retired situation, should be formed in the front of the houses, and their backs project into the street.

105 *Somerset Sunday*

A village-church on a Sunday I have always considered as a very impressive sight. I remained, therefore, at Porlock till the afternoon of yesterday, in order to partake in the social worship of the place. The simplicity of the service, the neat and cheerful appearance of the congregation, decked in their gayest attire to celebrate this 'rest of the Lord', when poverty relaxes from his labour, and industry is still, the attention and seriousness of the worshippers, all combined to form a scene in the highest degree interesting. This pleasing effect was greatly assisted by the manner in which the Rev Mr — performed the sacred offices of the day. No misplaced attempt at fine acting or fine speaking led the congregation to think that his thoughts were more employed about himself than the service of the church; but an energy and a solemnity marked his delivery, which, as they evinced that the speaker's own heart was affected by the truths he uttered, did not fail to produce a similar impression upon the hearts of his hearers. Indeed, here was no inducement to resort to stage-trick, or oratorical affectation; since Mr — and his audience stood much in the same relation to each other as Hamlet with Horatio:

> Nay, do not think I flatter;
> For what advancement may I hope from thee,
> That no revenue hast, but thy good spirits,
> To feed and cloath thee?

No patronage was to be obtained, no interest was to be acquired, for Mr —, like his great Master, preached the Gospel to the poor.

106   A Draught of Milk

After continuing five or six miles on these hills, with a noble view of the sea and the coast of Wales (which now began to fade away in distance) always before us, we turned our steps towards the coast, and descended a rapid steep to Culbone. On our way, about a mile from the hamlet, excessive thirst obliged me to enquire at an old stone cottage, about which I saw some cows, for a draught of milk. A squalid female figure, opening the door, informed me there was no such thing at the parsonage, but that a farm-house, about a quarter of a mile further, would supply me with a bowl of this beverage. The cordwainer [my guide] seeing me surprised at the term parsonage-house being applied to this wretched hovel, told me, with that sort of smile which superior information sometimes assumes, that this was the rectorial mansion, where the incumbent of Culbone formerly resided; adding, he had no doubt, miserable as it now was, that when it had a parson for its tenant, there was no lack of all the good things which could be stowed away in it.

107   A Lilliputian Church

In the centre of the little recess, thus surrounded and defended from the intrusion of the stranger, stands the Lilliputian church of Culbone, a Gothick structure, thirty-three feet in length and twelve feet in breadth, with a cemetery of proportionate dimensions stretching round it, appropriately ornamented with broken modest grave-stones, and the remains of an ancient stone-cross. Two cottages, planted just without the consecrated ground, are its only companions in this secluded dell.

Sure never was a spot better calculated for the indulgence of the meditative faculty than Culbone church-yard. Every circumstance around leads the mind to thought, and soothes the bosom to tranquillity. The deep murmur of the ocean tide rising from beneath, but softened in its lengthened course, falls gently on the ear, which lists with equal rapture to the broken mysterious whisper of the waving woods above. Here, whilst all without is wasteful war and raging horror, the thoughtful wanderer, as he treads the glen, will please himself with the conviction, that he has at least found one little spot, sacred to PEACE.

108   Culbone Revels

Quiet and sequestered as this romantic spot at present is, it has heretofore borne an honourable name in the annals of rustic revelry; its rocks have echoed to the shouts of multitudinous mirth, and its woods rung with the symphonious music of all the neighbouring village bands; in plain English, a revel or fair was wont to be held here in times of yore. I fortunately met with a garrulous old blacksmith, who had himself made a great figure on these festive occasions. He had been the Entellus of the place, and dwelt with great exultation on his many triumphs which the church-yard of Culbone had witnessed.

"About forty-five years agone, Sir," said he, "I was at a noble revel in this spot; three hundred people at least were collected together, and rare fun, to be sure, was going forward. A little warmed with dancing, and somewhat flustered with ale (for certainly Dame Matthews did sell stinging good stuff) I determined to have a touch at skittles, and sport away a sixpence or shilling, which I could do without much danger, as I had a golden half-guinea in my pocket. To play, therefore, I went, but the liquor getting into my head, I could not throw the bowl straight, and quickly lost the game, and two shillings and ninepence to boot. Not liking to get rid of so much money in so foolish a manner, and not thinking the fault was in myself (for too much ale, you know, Sir, is apt to make one over-wise) I resolved to win back the two and ninepence, and then leave off; and accordingly set to play a second time. The same ill-luck followed me, and in an hour and half I had not only lost the remainder of my money, but about sixteen shillings more out of a guinea which I borrowed of a friend. This terrible stroke quite sobered me; my wife was but just brought to bed, and I could not help thinking what a wicked scoundrel I must be, to go and run into ruin, and to deprive her and the child of food, merely to indulge myself in a game, which, instead of being an amusement, had put me into a terrible passion, and made me curse and swear more than ever I did in my life. Desperately vexed at my folly, I went into the wood hard by, and sat down by the side of the water-fall to reflect on my situation. I could plainly hear the singing and laughing of the revel, but it was now gall and wormwood to me; and I had almost resolved to escape from that, my own reproaches, and the distress

Clovelly—from the pier

Her swutelað on ðisse bec hwæt Leofric b. hæfð
ge don into sce petres mynstre on exancestre
þær his bisceop stol is þi is þe he hæfð ge innod þæm ge
incod þær þurh godes fultu. 7 þurh his pope sprece. 7 þurh
his gærsuma. þis ærost þland æt culmstoke. 7 þland
æt brancerscumbe. 7 æt sealtcumbe. 7 þland æt sce mariam
cyrcra. 7 þland æt storowotune. 7 æt sprancan wille. 7 þ
land æt moneterhille. 7 sretwulla hiwisc. 7 þland æt
byhterwices stant. 7 þland æt stoke. 7 þland æt storbirig.
7 þland æt nipan tune. 7 æt norðotune. Donne is his
se raca on landu þe he hæfð of his agenu þ minstre
inio ge todod for his hlaforda saplu. 7 for his agenre
þam godes ðeowu to biglcofan þe for heora saplum
þingian sceolon. þis ærost þland æt bem tune. 7 æt
iste tune. 7 æt ecommenige. 7 þland æt doflisc. 7 æt hola
cumbe. 7 æt suþ wuda. 7 þenexundt þa he to ðam minstre
feng nan manre landes þe ðiorn inn ge wilde pære
þonne ii. hida landes æt ror. 7 þær on næf onrkynnes
nan manre buton vi. hiwiderin Donne is sto on cnapen
ms þe he hæfð god mid ge cnapen 7 scm petru in to
þæ halgan mynstre on cyrclicu maðmum þ is þ he
hæfð þiorn inn ge don. ii. b. woda. 7 ii. mycele ge
bonite woda butan oðru litlu silwrenu sprs woðu.

of my wife, by throwing myself down the cliff upon the shore. Providence, however, was so good as to preserve me from this additional wickedness, and to put a thought into my head, which saved me from the consequences of despair. Cool and sober, for I had washed myself in the stream, and drank pretty largely of it, it struck me, that if I went back to the skittle-ground, and ventured the remaining five shillings, I should have a good chance of winning back my money from those who had beaten me before, as I was now fresh, and they all overcome with ale. Accordingly I returned to the church-yard, and took up the bowl, though pretty much jeered by the lads that had hitherto been winners. The case, however, was altered; I had now the advantage, could throw the bowl straight, took every time a good aim, and more than once knocked down all nine. To make short of my story, Sir, it was only night that put an end to my good-luck; and when I left off play, I found I had got back my own half-guinea, the guinea I had borrowed, and fifteen shillings in good silver, after paying my part of the charge for the day. You may suppose I was not a little happy at this change of fortune; in truth, Sir, I felt very grateful, and as soon as I had left my companions, fell down on my knees to thank GOD for saving me from ruin, and did not rise till I had made a solemn vow that I would never venture another sixpence in gambling again; a vow which I have for these five and forty years most religiously observed, and which I have found so much pleasure in keeping, that there is no chance I shall ever wish to break it."

I listened to the old gentleman's story, fraught with the wisdom of experience, with due attention; thinking, at the same time, that if the more exalted gamblers would imitate the wisdom and the virtue of this honest blacksmith, high-life, as it is called, would exhibit much fewer scenes of wretchedness and vice than it at present displays.

109 Simple Hinds

Early in the morning of the 7th I left Minehead, intending to reach Lynton, a village about twenty-five miles from that town, on the same evening. A deep shady road led me through Selworthy, and several other small hamlets, sequestered and picturesque in the highest degree. The inhabitants of these places, quiet in their manners, and ready in their offers of service, seemed to be formed for the peaceful retreats which they occupied. Far removed from the seats of refinement, as it is called, which is too frequently only an elegant modification of vice, the hinds pass their time, at least in honest simplicity; and having no artificial wants to supply, exhibit such an appearance of contentment, as gives them, in the eye of sober reason, a manifest advantage, when placed in comparison with the more refined classes of society.

110   Mineral Wealth

The mines of this country [Devonshire] have been also very profitable, which I the rather remember, for that they are not found generally in every country, and will therefore require a more particular description; most especially in regard of the species of them, as gold (in small quantity and little grains), silver, copper, tin, lead, iron, and the loadstone, with other minerals: all which have been (and some also are now) very commodious to our Sovereign, and the owners and workers of them.

111   Lanificium

Lanificium, the skill and knowledge of making cloth, is another most beneficial manufacture practised in this country [Devonshire], under which genus are contained the species of spinning, knitting, weaving, tucking, pressing, dying, carding, combing, and such like. This art, or hand-work, is laudable for antiquity, and needful for necessity in supplying our wants, with apparel to keep warm our weak bodies in extremity of weather, and cover decently our nakedness lest we should offend God, and be like beastly savages, or savage beasts. And this province, for quantity, quality, and variety (in these three kinds, I am confident to say), may compare with, if not exceed, most countries.

112   The Qualities of the Natives

This county [of Devon] as it is populous, so are the natives of a good and healthy constitution of body; of proportion and stature generally tall, strong, and well compact; active and apt for any forcible exercises (and if I may have leave to borrow a stranger's words in their encomium); bold, martial, haughty of heart, prodigal of life, constant in affections, courteous to strangers, yet greedy of glory and honour. And Diodorus Siculus saith the Danmonii were accounted most civil and courteous people.

   And our pleasant witted poet, Michael, extolleth them extraordinarily for valour and strength of body; and yet taketh not therein the liberty allowed to poets, to add to the subject whereof they write, but truly reporteth what is well known and seen by them performed; who in activity surmount many other people, especially at football, hurling, and wrestling, wherein they are generally equal with the best in any county. And I may boldly say of my countrymen as Horace did of his,

... In wrestling we
The skilful Greeks surpass in high degree.

A full report of their skill in wrestling and nimbleness of body whereof the Danmonii have been and still are so famous you may find in the Survey of Cornwall. But to make a question (as one hath done) whether they have it from their first planter, Corineus (that famous wrestler) or from the nature of the climate of the country, or (as I may best say) from their diurnal practice, I think it will not be answered without some difficulty, unless you say from all.

In knowledge of arts and variety of studies in all sciences and learning, very capable and ingenious; and hath yielded, and presently doth (whom in their convenient places I shall have fitter opportunity to remember), as many worthy divines, civilians, physicians, and men excellent in all other professions and arts as are elsewhere in any so small a compass to be found.

In matters of civil policy, causes of justice, judicature, and government of the common weal, wise, pregnant, and politic, discreet, and of sound judgment and integrity; so that the chief seats of justice have been very often most worthily supplied: which this our age can very sufficiently testify, as well as many former.

For martial affairs, by land or sea, forward and valiant; and, as a great and noble commander of late times said of one (intimating, as it seemed, the like in general), in service, painful; in peril, resolute; in action, industrious; in execution, quick and ready; in council, provident; fierce, yet with judgment: as their fierceness was nothing abated by advisement, nor their advisement dazzled by their fierceness, but both so equally compounded and conjoined, that they have been bold to take QUID NON? for a motto, (as Sir Humphrey Gilbert).

113 Dizzy Heights

The small church of Countisbury, perched upon a hill in solitary exposure, on my right, indicated that I was about three miles from Lynmouth, and here my guide of the preceding day had informed me I was to expect "a nation strange road". In truth, he had not excited my curiosity in vain, for perhaps this public way may be considered as one of the greatest wonders of North Devonshire. Narrow, rugged, and uneven, it creeps along the face of a prodigious rocky down, that runs with a most rapid descent to the ocean, which is roaring below, at the depth of five or six hundred feet. Formidable as the precipice is, the neighbouring inhabitants have not so much as erected a low wall, or stretched a friendly rail along its brink, to lend their aid in case of accident or darkness; so that should the traveller's horse become restive whilst treading this perilous path, or he himself mistake the way, nothing could probably prevent his immediate destruction. But this road, so alarming to the stranger, is totally divested of anything like horror to the Devonian. Custom, which reconciles all that is fearful or disagreeable, painful or terrible to the mind, enables him to travel it with perfect indifference; and whilst I was descending the most abrupt part with the greatest caution, a Devonshire peasant, seated upon a laden horse, and driving three others before him, passed by me down the declivity at the rate of a dashing postillion upon a good turnpike road.

Following this path to the bottom of the steep, I suddenly found myself in a village truly romantic; the little sea-port of Lynmouth crouching at the feet of august rocky hills which beetle over it in every direction, except where the bottom in which it stands unites with the shore. Unlike the usual formal arrangement of habitations in towns and villages, the houses here are not thrown together into regular groupes, or stretched out into rectilinear rows, but sprinkled over the little flat, as if dropped by the hand of chance, and concealed from each other by an abundance of shrubby trees, and high hedgerows. Two Alpine brooks, flashing over their craggy beds, rush from deep ravines that open upon the village to the east and south, and throw their waters under two small stone bridges, which, almost hidden in ivy, form happy and appropriate features in this very picturesque scene. A port, in epitome, lies at a small distance from the village, where the Lynmouth oysters, which here sell for two shillings per hundred, are shipped for other places, and necessaries from Bristol imported for the consumption of the place and its neighbourhood.

114   Jesus Christ of Venus

Fifteen years after what they believe was the arrival of Jesus Christ in his space ship on the top of a North Devon Hill, 200 pilgrims flocked to the shrine on Saturday....

Dr King was the only witness of Christ's arrival at Holdstone Down in July, 1958, but the society claims that several Combe Martin residents saw his space ship, and Dr King himself still has a clear idea of the appearance of Christ.

Dr King's Press officer described this yesterday. "He was dressed in a normal one-piece space suit, was more than 6ft tall, clean shaven and had shoulder-length hair.

"Dr King's special powers were given him by Christ, who charged Holdstone Hill with energy, using him as a medium," he said....

The Aetherius Society believe that Christ is a native of Venus and is still trying to solve the problems of the world. Members pay an annual subscription of £3·15.

115   A Rare Jewel

In this parish [Berrynarbor] we may not pass Bowdon; for if rare and admirable qualities of our ancestors do merit a grateful acknowledgment of posterity, then ought we most respectively to do the like to the singular natural endowments and supernatural graces of a most reverend prelate here born, that he may live and flourish in perpetual remembrance; by whom (as an especial means) the sincere religion we now profess received much vigour and strength in its new spring: John Jewel, Bishop of Salisbury, a perfect rich gem and true jewel indeed: for if I may allude to the name, there is one that saith, "the price, prosperity, and happiness of Aurelius Augustinus' labours and works; the industrious vigilance of Gregory; the heavenly gifts of Theodosius; the divine spirit of Ambrose; the golden mouth of Chrysostom; the sweet vein of Lactantius; the shining style of Fulgentius, are very conspicuous in their names:" so that if any where the observation of Chrysostom be true, that there lies a great hidden treasure in names, surely it may rightly be said to be here; grace in John and eminent perfection in Jewel. His life is already written in large volumes, and the light of my dim candle might be spared in such a fair sunshine, yet blame me not (intending to illustrate this province), to take this fit opportunity to enrich my barren discourse with an ornament of such value.

116 Wraxling

John Prowse, who had now taken me under his protection, was a good specimen of the North Devon peasant; lively and intelligent, stout and muscular, nearly six feet high, and with shoulders that would not have disgraced Hercules. Besides this, he was upright as a dart, a grace he had acquired by having been some time in Colonel Orchard's volunteer fencibles. As men are usually most attached to that art, pursuit, or employment in which they most excel, so John's ruling passion pointed towards wrestling, or as he called it, in the dialect of the country, wraxling; which he confessed to me he loved better than victuals or drink. Living near the confines of Cornwall, he burned with all the emulation of a borderer, and observed triumphantly, that the Devonians were at last confessed to be better men than their neighbours; for in a great wrestling-match, held at a Cornish town in the vicinity, a short time since, every Devonshire lad had thrown his Cornish antagonist, without receiving a single fall himself. He asserted it was the prettiest play he had ever seen; and on my asking him whether any accidents had occurred in the course of these amusements, he answered, nothing to speak of, only three ribs broken, and a shoulder dislocated! He would fain have tried a fall with me, whose skill, as an east-country-man, he wished much to experience; and I could perceive he did not hear me declare myself totally ignorant of the wrestling art, without some emotion of contempt.

117   Rosinante in Distress

It should seem that the Northern Devonians were not very anxious after the company of strangers, for they certainly take the best possible means of preventing them from visiting this part of England, by the execrable state in which they keep their turnpike-roads. Instead of making use of the advantages afforded them by their soil, and breaking the stone into small nodules, which, pressed together by the weight of horses and carriages, would form adamantine and impenetrable roads, they carelessly sprinkle these public ways with masses of stone larger than a man's head, and leave them to time and chance to be broken and scattered, to the great danger of the horseman, and the discomfort of him who is in a carriage. To me, indeed, an humble pedestrian, this produced small inconvenience; I had picked up a companion, however, who suffered somewhat more from it—a little pony, about eleven hands high, to carry my baggage; which, what with specimens and purchases, had increased to an inconvenient size. To this Lilliputian Rosinante the large stones and deep hollows, rendered still more dangerous by the wet which had fallen, produced most disastrous consequences; for he was, more than once, together with his burthen, prostrate in the mire.

118   A Very Superior Race

The peasantry of North Devon, as I have discovered for these two or three days past, are a very superior race to the labouring poor of the more eastern parts of the kingdom. Imbibing from the pure air of their native mountains mental vigour as well as corporal strength, they exhibit a sagacity and quickness which only require culture, to produce characters shining and energetic. The same faculties are observable in their children, who are not only ready in apprehending what is said to them but as quick in returning rational answers to questions asked. Instead of shrinking from the presence of the traveller, or looking scared and sheepish if he happen to address them, the young Danmonii generally are foremost in the conversation, with an "How d'ye do, Sir", "Your servant, Sir", or some such little colloquial civility. I confess I have been delighted with the respectful freedom of these little villagers; it becomes the sons of those who breathe the air of liberty, and indicates they have imbibed their manners from freemen, from men who feel their own weight in the scale of society, but who are at the same time as much aware of their duties as of their rights.

119   The Wind in his Face

Joining to the sea-shore is Mort, or Mort-hoe, remarkable for being the seat

of Sir William Tracy, knight, and the place where for a while he rested in
ease; until some ill-affected persons seeking for treasure, but disappointed
thereof, stole the leaden sheets he lay in, leaving him in danger to take
cold. This was the man that, accompanied with Sir Reynold Fitzurse, alias
Bearson, Baron of Braynes; Sir Hugh Morvill, alias Mortivile; and Sir
Richard Bryton, were the four knights who, hearing their lord and master,
King Henry II, complain of the unsufferable wrongs and affronts given him
by Thomas Becket (whom from mean degree he had advanced to be Lord
Chancellor of England, and afterwards to be Archbishop of Canterbury);
and yet no man revenged him of this insulting traitor, they came presently
for England, and on 29th December 1170, killed the said archbishop in
Canterbury church; for which fact they fled into divers remote places; and
this knight came into this place and here lived and his posterity; the Pope
banning, cursing, and excommunicating, then so formidable and powerful,
that it made the wind to blow always in his face; whereby grew a common
proverb in this tract to those who had adverse fortune or ill chances—thou
art like Sir William Tracy, wind and weather is always against thee.

120 Manurances

This soil, as is formerly said, being hilly and mountainous, cannot be by
nature fruitful (the meadows and marsh feedings only excepted), but
requireth and expecteth some help by the labours and manurance of the
husbandman; who spareth no cost, refuseth no pains, leaveth nothing
untried whereby he may, in any sort, enrich his land and make it more
bearable, profitable, and fruitful: and therefore, according to the nature of
the soil where he inhabiteth, accommodateth his manurance, which is very
diverse and of sundry sorts.

Those that are near neighbours to the sea, on either side, gather a certain
weed growing on the rocks, which they name oare, spreading it on the earth,
whereby it yields a rich crop.

Others, at low water, gather the sea-sand that by some storm or violent
tide is thrown and forced into the creeks, and therewith quicken their land;
than which there is no better manurance for grass, and good also for corn.

In very coarse and barren heathy and furze ground, remote from the
sea, they cut the superficies, upper face, or spine of the soil with mattocks
into turf, which, after it hath lain some while and is withered and dried by
the heat of the sun, they cast together into small hillocks, like little haycocks,
and with some combustible matter (as furze, ferns, straw, or such like),
fire it; which, burnt to ashes, they spread them for manurance, which for
one harvest yields profit: and this they name pear-burning.

Another very ancient improvement is also yet used among them: whereof
Pliny wrote in his time thus—"they dig marle out of deep pits like unto
tin-works, and the land therwith covered will be bettered some 80 years

following." We use the same, but it will hardly hold out the fourth part of that long time. This is of divers sorts both in colour and substance; but not to be particularly remembered here.

Late practices we have begun within the memory of old men, as chimney ashes, soap ashes (dear and much in request), salt also; and now newly and most in use, lime, which is employed many several ways. All these, with fallowing, folding, compost, and such like, do yield (though with no small charge) good increase at harvest, and better the succeeding pasture.

They are also very ingenious and careful for conveying and converting of watercourses, whereby they reap good benefit for increase of pasture in dry land, which is commonly effected with less charge than any of the former, for this once perfected needs little further cost nor much labour.

They have of late years much enlarged their orchards, and are very curious in planting and grafting all kinds of fruits, for all seasons, of which they make good use and profit, both for furnishing their own table as furnishing of the neighbour markets.

But most especially for making of cider, a drink both pleasant and healthy; much desired of seamen for long southern voyages, as more fit to make beverage than beer, and much cheaper and easier to be had than wine.

All these, with many other kinds of manurances, as dressing of corn for seed by steeping it in certain liquors, mixtures, and powders (at first like new fruit much longed for and sought after, but that desire was soon satisfied); setting corn also, and other like, far too tedious to be spoken of. Yet all these are the more beneficial in that the land is enclosed and severed with strong fences, hedges, and dykes; which bringeth with it these farther several commodities, as sheltering cattle and sheep in violent storms and extremity of wind, snow, and such like weather; and their beasts also, by their sundry changes in divers pastures, feed still as in a new spring, needing neither cowherd nor shepherd; and at the plashing and stooping down of their hedges it yields to the owner sufficient fuel for their fire all year long.

121   A Genteel Town

A long hill now gratified me with an extensive prospect, and displayed Barnstaple and the country round it, with some of the riches and fertility of Devonshire; a different view to any I had hitherto seen, as the Northern part of the county exhibits only rugged beauties, and majestic features. From this elevated spot Barnstaple appeared to great advantage, situated in a broad and fertile vale, which is belted with high hills, watered by the river Taw, and adorned with many elegant gentlemen's seats. A woollen trade, formerly carried on here with considerable spirit, threw a large sum of money into the town, and enabled its inhabitants to beautify it with many very respectable houses; this trade has of late failed, but baize, silk-stocking, and waistcoat manufactories still give life to the place, which contains above four thousand inhabitants. Besides this source of wealth and population, the pleasing character of the country around, and the comparative cheapness of this part of England, have added to its inhabitants, by inducing many independent families to settle here entirely; a circumstance that renders Barnstaple by far the most genteel town in North Devon. It boasts, indeed, some of the marks of a metropolis, balls every fortnight, and a regular theatre; and nothing is wanting to render it compleatly agreeable, save a decent pavement, the little oval pebbles with which its streets are studded, being not only extremely unfavourable to the shoes, but what is much worse, very injurious to the feet. A noble quay stretches along the river-side to a great length, terminated at one end by a handsome piazza, over the centre of which stands the statue of Queen Anne.

122 Not So Genteel

Be us *down*, sir?
Be us buggery!
Us be *up*—to Barum:
Where all the whores
Wear calico drawers—
And us knows 'ow to tear 'un.

123 Barnstaple Graced

A Riveret called *North-Yeaw*, sheddeth itself into the *Taw* on the one side of this Town, by whose Confluence it is in some sort incircled, whereof one wrote thus:

> To a Town for Situation, delightsome to the eye,
> Thro' pleasant Meads and Marishes, *Tawe* merrily doth hye;
> Which furnished with Traffick is, and Merchandice so good,
> For that her Stream is intermix'd with *Severn's* swelling Flood.
> Yet *Barnstaple* grac'd, tho' thou be by the brackish *Tawe*,
> In all thy Glory see thou not forget the little Yeaw.

124 A Little White Town

All who have travelled through the delicious scenery of North Devon, must needs know the little white town of Bideford, which slopes upwards from its broad tide-river paved with yellow sands, and many-arched old bridge where salmon wait for autumn floods, towards the pleasant upland on the west. Above the town the hills close in, cushioned with deep oak woods, through which juts here and there a crag of fern-fringed slate; below they lower, and open more and more in softly-rounded knolls, and fertile squares of red and green, till they sink into the wide expanse of hazy flats, rich salt marshes, and rolling sand-hills, where Torridge joins her sister Taw, and both together flow quietly towards the broad surges of the bar, and the everlasting thunder of the long Atlantic swell. Pleasantly the old town stands there, beneath its soft Italian sky, fanned day and night by the fresh ocean breeze, which forbids alike the keen winter frosts, and the fierce thunder heats of the midland; and pleasantly it has stood there for now, perhaps, eight hundred years, since the first Grenvile, cousin of the Conqueror, returning from the conquest of South Wales, drew round him trusty Saxon serfs, and free Norse rovers with their golden curls, and dark Silurian Britons from the Swansea shore, and all the mingled blood which still gives to the seaward folk of the next country their strength and intellect, and even in these levelling days, their peculiar beauty of face and form.

But at the time wherof I write, Bideford was not merely a pleasant country town, whose quay was haunted by a few coasting craft. It was one of the chief ports of England; it furnished seven ships to fight the Armada: even more than a century afterwards, say the chroniclers, 'it sent more vessels to the northern trade than any port in England, saving (strange juxtaposition!) London and Topsham', and was the centre of a local civilization and enterprise, small perhaps compared with the vast efforts of the present day: but who dare despise the day of small things, if it has proved to be the dawn of mighty ones. And it is to the sea-life and labour of Bideford, and Dartmouth, and Topsham, and Plymouth (then a petty place), and many another little western town, that England owes the foundation of her naval and commercial glory. It was the men of Devon, the Drakes and Hawkins, Gilberts and Raleighs, Grenviles and Oxenhams, and a host more of 'forgotten worthies', whom we shall learn one day to honour as they deserve, to whom she owes her commerce, her colonies, her very existence. For had they not first crippled, by their West Indian raids, the ill-gotten resources of the Spaniard, and then crushed his last huge effort in Britain's Salamis, the glorious fight of 1588, what had we been by now, but a Popish appanage of a world-tyranny as cruel as heathen Rome itself, and far more devilish?

It is in memory of these men, their voyages and their battles, their faith and their valour, their heroic lives and no less heroic deaths, that I write this book; and if now and then I shall seem to warm into a style somewhat too stilted and pompous, let me be excused for my subject's sake, fit rather to have been sung than said, and to have proclaimed to all true English hearts, not as a novel but as an epic (which some man may yet gird himself to write), the same great message which the songs of Troy, and the Persian wars, and the trophies of Marathon and Salamis, spoke to the hearts of all true Greeks of old.

125 Bideford Desolate

Bideford, however, did not always make the desolate figure it now exhibits. Before our unfortunate dispute with the Americans, which, after absorbing one hundred millions of our money, and destroying one hundred and fifty thousand of our countrymen, terminated in the loss of an immense portion of the British empire, this place enjoyed a considerable commerce with Virginia. Trade, however, like love,

> At sight of human ties,
> Spreads its light wings, and in a moment flies.

Restrictions took place, the war broke out, and the American trade of Bideford was wafted into foreign ports. A manufactory of coarse pottery at this place, from clay found in the neighbourhood of Barnstaple, keeps up a languid exportation at its quays.

126 Poor Little Come-by-Chance

Poor little Come-by-chance
    Wept in the rain!
Starving and shivering,
    Weary with pain,
Ragged and shoeless,
    Pallid and lean,
Poor little Come-by-chance
    Stood in the rain.

Poor little Come-by-chance!
    Nobody knew
Who were her parents,
    They cared little, too.
Wild was the tempest,
    Fast fell the snow,
And winter had bitten her little feet raw.

By little Come-by-chance
    Swung an old gate;
Inside, a palace
    Where Death sat in state.
A mud-pool and hovel
    Where swine held the sway;
With old wooden windows to bar out the day.

Wild blow the hailstones
  Over the snow;
Hark! there's a groan
  From a pallet of straw!
Darkness within,
  And a heap on the floor,
Where her poor grandmother
  Dies by the door.

Wealth in its chariot
  Sees nothing wrong;
Waggons, corn-laden,
  Are rumbling along:
Poor little Come-by-chance
  Sits by her home,
The ghost of a little one
  Ripe for the tomb.

Her eye is unclosed,
  Yet dumb is the maid;
And dropped on her bosom
  Her innocent head!
Her sorrow is over,
  Her suffering and wrong—
Her soul is an angel,
  Her wail is a song.

A hole in the grave-yard
  Is dug the next day;
And both, without mourners,
  Are buried straightway.
A 'shell' is let down—
  Then, a small wooden chest—
And Come-by-chance sleeps
  On her grandmother's breast.

127   Tarka's Death

Below the island the river widened, smooth with the sky. Tarka swam down slowly, bleeding from many wounds. Sometimes he paddled with three legs, sometimes with one, in the water darkening so strangely before his eyes. Not always did he hear the hounds baying around him. At the beginning of the tenth hour he passed the banks faced with stone to keep the sea from the village, and drifted into deeper water, whereon sticks and froth were floating.

Hounds were called off by the horn for the tide was at flood; and there is no scent in salt water.

But as they were about to leave, Tarka was seen again, moving up with the tide, his mouth open. The flow took him near the bank; he kicked feebly, and rolled over.

Tally-Ho!

Deadlock saw the small brown head, and bayed in triumph as he jumped down the bank. He bit the head, lifted the otter high, flung him about and fell into the water with him. They saw the broken head look up beside Deadlock, heard the cry of Ic-yang! as Tarka bit into his throat, and then the hound was sinking with the otter into the deep water. Oak-leaves, black and rotting in the mud of the unseen bed, arose and swirled and sank again. And the tide slowed still, and began to move back, and they waited and watched, until the body of Deadlock arose, drowned and heavy, and floated away amidst the froth on the waters.

They pulled the body out of the river and carried it to the bank, laying it on the grass, and looking down at the dead hound in sad wonder. And while they stood there silently, a great bubble rose out of the depths, and broke, and as they watched, another bubble shook to the surface, and broke; and there was a third bubble in the sea-going waters, and nothing more.

128   The Burial of Salvation Yeo

It was the First of October. The morning was bright and still; the skies were dappled modestly from east to west with soft grey autumn cloud, as if all heaven and earth were resting after those fearful summer months of battle and of storm. Silently, as if ashamed and sad, the *Vengeance* slid over the bar, and passed the sleeping sandhills, and dropped her anchor off Appledore, with her flag floating half-mast high; for the corpse of Salvation Yeo was on board.

A boat pulled off from the ship, and away to the western end of the strand; and Cary and Brimblecombe helped out Amyas Leigh, and led him slowly up the hill towards his home.

The crowd clustered round him, with cheers and blessings, and sobs of pity from kind-hearted women; for all in Appledore and Bideford knew well by this time what had befallen him.

"Spare me, my good friends," said Amyas, "I have landed here that I might go quietly home, without passing through the town, and being made a gazing-stock. Think not of me, good folks, nor talk of me; but come behind me decently, as Christian men, and follow to the grave the body of a better man than I."

And, as he spoke, another boat came off, and in it, covered with the flag of England, the body of Salvation Yeo.

The people took Amyas at his word; and a man was sent on to Burrough to tell Mrs Leigh that her son was coming. When the coffin was landed and lifted, Amyas and his friends took their places behind it as chief mourners, and the crew followed in order, while the crowd fell in behind them, and gathered every moment; till, ere they were halfway to Northam town the funeral train might number full five hundred souls.

They had sent over by a fishing-skiff the day before to bid the sexton dig the grave; and when they came into the churchyard, the parson stood ready waiting at the gate. . . .

The Burial Service was done; the blessing said; the parson drew back: but the people lingered and crowded round to look at the coffin, while Amyas stood still at the head of the grave. It had been dug, by his command, at the west end of the church, near by the foot of the tall grey wind-swept tower, which watches for the beacon far and wide over land and sea. Perhaps the old man might like to look at the sea, and see the ships come out and in across the bar, and hear the wind, on winter nights, roar through the belfry far above his head. Why not? It was but a fancy; and yet Amyas felt that he too should like to be buried in such a place; so Yeo might like it also.

129   Clovelly Perilous

The descent of the High Street of Clovelly, at night, turned out to be a matter of more difficulty than we had anticipated. There was no such thing as a lamp in the whole village; and we had to grope our way in the darkness down steps of irregular sizes and heights, paved with slippery pebbles, and ornamented with nothing in the shape of a bannister, even at the most dangerous places. Halfway down, my friend and I had an argument in the dark—standing with our noses against a wall, and with nothing visible on either side—as to which way we should turn next. I guessed to the left, and he guessed to the right; and I, being the more obstinate of the two, we ended in following my route, and at last stumbled our way down to the pier. Looking at the place the next morning, we found that the steps to the right led through a bit of cottage-garden to a snug little precipice, over which inquisitive tourists might fall quietly, without let or hindrance. Talk of the perils of the deep! what are they in comparison with the perils of the shore?

130   Somewhere for the Sea Horse

Seafaring men and means, I intend mariners and shipping, is another and no slender (assure you) commodity to the kingdom in general, and this county in particular, in time either of war or peace, for merchandising or fishing; with whom, from hence, upon all occasions, our sovereign's navy (the sinews of our strength) is partly manned and furnished; for our havens are well replenished with shipping fit for war or peace; and them employed in merchants' affairs or in fishing voyages, upon our own coasts, and elsewhere in many fair remote countries, as Canada, Virginia, Newfoundland, and other regions, whence much fish is brought home; or, in times of peace, into the Straits, Spain, or Portugal, with profitable return; and in Ireland, and Clovelly and Linmouth upon our own northern coasts for herring, the king of fishes; and upon our southern coasts, generally throughout all, for pilchards, preserved and sundry ways prepared is a very vendible and profitable commodity. The variety of sundry other dainty fish taken on our coasts are elsewhere spoken of. Concerning their adventuring for whales upon the coasts of Iceland, and somewhere for the sea horse, how it is now in practice I can say little, but in former times good use hath been made thereof.

131   Tristram Risdon

Tristram Risdon, a painful and industrious *Antiquary*, was born at *Winscot* in *Devonshire*, in the little Parish of *St Giles*, near *Great Torrington* in the said County ... and he resolved that neither the Business nor Pastimes of the Country should engross his Time and Pains; and therefore applied himself to Study, in which he greatly delighted. He betook himself to what is most ornamental to a Gentleman, *viz.* the *Study of History and Antiquities*; more especially those of his own Country....

132   Cornu: a Horn

... That Region which Geographers account the first of all *Britain*, and shooteth out farthest into the *West*, was once reputed the fourth Part of this Island, and supposed to be a Kingdom before the Sea swallowed up the Land between St *Burian* and the Islands of *Scilly*, included under the name of *Danmonia*, is of later Times divided into two Parts, known by the Names of *Denshire* and *Cornwall*, a Country which contained one Province, and was inhabited by one Nation, 'till those *Britons*, which *Ptolemy* called *Danmonii*, before the reign of *Athelstane*, that mighty Monarch; at which Time the Britons, impatient of Servitude, repined against his Government, and after sundry Conflicts, were chased beyond the River, then called *Tambra*, now *Tamar*, into the utmost Parts of this Island, and made that River to be the Bounds between the *English*-Men and those *Britons*, which at this Day, for the most part is the Bound of both Shires; since when, they have there remained, and were from thenceforth no more called *Britons*, but *Cornwallians*; for that they were singled from the Saxons, and driven to dwell in a narrow Nooke or Corner (as they call it) of the Land; for so doth (as some do derive) the Word *Cornwall* signify, being compounded of *Cornu*, a Horn, which is broad at the one End, and narrow, crooked, and smaller at the other; even so is that Country, and *Wall*, which in the *Saxon* Tongue doth signify strange and foreign. . . .

133   Bare-footed and Bare-legged

It is ordered that Mary Cutting of Pyworthy in the County of Devon . . . shall upon some Sunday before the Day of the Return hereof in the forenoon immediately after the reading of the second Lesson come into the Parish Church aforesaid, bare-headed with a white sheet about her shoulders, bare-footed and bare-legged, with a white rod in her hand, and shall stand before the Minister's seat or pew until the end of the Nicene Creed, and shall openly confess and acknowledge that she hath been delivered of a male child unlawfully begotten on her body, and shall show her hearty sorrow and repentance and shall desire God to forgive her, and the Minister and the People to pray for the amendment of her life for the future, Promising by her own endeavours to certify her repentance by a Holy and Circumspect Conversation, and no more to give the like occasion to the Church.

134   Moorland Waters

But leaving the name, let us for your more ease, and the sooner to be quit of this barren soil, cold air, uneven ways, and untrodden paths, swim with the stream [the Exe] the better to hasten our speed; so we are sure not to deviate, though we walk the farther way about, yet it may prove the nearest way home. In his small beginning he keeps Somersetshire; and passing by Exford, a place where he is fordable, he leaveth his name; and at Exton he doth the same after his passage by Winsford; and there received a small nursling from Carhampton and Cutcombe: he hath further augmentation from a rill that ariseth beyond Brompton-Regis; then, grown somewhat in strength, hasteth to Dulverton to meet his fair sister Barle; hoping, with her rich portion, to better and enlarge his state. They were, at their first springs, congenuited, being sprung not 500 paces distant one from the other.

Barle yields nothing to Exe in quantity, and seems as if she would strive for superiority, as having the first bridge of stone, as otherwise unpassable, and that in the midst of the forest; near which is a large deep pool which they name Symon's Bath, as a place where one Symon used to bathe himself, and is said to have been (but upon what small colour of warrant) another Robin Hood, and standing in outlawry, kept this forest: and in the moors of Somerset there is a burrow or fort called, by the inhabitants, Symon's

Exeter Cathedral

Exeter

Burrow, which he made his winter strength to retire unto. But for that I can tell no Robin Hood's tales of him, I will follow Barle, which washeth the feet of an ancient castle, (so they called it) Cowcastle; which was there cast up for some (long since) forgotten occasion, whereof neither tradition nor writing maketh mention. There is also another such fort, south-west from Challacombe, called Solsbury Castle. We will not stay so long as to describe the site thereof, yielding no matter worthy the remembrance; only Barle by this time is come to Longacre [Landacre] his second bridge, and draweth near to Withy-Pool and Hawkridge, to meet Dunsbrook, and both together to subscribe to Exe; which at Exbridge receiveth the whole of another pretty brook.

135   The Wizard's Slough

For there was the Wizard's Slough itself, as black as death, and bubbling, with a few scant yellow reeds in a ring around it. Outside these, bright watergrass of the liveliest green was creeping, tempting any unwary foot to step, and plunge, and founder. And on the marge were blue campanula, sundew, and forget-me-not, such as no child could resist. On either side, the hill fell back, and the ground was broken with tufts of rush, and flag, and marestail, and a few rough alder-trees overclogged with water. And not a bird was seen, or heard, neither rail nor water-hen, wagtail nor reed-warbler.

Of this horrible quagmire, the worst upon all Exmoor, John had heard from his grandfather, and even from his mother, when they wanted to keep him quiet; but his father had feared to speak of it to him, being a man of piety, and up to the tricks of the evil one. This made John the more desirous to have a good look at it now, only with his girths well up, to turn away and flee at speed, if any thing should happen. And now he proved how well it is to be wary and wide-awake, even in lonesome places. For at the other side of the Slough, and a few landyards beyond it, where the ground was less noisome, he had observed a felled tree lying over a great hole in the earth, with staves of wood, and slabs of stone, and some yellow gravel around it. But the flags of reeds around the morass partly screened it from his eyes, and he could not make out the meaning of it, except that it meant no good, and probably was witchcraft.

136   Old Exmoor

Today, one of Walter Raymond's forgotten books fell into my hands. He is, I think, Somerset's only 'regional' writer and seems to have had considerable insight into the character of the Somerset countryman.

7

In 1905 Walter Raymond came from the Somerset village of Preston Plucknett, famous for its medieval buttressed tithe-barn, to the Somerset village of Withypool, a minute thatched village folded in a hollow of Exmoor, approached by climbing trackways, encircled by moorland and by fields of grass and corn that generations of Withypool men had snatched from the barren moor. Here he stayed for over a dozen years writing essays about this corner of Somerset for *The Nineteenth Century*, *The Spectator*, *The Westminster Gazette* that he collected in two volumes, *The Book of Simple Delights*, and *The Book of Crafts and Character*.

Reading these sketches forty years later, the country-lover realizes that although to outward view the Somerset scene, the Exmoor scene in particular, has not changed enormously during the last half-century, these books of Walter Raymond's portray a vanished world.

At Withypool he found, for the weekly rent of one shilling, a cottage with old beams, half-door, chimney seats and bread oven. It was cleaned for him daily by a zealous Mrs Critchell who took an artist's pride in her work, kept his accounts, supplied him with eggs at sixteen a shilling and chickens at four and sixpence a pair. At the village inn he drank in a kitchen furnished with oak settle and rush-bottomed chairs. The landlady came from her dairy to serve him, the windows looked on a cow-barton and lichened buildings, for the host was farmer as well as publican. Some Exmoor innkeepers still combine the two vocations, but the combination was more common when their customers were exclusively the labourers of the farms, the craftsmen of the village.

The men who foregathered at the inn in Raymond's time still cast a libation upon the ground before drinking, fastened their door with a horseshoe for protection, were not incredulous of pixies and witches, while their children played unsophisticated games like 'London Bridge is fallen down', and picked up acorns for the pigs. Who were they, the proud skilled men Walter Raymond met by the inn fireside and along the moorland ways?

Among them was the thatcher who with bat and hazel spars laid upon the roof the wheaten reed, supplied free by the landlord of the cottage, loaded upon a yellow wagon. Such wagons were fashioned by the village wheel-wright, superb master of a difficult craft, whose name 'Noah Pike' was emblazoned in red upon the tailboard. Significant name. If Pike were really his name the Withypool wheelwright may have been related to the family of Pike of Tinhead whose wagons were masterpieces of the craft; if the name is fictitious Mr Raymond must have thought him worthy to rank in famous company. The frames of his carts were oak, sides and rave-boards of elm, felloes of elm, spokes of oak, floor of deal, the hanging-pillar of ash. In his own forge this man fashioned the metal bonds or 'tires' and the very fire on his hearth was fed by old tailboards and felloes.

These wagons were driven by a carter who decked his fore-horse with brass bells, crimson tassels, a protective crescent moon in brass, and polished his harness-brasses to the lustre of gold. The thatcher's spars were made of hazel or withy sorted out by the hedger who also found poles for farm rails, selected rods of ash and maple for garden sticks, bound faggots for the bake-house as well as accomplishing the jobs of ditching and 'laying' hedges.

The hurdler made his hurdles with a frame of ash or birch which he wreathed with hazel or green withy, all cut by the Exmoor woodman. Such men wove a splendid living tapestry, their interdependent occupations its criss-crossing threads.

Around Withypool Raymond also encountered men of various humbler occupations that are practically extinct: the mole catcher in moleskin cap and waistcoat; the tranter whose jogging cart carried parcels, letters, merchandise and passengers along the roads to Dulverton and Wiveliscombe; the snail-catcher who sold his wares to Bristol glass blowers because snails were 'good for the chest'; the strapper or itinerant hired labourer; the wandering hawker whose cart brought pans and brooms to village doorways.

In Withypool in 1905, small farmers still cut corn with the sickle and a few of the older women still came to bind the sheaves. But on bigger farms the miraculous 'reaper' had arrived to do both jobs, a machine that had beauty in Raymond's eye because as yet it was drawn by a team of great sweating horses. Sheaves were set up ten to a 'stitch', the Somerset name for a shock, as in the days when Parson took every tenth sheaf. After harvest came Thanksgiving with a gargantuan tea that included jam of Exmoor whortleberries, Exmoor honey, clotted cream, and afterwards the company danced traditional dances, 'Hunt the Squirrel' and 'Wave the Handkerchief', and sang old songs like 'The trees they do grow high and the leaves they do grow green'.

137 Hot Mutton Pasty

But now, at Dulverton, we dined upon the rarest and choicest victuals that ever I did taste. Even now, at my time of life, to think of it gives me appetite, as once and awhile to think of my first love makes me love all goodness. Hot mutton pasty was a thing I had often heard of from wealthy boys and men, who made a dessert of dinner; and to hear them talk of it made my lips smack, and my ribs come inwards.

And now John Fry strode into the hostel, with the air and grace of a short-legged man, and shouted as loud as if he was calling sheep upon Exmoor—

"Hot mootton pasty for twoo trarv'lers, at number vaive, in vaive minnits! Dish un up in the tin with the grahvy, zame as I hardered last Tuesday ."

Of course it did not come in five minutes, nor yet in ten or twenty; but that made it all the better when it came to the real presence; and the smell of it was enough to make an empty man thank God for the room there was inside him. Fifty years have passed me quicker than the taste of that gravy.

138   The Beauty of Staghounds

As far as I am aware North Devon and West Somerset are the only localities not only in the British Isles but also in the world, where Wild Red Deer are hunted with packs of hounds. The Devon and Somerset Staghounds is the oldest pack and for many years consisted of doghounds only, which were drafted, because they were too big, from other foxhound packs. Some of these hounds stood quite 26 inches at the shoulder. These doghounds had not only poise but elegance and rhythm as well: their main characteristics were that, when laid on to the line of a deer, they would string out in single file as well as running practically mute. Both qualities were of course completely foreign to the foxhound fraternity. The way in which they hunted was thus unusual, but none the less it was most attractive. They would not speak across the Commons and out over the Forest, but would do so spasdmodically when coming into the wooded valleys. It was not until after the first war and around the early 1920s when hounds had become somewhat scarce that the D and S Staghounds began breeding hounds of their own. The turning point came in April 1927 when Ernest Bawden, then huntsman, brought to a meet at Dulverton an all bitch pack, a hitherto unheard of event in the annals of staghunting!

Froude Hancock, a rugger international and probably the most renowned staghunter of all time, wrote in his diary: "The bitches are too fast for my style of hunting." I entirely agreed with him; but most people today appear to disagree with both of us: I never know quite why, because staghunting is essentially for doghounds with their beautiful deep voices.

The principal and clear distinction between those far-off days and now, that is to say the Sidney Tucker–Ernest Bawden era roughly up to 1930 and the period thereafter, is that we were completely dedicated in those former years, especially the younger group. No such dedication existed after the last war; it is unknown today. This group knew all about deer and they knew the names of all the hounds. They hollood and vied with each other as to whose voice carried furthest: and when hounds and huntsman arrived we were expected to give every detail of what we had seen. The crossing places and tracks of deer were avoided like the plague, but we would watch them from concealment under a nearby fence, since it was an outrageous and heinous sin to head an autumn stag—if ever it happened we would slink away as fast as possible out of sight! As young men, Tucker, Bawden, Earnest Hancock, Will Tame and others were our heroes just as today Bobby Moore, Peter Lorimer and other footballers are to teenagers. To be allowed to ride for a short distance on the way home amidst the big doghounds was sheer bliss.

Since the early 1930s the Devon and Somerset have had two separate packs, the dog pack and bitch pack. Hounds thrill me, they always have since an early age, by their beautiful, rhythmic balanced movement. It is the dog pack who usually steal the show and capture the eye in the field—it is they whom the huntsman really in his heart of hearts prefers, because they are more sagacious and more reliable than the bitches, who are flashy and unpredictable. Many people who hunt will no doubt arise in wrath over these words of mine, but Ernest Bawden confessed to me his agreement as did Alfred Lenthall later on.

Nureyev and Margot Fonteyn are both superb ballet dancers, but the real controlled and balanced grace belongs to Nureyev.

To be with the doghounds across Anstey Common, Winsford Hill or on the Forest is a truly wonderful experience—they deceive by their effortless grace of movement; they glide and bit by bit edge away leaving even a good horse struggling. All this joy I gained and learned from personal experience on the running track. Strained effort produces ungainly and unbalanced movement: it is only when harmony and rhythm meet that beauty is born in whatever field it may be.

Since the day when two separate packs came into being, hunting in single file and running almost mute is something which belongs to the past. Now both packs run up together like foxhounds and their music when in full cry is superb. Even folk who do not hunt cannot fail to be thrilled and enchanted on hearing either pack running up the Barle valley or out across the Commons.

I make no secret of the fact that from my early days I have always reached the end of a hunt, when the stag is brought to bay, with very mixed feelings; as the years went by I became increasingly saddened and disliked what I may term the climax.

There was the thrilling find, when all was fresh, alert and active in every muscle and limb. One became entranced and enraptured as the pack was let go upon the line—streaming like pigeons racing—over moor, heather, bogs and combe to the enclosed fields.

And so down to the stronghold coverts of Horner, the Barle or Exe and to the river itself. Old hounds pausing to sniff overhanging branches and twigs jutting out from the bank of the stream. Sterns thrashing from side to side—and then suddenly a deep note loud and long from 'Comus'—"He has passed this way". And then finally, face to face in a deep pool further down, Elegance and Rhythm meet: one or the other must become as dust. For an hour or more I have been living in a glorious and enchanting dream; but now with a start I awake to reality—all is completely shattered.

Every individual of course holds his or her view upon this matter and is entitled to it.

The two following remarks made in the hunting field and in my presence are perhaps of interest because they are such poles apart.

A farmer well known to me said to those around him and towards the end of a hunt, "One can't help feeling sorry for that stag".

The other was a female, who said to me, "What a lovely smell of dead stag."

The latter remark struck me as revolting.

It has been ever thus: the climax in the arena of old was similar to the climax or bringing to bay of the stag. The gladiator holds his enemy at his mercy, his hand raised—but he is not looking at his victim. He is looking backward with a strange haunted expression. The great moment has come and it is nothing.

His desire is granted and it is dust.

'Our desire like a butterfly is alluring only while it eludes; captured it is a dead thing through which we stick a pin.'

139   Richard Huxtable of Challacombe

Richard Huxtable and his wife Elizabeth probably married in or about 1795 and went to live in Challacombe almost at once. Here, he soon acquired the leaseholds of several houses, mostly small cottages which have now disappeared, at Challacombe Mill. He may also have held the mill itself, though he did not himself work it. But his second son, William, was certainly the miller for several years before 1840. About the same time his eldest son, another Richard, born in 1797, kept the New Inn, which almost adjoined the mill.

The elder Richard, who died in 1855, was in business as a millwright and carpenter for many years, and a few pages of a daybook or diary which he kept, covering nine months from July 1824 to March 1825, have been preserved and are now in the possession of his great-great grandson, Mr J. F. Huxtable of Swincombe in Challacombe, by whose permission a transcript is appended. The combination of very individual spelling and a difficult script, as well as the inclusion of many dialect words now extinct, make decipherment of the manuscript no easy task, and the present writer would have been forced to abandon it but for the help of Mr J. F. Huxtable.

The very first entry, for 1 July 1824, is: *Martinaw droing timber*, that is 'At Martinhoe, throwing (i.e. felling) timber'. Two days later Richard Huxtable was *Soying geat stof for Axton*, in other words 'Sawing gate material for Haxton' (in Bratton Fleming). Later in the month he was *Hom moing* (At home, mowing) or *Hom to hay* (At home, haymaking). One day he spent *boring turf and soying* ('stoping' or cutting peat and sawing). In August he *Spok and veled a well* (spoked and fellœd a wheel) and two days later he *Mad a cofin for Susanna Joans*.

140   The Great Exmoor Snow

It must have snowed most wonderfully to have made that depth of covering in about eight hours. For one of Master Stickles' men, who had been out all the night, said that no snow began to fall until nearly midnight. And here it was, blocking up the doors, stopping the ways, and the watercourses, and making it very much worse to walk than in a saw-pit newly used. However we trudged along in a line; I first, and the other men after me; trying to keep my track, but finding legs and strength not up to it. Most of all, John Fry was groaning; certain that his time was come, and sending messages to his wife, and blessings to his children. For all this time it was snowing harder than it ever had snowed before, so far as a man might guess at it; and the leaden depth of the sky came down, like a mine turned upside down on us. Not that the flakes were so very large; for I have seen much larger flakes in a shower of March, while sowing peas; but that there was no room between them, neither any relaxing, nor any change of direction.

Watch, like a good and faithful dog, followed us very cheerfully, leaping out of the depth, which took him over his back and ears already, even in the level places; while in the drifts he might have sunk to any distance out of sight, and never found his way up again. However, we helped him now and then, especially through the gaps and gateways; and so after a deal of floundering, some laughter and a little swearing, we came all safe to the lower meadow, where most of our flock was hurdled.

But behold, there was no flock at all! None, I mean, to be seen anywhere; only at one corner of the field, by the eastern end, where the snow drove in, a great white billow, as high as a barn and as broad as a house. This great drift was rolling and curling beneath the violent blast, tufting and combing with rustling swirls, and carved (as in patterns of cornice) where the grooving chisel of the wind swept round. Ever and again, the tempest snatched little whiffs from the channelled edges, twirled them round, and made them lie like herring-bones, or the seams of sand where the tide had been. And all the while from the smothering sky, more and more fiercely at every blast, came the pelting pitiless arrows, winged with murky white, and pointed with the barbs of frost.

But although, for people who had no sheep, the sight was a very fine one (so far at least as the weather permitted any sight at all); yet for us, with our flock beneath it, this great mount had but little charm. Watch began to scratch at once, and to howl along the sides of it; he knew that his charge was buried there, and his business taken from him. But we four men set to in earnest, digging with all our might and main, shovelling away at the great white pile, and fetching it into the meadow. Each man made for himself a cave, scooping at the soft cold flux, which slid upon him at every stroke, and throwing it out behind him, in piles of castled fancy. At last we drove our tunnels in (for we worked indeed for the lives of us), and all converging towards the middle, held our tools and listened.

The other men heard nothing at all; or declared that they heard nothing, being anxious now to abandon the matter, because of the chill in their feet and knees. But I said, "Go, if you choose, all of you. I will work it out by myself, you pie-crusts." And upon that they gripped their shovels, being more or less of Englishmen; and the least drop of English blood is worth the best of any other, when it comes to lasting out.

But before we began again, I laid my head well into the chamber; and there I heard a faint 'ma-a-ah,' coming through some ells of snow, like a plaintive buried hope, or a last appeal. I shouted aloud to cheer him up, for I knew what sheep it was, to wit the most valiant of all the wethers, who had met me when I came home from London and been so glad to see me. And then we all fell to again; and very soon we hauled him out. Watch took charge of him at once, with an air of the noblest patronage, lying on his frozen fleece, and licking all his face and feet, to restore his warmth to him. Then fighting Tom jumped up at once, and made a little butt at Watch, as if nothing had ever ailed him, and then set off to a shallow place, and looked for something to nibble at.

Further in, and close under the bank, where they had huddled themselves for warmth, we found all the rest of the poor sheep packed as closely as if they were in a great pie. It was strange to observe how their vapour, and breath, and the moisture exuding from their wool had scooped, as it were, a coved room for them, lined with a ribbing of deep yellow snow. Also the churned snow beneath their feet was as yellow as gamboge. Two or three of the weaklier hoggets were dead, from want of air, and from pressure; but more than three-score were as lively as ever; though cramped and stiff for a little while.

"However shall us get 'em home?" John Fry asked in great dismay, when we had cleared about a dozen of them; which we were forced to do very carefully, so as not to fetch the roof down. "No manner of maning to draive 'un, drough all they girt driftnesses."

"You see to this place, John," I replied, as we leaned on our shovels a moment, and the sheep came rubbing round us: "let no more of them out for the present; they are better where they be. Watch, here boy, keep them!"

Watch came, with his little scut of a tail cocked as sharp as duty; and I set him at the narrow mouth of the great snow antre. All the sheep sidled away, and got closer, that the other sheep might be bitten first, as the foolish things imagine: whereas no good sheep-dog even so much as lips a sheep to turn it.

Then of the outer sheep (all now snowed and frizzled like a lawyer's wig) I took the two finest and heaviest, and with one beneath my right arm, and the other beneath my left, I went straight home to the upper sheppey, and set them inside, and fastened them. Sixty and six I took home in that way, two at a time on each journey; and the work grew harder and harder each time, as the drifts of the snow were deepening. No other man should meddle with them: I was resolved to try my strength against the strength of the elements; and try it I did, ay and proved it. A certain fierce delight burned in me, as the struggle grew harder; but rather would I die than yield; and at last I finished it. People talk of it to this day: but none can tell what the labour was, who have not felt that snow and wind.

Of the sheep upon the mountain, and the sheep upon the western farm, and the cattle on the upper burrows, scarcely one in ten was saved; do what we would for them. And this was not through any neglect (now that our wits were sharpened), but from the pure impossibility of finding them at all. That great snow never ceased a moment for three days and nights;

and then when all the earth was filled, and the topmost hedges were unseen, and the trees broke down with weight (wherever the wind had not lightened them), a brilliant sun broke forth and showed the loss of all our customs.

All our house was quite snowed up, except where we had purged a way, by dint of constant shovellings. The kitchen was as dark and darker than the cider-cellar, and long lines of furrowed scallops ran even up to the chimney-stacks. Several windows fell right inwards, through the weight of the snow against them; and the few that stood bulged in, and bent like an old bruised lanthorn. We were obliged to cook by candlelight; we were forced to read by candlelight; as for baking, we could not do it, because the oven was too chill; and a load of faggots only brought a little wet down the sides of it.

For when the sun burst forth at last upon that world of white, what he brought was neither warmth, nor cheer, nor hope of softening; only a clearer shaft of cold, from the violet depths of sky. Long-drawn alleys of white haze seemed to lead towards him, yet such as he could not come down, with any warmth remaining. Broad white curtains of the frost-fog looped around the lower sky, on the verge of hill and valley, and above the laden trees. Only round the sun himself, and the spot of heaven he claimed, clustered a bright purple-blue, clear, and calm, and deep.

That night, such a frost ensued as we had never dreamed of, neither read in ancient books, or histories of Frobisher. The kettle by the fire froze, and the crock upon the hearth-cheeks; many men were killed, and cattle rigid in their head-ropes. Then I heard that fearful sound, which never I had heard before, neither since have heard (except during that same winter), the sharp yet solemn sound of trees, burst open by the frost-blow. Our great walnut lost three branches, and has been dying ever since; though growing meanwhile, as the soul does. And the ancient oak at the cross was rent, and many score of ash trees. But why should I tell all this? the people who have not seen it (as I have) will only make faces, and disbelieve; till such another frost comes; which perhaps may never be.

141   Ring Him In

Incidentally, Oare church provides the most charming (strange adjective!) ghost story I have come across—the antithesis of the grim or grisly which the 'ghost' term conjures up. The Rev. H. J. Marshall, who went to Porlock in 1895 to work as a curate under Prebendary Hook, has told the story. It concerns an inexplicable incident involving his brother, the Rev. Paul Marshall, who became Rector of Oare. On the evening of his induction, while sitting in his study, he heard the sound of the church bell. As there was no reason for this, and assuming some trippers had gone into the church and were playing with the bells, Mr Marshall walked up the lane to the church to investigate. It was twilight, and on the way Mr Marshall met an old clergyman who passed by in silence but gave him a smile. Mr Marshall went on to the church and found everything in order and the door shut. Later, he mentioned the incident to an old parishioner and was amazed to be told that when a rector was inducted at Oare a certain predecessor was "wont to come back and ring him in." Former rectors had seen this old clergyman coming down the lane, and Mr Marshall was able to describe his appearance and dress exactly as his predecessors had seen him. Local tradition connected the strange figure with a rector who had long and devotedly served the parish, and whose monument was in the church. I say a 'charming' ghost story, because it is. A happy thought—an old rector coming back to welcome a new one!

142   Hunted Henry

I have known a stag, whom I shall call Henry, for a great many years. He has now reached a ripe old age due to his intelligence and craftiness. As only to be expected his face is weather-beaten and grey, yet he still walks with elegance and grace—two characteristics invariably to be found amongst all red deer. He has often told me about his many and varied experiences throughout his exciting life and so I now hand over to him to recount perhaps his most terrifying.

Henry: I shall probably shake all over when I tell you this tale. It was truly frightening. I had been asked by Aunt Fanny to spend the weekend with her near Wallover Barton several miles south of Lynton. She had also invited a charming young hind; she was an absolute peach, whom I fell for in a big way. At that time I was in my prime and a pretty handsome fellow with a superb head. On the Tuesday morning we were both lying tucked up all snug in the bracken, when I heard the horn. Then a few moments later I suddenly saw the face of a big light-coloured hound peering into our bedroom and straight at us. He lifted his head and bayed deep, loud and long. I jumped up and lunged at him, but he was crafty and avoided me. Out I bounded into the full glare of daylight to be greeted with tremendous and resounding shouts on every side of the valley. My immediate thought was that I must return home to the Barle valley as speedily as possible. I soon left all the shouting and hullabaloo behind, crossed the road at Five Cross Ways and set sail via North Radworthy into Long Wood. Here I had a bit of time to spare and so started to look around for help; I soon found it in the shape of an ignorant looking two-year-old, who was basking in the sun. I gave his behind a sharp jab with my brow point; he awoke with a start and his expression had to be seen to be believed. Then he shot off at the rate of knots and I lay down in his soft inviting bed.

  For the time being all was peace, but not for long, because in the distance I could hear those devils coming. They crossed the small stream and entered Long Wood, driving on relentlessly and making the most hideous noise any stag can experience. My heart was pounding as I threw my head back and waited: they seemed to be all round and almost on top of me, but my trick had worked—on they went on the line of the two-year-old. For the doghounds to be foxed in this way was unbelievable—the bitch pack yes, but not this lot!

There was only a brief interval, however, before my worst fears were confirmed.

The horn sounded quite close in the path at the bottom of the wood; and then it happened, I was again face to face with that vile, revolting, big light-coloured hound. He had winded me lying in the two-year-old's bed, had me at a disadvantage and knew it. He gave one bound and was on me; but realising his intention, I suddenly brought my head forward and caught him with my bay point and with the strength of my great neck hurled him into the bushes. He yelled with pain, which of course had the effect of bringing all his pals rushing to find out what his trouble was. I was now standing and amidst pandemonium set off up Long Wood. It was no earthly use going the usual way up the North Molton ridge combe to Three Corner Allotment because masses of goggle-eyed humans would be waiting for me there: so I swung left to Shortacombe, Sherdon Water, Brightworthy, Westwater and to the Barle below Tarr Steps. I was tired, very tired, and my head was muzzy and swimming, but I could still remember a deep secluded pool below Three Waters tucked in under Slade Wood.

As I reached it, I could hear those infernal doghounds roaring on down the valley after me not very far away. I just had time to select the pool I wanted; it was under an overhanging part of the bank where the river curved and the water was about three feet deep. To this I went and sank my whole body slowly and silently into the water; then, throwing my head back under the bank, left only my ears and eyes and nose visible—my ears, because deer just abhor getting them wet in the river.

Hounds came down the river on both banks, passed me and went on; the horn sounded further and further away. I lay there motionless, it was my only hope, when to my horror I noticed the old light-coloured devil coming up the river again on his own. Clearly he was not satisfied that I had gone down—he knew I was somewhere around and close at hand. Instinctively I sensed him feathering on the bank just above me—the suspense was appalling, because had he spotted me, it would all have been over.

My joints and whole body had become stiff through lying in the cold water after galloping from Long Wood; had I been turned out of the river, I should not have been able to travel more than a short distance.—

But at that very moment a miracle occurred! I heard the unmistakable bump, bump, bump of a horse coming down beside the river close to where I was lying and then a voice: "What are yer doin' 'anging around there? Get on to 'im, get on to 'im." Followed by a loud crack of the whip.

After they had passed on down stream, I waited a short while and then decided to take a chance, because my whole body was becoming numb from the cold water. With a great effort I rose out of the pool, shook myself and crossed to the other bank, where I heaved myself out of the water and almost crawled up into the thick undergrowth of Slade Wood; about halfway up I lay down to wait and hope. To hope that I was at last safe, saved by the friendly stream, which had helped so many deer in the past and by the fact that daylight was slowly fading.

From down the valley there came to me the notes of the horn again, but this time it no longer worried me. The notes were long, drawn out and at intervals. I had been told about this by my mother, when I was very young. It meant that all was over for the day and that hounds are being taken home to kennels. What wonderful relief I felt! The horn now was just below me. "So near and yet so far—did they but know," I whispered to myself. On it went further and further up the valley, finally to be lost and replaced by the lovely song of the Barle.

The moon rose and shone down upon me through the trees. All was silent and very peaceful until an owl hooted close by to announce and herald the departure of humans and the arrival of night.

Joy came to me and my spirits revived, even terribly tired as I was. I had triumphed and beaten the doghounds; now I was safe for a full nine months. Safe and free to roam at will, to wander over farms and take the best of food, that these farmer fellows could produce.

I'd show 'em that it was not all one way traffic; if they wanted their fun next autumn then I would give it them. But in the meantime I intended to take it out of them and it was no good their going about moaning and saying "Thiccy there stag's ruining me—'ees eat most ov me corn and now 'ees pullin' the taters abroad." After all one simply must have something to gallop on!

143   The Wild Red Deer

Obviously it is quite impossible to procure an accurate census of the Red Deer population throughout the lovely wooded valleys, the outlying commons, the combes and Forest of Exmoor itself; however, an approximate guess of between 700 and 800 would probably not be very wide of the mark.

A lovely autumn stag with a wide spread of antlers possessing all his rights on both horns and with three points atop both sides, standing with some twenty hinds around him on open moorland is a glorious sight.

But seen individually throughout the year, a Red Deer of either sex does not fill the eye as does a superb racehorse.

That is of course a personal opinion arrived at after having seen innumerable deer.

But strangely enough once both the horse and the deer are set in motion, there is no question as to which is the more elegant, the more graceful.

The amazing grace and effortless ease with which a hind trots has to be seen to be believed. The nearest approach to this is to be found in a charming slender steeplechaser of today called Pendil—he stirs the heart every time

I see him in action; he is a champion. I had the good fortune to train on the track a very great deal with Bevil Rudd the South African Olympic quarter-mile champion. When running behind him his feet never seemed to touch the track, it was as though he was airborne. And so it is with Red Deer, who never cease to lead me to that secret well of joy at which I can drink for ever. . . .

Their jumping powers are quite astonishing and so are some of the obstacles they surmount not only when travelling at night in search of food, but also when being hunted and under pressure. Over the many years that I have watched them, I cannot recollect an occasion when they have put a foot wrong—it is really quite incredible.

The damage inflicted by deer in the past was very considerable and farmers were compensated for this loss by the hunt. Stags in particular often rejoice in lying in corn fields and eating whenever the spirit moves them. In this respect the damage nowadays is not as much as it used to be, since barley has largely taken over from oats. Again, the advent of the combine harvester has dispensed with the need for ricks, which were often targets for deer in hard winter weather.

Root crops too are attacked, sometimes with devastating results. Here stags are the chief offenders, since they will take one bite out of the mangold, swede or turnip and then pull it up; hinds are not quite so fastidious, they usually consume the whole thing.

The controversy still rages as to the best method of keeping the Red Deer herd within reasonable limits: I feel I cannot do better than to hand over to 'Henry' and ask his opinion on the question—should Staghunting be abolished?

Henry: I am so glad you have asked me this question—the most important of all. Up till now there has been solely incessant wrangling by you humans about it; what is astonishing is that the views and opinions of a stag have never been sought. I have had many chats with my fellow stags: if asked one and all of us would reply with a very emphatic *No*. Our reasons fall under three main headings.

In the first place the chief error lies in the fact that we deer do not experience the same forms of anguish, sorrow, despair etc. as you humans. Secondly, we feel there is a definite parallel between hunting and modern football; both have a set of rules, both rely upon large sums of money to function and both are brought into disrepute by the stupidity and thoughtless behaviour of spectators. It is the followers in cars, so few of whom know the rules of hunting, whose interference with the hunt staff often causes ugly scenes at the end of a hunt; and these scenes are seized upon by the Press and usually exaggerated.

Finally we stags are perfectly satisfied with existing conditions. Not for us the imported crack marksman to keep our numbers in check, snooping through our covert homes and hiding behind trees to take a shot at us: what an appalling thought! Such a situation would be unbearable and keep us on tenterhooks. With hounds and huntsman we know exactly where we are and are given due notice.

All we want is the preservation of our freedom; to be allowed to roam at will far and wide and in so doing partake of any food we like. We know all too well that the abolishment of hunting would curtail all this and that farmers would no longer tolerate our raids upon their crops. A salient point often overlooked is that after three years old a stag is seldom, if ever, hunted until around seven years old. Furthermore from November to the following August a mature stag is in no danger of being hunted—and what is more the stags know it!

144   Not Worth the Rearing

And now we are happily come, being Friday, to the market at Chulmleigh, briefly Chymley, where we may chance to meet good company. This was the land of Bomeleston, and after the Earl of Richmond had the manor and the Earl of Devon the borough. Of one of their noble ladies (which should be the Countess of Devon, for never can I find an Earl of Richmond inhabiting here) is left unto us this tale, (commonly spoken and constantly believed)—a poor labouring man, inhabiting this town, had many children, and thinking himself over-burdened by such a multiplied blessing of God in that kind, intended, by a politic natural course, to avoid all such future charge, and therefore absented himself from his wife and home seven years; at the end whereof he returned, and accompanying with his wife as formerly, she (see the vanity of man's natural wisdom to prevent God's purpose) conceived, and in due course of time was well delivered of a very fruitful birth, *viz*, seven sons; which being so secretly kept as but known to himself and his wife, he, despairing of Divine Providence (which never deceiveth them that depend thereon, but giveth meat to every mouth and filleth with his blessing every living thing), resolveth to let them swim in our river, and to that purpose puts them all into a large basket and takes his way towards the river. And here again, he is here prevented. The countess having been somewhere abroad to take the air, or doing rather some pious work, meets him with his basket, and by some, no doubt, Divine Inspiration, demands what he carried in his basket. The silly man, stricken dead well near with that question, answered they were whelps. "Let me see them," quoth the lady. "They are puppies," replied he again, "not worth the rearing." "I will see," quoth the good countess; and the loather he was to show them, the more earnest was she to see them: which he perceiving, fell on his knees and discovered his purpose, with all former circumstances: which understood, she hasteth home with them, provides nurses and all things else necessary. They all live, are bred in learning, and being come to man's estate gives each a prebend in this parish. Which I think are vanished not to be seen, but the seven crosses near Tiverton, set up by this occasion, keeps it yet in memory, unless they are appropriated to the free-school there erected.

145   Boniface the Blessed

Boniface, perhaps the greatest figure in this missionary movement, was a West Saxon said to have been born near Crediton about 675. He was received into the monastery at Exeter while still a child and from there he went to Nursling near Southampton, where he was able to profit both from the new learning which had been brought to Canterbury by Theodore and Hadrian and from the teaching and writing of Aldhelm by whom he was strongly influenced. His first visit to Frisia was in 716, but the times were not propitious and he returned to England in the next year. He set off once more in 718, never again to return to his own country. He visited Rome in 719 to receive a general commission from the Pope to preach to the heathen and again in 722 to receive episcopal consecration. He was consecrated in 732 and after working for more than twenty years among Germans and Franks he went back to Frisia and here, at Dokkum near the coast, he and some fifty of his companions were massacred by a band of pagans in June 754. Such in its barest outline was the most remarkable career of this man.

146   Kirton and its Praty Market

Ther is a praty Market in Kirton. The Toun usith Clothing, and most therby lyvith. The Place wher the old Cathedrale Chirch of Crideton stoode is now occupied with buildinges of Houses by the New Chirch Yarde side. The olde Chirch was dedicate to S. Gregory. The Chirch ther now standing hath no maner or token of Antiquite. One Sir John Scylley, a Knight, and his Wife, sumtyme dwelling in that Paroche, be buried in the North Part of the Transept of this. The Bishop of Excestor hath a Maner Place or Palace by the Chirch Yarde, and to this Maner Place there longith a Parke. Ther is a Deane, and he is as the Curate, but he is no Prebendarie of Course. Ther be xij. Good Prebendes in Kirton, besides certen Bursaries, Ministers and Choristes.

147   Creedy and Kirton

But now our river [the Creedy] thinks somewhat better of himself, and gives his name to his chief son, a borough, a market town, yea more, a bishop's see, Creedy-town, [Crediton] or the town upon Creedy; which may be said to be two towns, or rather one made of two joined, yet distinguished by the names of the east and west towns—the bishop's see and the borough. The Saturday market being always (two or three days excepted) kept in the borough, or the western town. It is sited seven miles from Exeter, and was the cathedral church of the bishops divers ages; and the fairest, in his chief state, of thirteen palaces, and richest demesnes: for here he was said to have three fairs, a fair palace to inhabit in; a fair park to sport in; and a fair demesne to walk, thrive, feed, and keep hospitality in. The whole manor and hundred, with the royalty thereof, to which it gives name, and contains five parishes, valued anciently at 1,000 marks annuatim, and with the sheaf it is little less worth now, you may be well assured. But they are now separated: for a bountiful (that I say, not wasteful) bishop thinking it to be too much to be left to his successors, alienated it, yet was it again recovered, and then again so assuredly reconveyed, that, though proof hath been made, yet it is thought passed all hope of recovery; and is now the inheritance of Sir Robert Killigrew, knight, vice chamberlain to the queen's majesty; and the sheaf in the corporators of Crediton. They keep three fairs; one the third of May, another the feast of St Lawrence, and the third holy-cross day in September.

Their market for kersies hath been very great, especially of the finer sort (and before the perpetuanos were wrought); for the aptness and diligent industry of the inhabitants (for making such cloth), did purchase it a supereminent name above all other towns, whereby grew this common proverb—as fine as Kirton spinning (for we briefly call it Kirton); which spinning was very fine indeed: which to express the better to gain your belief, it is very true that 140 threads of woollen yarn spun in that town were drawn together through the eye of a tailor's needle; which needle and threads were, for many years together, to be seen in Watling Street in London, in the shop of one Mr Dunscombe, at the sign of the golden bottle.

The soil is very fertile both for corn and pasture, insomuch as it is grown to a general proverb throughout the whole kingdom—as good hay as any in Denshire; and here in the country—as good hay as any in Kirton; and there—as good as any in my lord's meadow, than which there can be no better; for, considering the quantity of the field, it is a rich plot of land.

148   A Blessed Land

There be within the province XXXVIII market towns besides the city of Exeter of which XI be incorporated. The number of parks be very much impaired and of many remain not above or about XX, besides the two forests of Dartmoor and part of Exmoor, which some times were replenished with red deer, but now the game is very small and little regarded. And as for waters no one particular province in this land is more or better stored than is this county, for of rills, brooks, lakes, and springs, the number is as it were infinite or very hard to be numbered. And these by reason they do fall into great streams and rivers they do make them very great and some of them to be navigable; as namely, Exe, Dart, Plym, Tamar, Taw. In these rivers is great abundance of sundry fish. . . .

As for the country itself it is very strongly seated . . . if the loyalty, faith, and obedience due unto the sovereign be yielded. It is not then very safe begotten nor invaded. For on the north and south sides it is . . . hedged with . . . British seas and on the west it bords . . . upon the river Tamar which is now the . . . boundary between the two provinces of Devon and Cornwall; . . . only the East part lyeth open upon the main land . . . and these marches being also full of vales, hills, rocks, and stone is very safely to be made strong and fortified against the invasion of any enemy if the disloyalties of the subjects do not cause the contrary.

The whole province and country within these boundaries is in greatness the second to the greatest in this land and is altogether or for the most part wild, full of wastes, heaths, and moors, uphill and downhill among the rocks and stones . . . long, craggy, and very painful for man or horse to travail as all strangers travelling the same can witness it. . . . And therefore so much the less passable for the enemy with his troops and impediments of war. The soil itself which was full of craggy hills and altogether full of stones and plains which were full of heather and sedges and the valleys which were altogether full of briars and brambles are by mans travail and industry . . . become fertile and fruitful and do yield great varieties and plenties and plenty of herbs, fruits, and corn for the ease of man and goodly feeding and pasture for beasts of the field, great abundance of all kinds of fruits. . . . Great store of cattle both for necessity and for pleasure. The abundance of fowl both wild and tame, and of sea fish and of the like variety and abundance as in no other country. . . . And likewise in the belly of the earth there be found and digged sundry rich mines, some of gold and silver, some of tin and lead, some of iron and other metals. . . .

And if I might speak without offence I dare avouch that which one writeth of generally of this land. That England may better live of self without any other nation than any other nation without it. And even so also this little corner of this land can live better of itself without the rest of the land than all the residue can live without it.

149 Axe-Land

Ax then rennith to Axminstre, a pratie quik Market Toun a 3. Miles lower *ripa citeriori*; this Toun is in Devonshir. The Personage of Axminster, so I lernid, is impropriate to the Chirch of York. The Chirch of Axmistre is famose by the Sepultures of many Noble Danes slain in King Atthelstane's

8

Time at a Batel on Brunesdoun thereby, and by the Sepultures likewise sum Saxon Lordes slain in the same Feld.

Ax thens rennith thorough Bridge of Stone about a Quarter of a mile lower than Axmistre Toun; sumwhat lower then this Bridge enterith Artey [Yartey] Ryver, being sumtyme a Raging Water, into the Ryver. Ther is a Stone Bridge on Artey about half a Mile from the Place wher it enterith into Ax; this Bridge of sum is caullid Kilmington Bridge, (from) a village not very far it. About half a Mile lower then Axmistre Bridge is Newenham, sumtyme an Abbay of Bernardines, of the Foundation of Mohun, Erle of Somerset. Ax rennith a Mile dim. lower thorough Ax Bridg of 2. Archis of Stone; this Bridg servith not to pass over at High Tides, otherwise it doth. Thens Ax rennith half a Mile lower to Axmouth Town, and a Quarter of a Mile lower undre White Clif into the Ocean Se, ther caullid Ax Bay.

150   Mud and Straw

Axminster is a collection of two hundred houses, many of which are made of mud, and thatched with straw. It contains nothing considerable, except the parish church, which has a tower, in which bells so well tuned, that their sound is exceedingly harmonious and agreeable. The trade of the inhabitants consists in the manufactory of woollen cloth.

151   Blackdown Prospects

Beyond Chard to Honiton is a very bad road of stones and sand, over brooks, spring-heads, and barren downs. From the hill-tops about Stockland I first had sight of the southern ocean; a most solemn view, a boundless extent of water thrown into a mighty horizontal curve. Beyond Honiton the scene of travelling mended apace, and the fine Devonshire prospects entertained the eye in a manner new and beautiful; for here the hills are very long and broad, the valleys between proportional, so that the vastly extended concavity presented an immense landscape of pastures and hedge-rows distinct, like a map of an actual survey, and not beyond ken: these are full of springs, brooks and villages, copses and gentlemen's seats; and when you have passed over one hill, you see the like repeated before you, with Nature's usual diversity. They told me of a great cairn, or heap of stones, on Black Down, called Lapper-stones; probably a sepulchral monument.

152   Fat Mould

. . . for the red Marle hath this Property to fructify the barenesst Ground, and little to benefit the good Land; nevertheless, this Soil is a great Enemy to Sheep, whose Fat it melteth, and whose Flesh it corrupteth, though it feedeth them speedily. In the Spring and Fall of the Year, after a Shower of Rain, you can hardly endure to sit on the Ground the Heat will be so piercing, which proceedeth from the Fatness and Binding of the Ground, that suffereth not any Heat to descend, but calleth all upwards; Amongst this fat Mould they have high Grounds call'd Downs, containing not much in Breadth, yet running out in Length even to the Borders of *Somersetshire....*

153 Country Borders

I entered into Devonshire five miles off from Wellington, just on a high ridge of hills which discovers a vast prospect on each side full of enclosures and lesser hills, which is the description of most part of the West. You could see large tracts of grounds full of enclosures, good grass, and corn, beset with quicksets and hedgerows, and these lesser hills which are scarce perceivable on the ridge of the uppermost, yet the least of them have a steep ascent and descent to pass them.

Culimton [Cullompton] is a good little market town, and [has a] market cross and another set on stone pillars. Here was a large meeting of near four or five hundred people; they have a very good minister, but a young man. I was glad to see so many, though they were but of the meaner sort, for indeed it is the poor [that] receive the gospel, and there are in most of the market towns in the West very good meetings. This little place was one continued long street, but few houses that struck out of the street.

154 Underfoot

An old Devonshire farmer who was very fond of cheese was once given a really ripe Limburger as a treat. Some days later, the donor met him.

"Well, Harry," he asked, "have you ever eaten anything like that in your life?"

"No," came the reply. "Us reckons us never 'as eaten 'un before; but us 'as often trodden in 'un!"

155 Death at Feniton

Feniton is memorable only for that in the 3rd year of King Edward VI, some 6,000 hair-brained simple (no cowardly) commotioners (no more said our fathers that then lived), but the history 10,000 tall soldiers, first made insurrection in Cornwall and by degrees begirt the city of Exeter with a siege; yet unable by divers (and those sharp and desperate) assaults to prevail, proceeded eastward to this place, hoping their bulk would, like a snowball (for like that it soon melted), increase and multiply as it rolled forward. Hither they came, and in a fair meadow spread their colours. To encounter whom Lord Russell was ready, with the Lord Gray of Wilton. (Under whom served a band of Italians, 300 strong.) The general having the better cause, thought it to stand with his honour to give the assault, and offered to enter their fortifications which they had made at the bridge, which was courageously attempted, and with like violence resisted; the like they did valiantly divers sundry times, and so often strongly repulsed: but in fine the bridge was taken; then forcing the main battalion of the commotioners, the fight for a while was sharp, cruel, and full of blood; but (as it is most often) the worser cause had the worst success; they were put to the rout and fled. The chase was not long followed, for the Italians disbanding, fell to the spoil; which soon the rebels perceived, they suddenly reordered themselves, and wheeling about began a second more sharp fight, furious and violent, full of desperate resolution; but their arrows spent, and the general supplying his men with fresh troops, they were again scattered, leaving 300 dead in the place, and then retired to Clist; where what was their catastrophe you have already understood. But for a conclusion of this matter, if I should relate what hath been vulgarly reported (and verified by some that felt it), of the strength, and force, and resolution of these commons (the archers especially) you might, peradventure, take it with some doubt lest it increased somewhat by time or penning, but I intend to gather no more harvest than comes of the seed of truth.

156   A Lost Cause

The Rising in the West is usually called the Prayer-Book Rebellion; as if it were only a spasmodic outbreak against the introduction of a new form of church service on the part of the benighted Westerners. It was that; but it was also a great deal more. The new Prayer Book was a symbol to the adherents of the old faith in the West of the encroachments of the new order upon their old beliefs and usages; and they determined to use the occasion of its being launched for taking up arms on behalf of the old ways. They were conservative; they were reactionary; they were a lost cause before they started.

The movement came to a head in 1549, under the mild government of Somerset, and it found leaders of some standing in Humphrey Arundell of Helland, who was the acknowledged captain of the Cornish ranks, and in John Winslade of Tregarrick, and his brother William, who lived at Mithian in St Agnes: all of them men of property. Sweeping into their ranks various

Devon contingents, such as that from Sampford Courtenay where first
the Rising broke out, they advanced on Exeter and besieged it for four or
five weeks; and during the summer months of 1549 the Government was for
the time paralysed by the struggle.

Lord Russell was sent down to the West and made his headquarters at
Honiton against the Cornish camp around Exeter. He had with him a
contingent of German mercenaries, trained to formal warfare; and when
reinforcements had made him overwhelmingly superior in force, he advanced
along the Honiton–Exeter road. But his passage was fiercely contested; for a
time his army was held up and even beaten into retreat. The advance of the
Royal troops was resisted all along the old road crossing the Clyst valley;
Clyst St Mary itself was set on fire, and by Russell's orders the prisoners
taken were killed higher up the valley on Clyst Heath.

As I sat eating my lunch peaceably to myself, in a window looking out
on the main street of the village, I could not but think of that other August
day, so long ago now all knowledge of it must have perished out of mind
among the villagers. And yet here was the same street, and the slope down
which the troops came amid the burning houses; and at the bottom of the
hill the bridge and the long raised causeway of red sandstone across the
marshes where the Clyst breaks into two branches and spreads itself out
over the flats. Here there were bright saffron and purple marsh-flowers to
be seen among the weeds and sedge.

157 Perlycross

That grand old church of Perlycross [Culmstock] (standing forth in grey
power of life, as against the black ruins of the Abbey) had suddenly been
found wanting—wanting foundation, and broad buttress, solid wall, and
sound-timbered roof, and even deeper hold on earth for the high soar of the
tower. This tower was famous among its friends, not only for substance, and
height, and proportion, and piercings, and sweet content of bells; but also
for its bold uplifting of the green against the blue. To wit, for a time much
longer than any human memory, a sturdy yew-tree had been standing on
the topmost stringing-course, in a sheltering niche of the southern face,
with its head overtopping the battlements, and scraping the scroll of the
south-east vane. Backed as it was by solid stone, no storm had succeeded in
tugging its tough roots out of the meshes of mortar; and there it stood and
meant to stand, a puzzle to gardeners, a pleasure to jackdaws, and the pride
of all Perlycrucians. Even Mr Penniloe, that great improver, could not get a
penny towards his grand designs, until he had signed a document with both
Churchwardens, that happen what might, not a hair of the head of the sacred
yew-tree should perish.

158   A Gloomy Rectory

Moreover the rectory, a long and rambling house, was not a cheerful place to sit alone in after dark. Although the high and whitewashed back abutted on the village street, there was no door there, and no window looking outwards in the basement; and the walls being very thick, you might almost as well be fifty miles from any company. Worst of all, and even cruel on the ancient builder's part, the only access to the kitchen and the rooms adjoining it was through a narrow and dark passage, arched with rough flints set in mortar, which ran like a tunnel beneath the first-floor rooms, from one end of the building to the other. The front of the house was on a higher level, facing southwards upon a grass-plat and flower-garden, and as pretty as the back was ugly.

Even the stoutest heart in Perlycross [Culmstock] might flutter a little in the groping process, for the tunnel was pitch-dark at night, before emerging into the candlelight twinkling in the paved yard beside the kitchen-door.

159   As It Was

At the beginning of the eighteenth century Devon was the fourth most populous county in England. Plymouth, its largest town, had a population of 43,194; Exeter came next with 16,827, followed by Tiverton with 6,505 and Crediton with 4,297. There was also a score of market-towns or seaports such as Tavistock, Ashburton, Ottery St Mary, Colyton, Cullompton, Dartmouth, Brixham, Barnstaple, and Bideford, each with two to four thousand inhabitants, and another score like Holsworthy, Chulmleigh, and Chudleigh with one to two thousand. This population remained remarkably steady through the century.

Coastline and rivers were important factors in the commercial and industrial life of the county. The manufacture of wool, which depended on an abundance of sheep and water, was the chief industry, and continued to flourish until the middle of the century. Devon's serge industry was the most important branch of England's woollen export trade. Not only was local wool sold in most of the market towns, but Irish wool was imported through Barnstaple. Tiverton was the main centre of manufacture, and Exeter, with the River Exe as the export outlet to the continent, was the finishing centre and market. The continual wars of the century gradually deprived the industry of its overseas markets, and the expansion of the Yorkshire woollen industry later in the century completed its decline. The industries of the county steadily reverted to the size of small local industries, while the bulk of the population, dependant on agriculture, lived in villages and small isolated farms.

160   Johannes de Bampton

Here [at Bampton] Marianus and Florentius report that anno domini 620 there was a great conflict between Cynegils, first Christian king of the West Saxons and the Britons, where the king put 20,000 to the sword: the original nameth a far larger number by one cipher. They keep a weekly market, Saturdays, and two yearly fairs, one in the Whitsun week and the other at Luke's feast. As this place may glory of many worthy lords in succession of divers families (whereof some of either name have been here interred), though we know not how to distinguish them but by their armories; yet that is not his only honour, for it also bred a worthy and great scholar in the time of Edward I, a native of this place, whence he took his addition Johannes de Bampton, a monk of the Carmelite order. He is the first that read Aristotle publicly in the schools in Cambridge, when he lived there; was after Doctor of Divinity, and wrote sundry good books.

161   Hoe, Hoe, Who Lyes Here?

In the Church-yard [of St Peter's, Tiverton] is a Chapel built by the Earls of this County, and appropriated for their Burials, now demolished, where there is a Tomb under which *Edward Courtney*, Earl of *Devonshire*, and his Countess were interred, having their Effigies of Alabaster, sometime sumptuously gilded, and was about 40 Years ago to be seen, and which lamenteth me to write. Time hath not so much defaced, as Men have mangled that magnificent Monument, which had this written thereon, as some have seen:

> Hoe, hoe, who lyes here?
> 'Tis I, the goode Erle of Devonshire,
> With Kate my Wyfe, to mee full dere,
> We lyved togeather fyfty fyve Yere.
> That wee spent, wee had;
> That wee lefte, wee loste;
> That wee gave, wee have.

162   Weather Lore

Exmoor the tea-pot: Tiverton the spout.

163   Phoenix

This borough [of Tiverton] is much benefited by its weekly market of kersies of all sorts, and mixed and coloured cloths, which are either transported thence beyond the seas, or conveyed to London and there profitably sold, which may be easily conceived by considering the great wealth gotten by an inhabitant thereof not long since deceased; who, for his bountiful large legacies to pious uses, is right worthy of a perpetual remembrance, and the particulars thereof (if I could relate them) fit to be registered, never to be forgotten. A worthy living monument is the fair free school by him erected and perpetually stipended. His name is Peter Blundell; in whose memory, on St Peter's day, there is yearly, there and in other places, a feast kept.

But I must now pass to a subject of sadness. This town had a woeful market on the 3rd of April, 1598, when the whole town, consisting of 600 houses, was, in less than two hours, utterly consumed, with divers persons to the number (as I am told) of fifty. This sudden fire began in the western part of the town over the river, called thereby West-Exe, about one of the clock in the afternoon, and kindled with so violent a wind that, to the great terror and amazement of all the spectators, it was suddenly blown over the large river, and all the town generally and instantly in one flame, and consumed to ashes, the church and two alms-houses only (and not without wonder) preserved; the last being in the midst of the fire and the flame kindled therein, and yet quenched of itself without help of man. So powerful is the great God of Heaven, and so prone to mercy, and so vigilant and watchful of those whom he taketh into his protection.—

> As at his side as he doth stand
> A thousand dead shall be;
> Ten thousand eke at his right hand,
> And yet he shall be free.

Great were the riches and wealth consumed in these flames, yet God enabled them in a short time to re-edify it again as fair (that I say not fairer) than before; and it flourished again with great trade for some fifteen years; and then again, on the 5th of August, 1612, it pleased God to try their patience again with the like sudden fire, to their greater hindrance, yea, even to the utter impoverishing of the whole town, and to the great grief and sorrow of the good men of the same (this last leaving it almost hopeless of recovery), who, duly considering the cause of this their punishment, without murmuring or repining, mourned forth with patient Job,—

> Ah! naked came we from our mother's womb,
> And naked shall we return unto our tomb;
> The Lord hath taken what himself hath given:
> Blessed be God Almighty, Lord of Heaven.

And God, remembering his mercy, hath again, the second time, enabled them to rebuild it much fairer than any time before: so that it may comfortably be applied to this borough what is written of the re-engendering of the Phoenix by fire—

> Worn out with age, wishing her endless end,
> To shining flames she doth herself commend,
> Dies to revive, and goes unto her grave
> To rise again more beautiful and brave:
> Just like the first, or much more fair indeed,
> Though re-engend'ring of the self-same seed.

164 Ashes

It was on the 5th of *June* 1731, about Six a-Clock in the Evening, that the Fire, of which I am about to give an Account, broke out in the Town of *Tiverton* in the County of *Devon*; first discovering itself at a Baker's House near the East-end of the Town: And most of the Buildings thereabout being covered with Thatch, which through the extraordinary Drought of the Season was apt to take Fire from the smallest Sparks, the Flames in a few Minutes rose to a great Height, and by means of a brisk Northerly Wind spread themselves with such Fury, that several Houses were instantly on Fire.

The Fire-Engines being usually kept in the Church, at a considerable Distance from the Place where the Fire began, it was some time before they could be brought thither and put in order to do any Service, and through the Hurry and Confusion which the People were in upon this Occasion, one of the largest of them was brought without the Arms necessary for working it; and before the Persons, who were sent to fetch them, could return, the Houses on both sides being in Flames, and a great Quantity of Thatch and lumber Goods taking Fire in the Middle of the Street, and burning with extreme violence, the People were forced to fly off and leave their Engine, which though filled with Water was soon consumed. Nor had they better Success in other Parts of the Town, but the Fire spread itself into all Quarters, and put them into such a general Consternation, that they knew not where to apply their Endeavours; so that by this Means the Flames took their own Course for some Hours together, without any considerable Resistance; and being extended for more than a Quarter of a Mile in Length, and almost as much in Breadth, near Three Hundred Dwellings, besides Stables and other Out-Houses were burning all at once; from which dismal State of Things nothing less could be expected than the utter Ruin of this large and populous Town. But when the Fire was advanced on each Side to the Houses of some considerable Merchants, which were high and strongly built with Brick or Stone Wall, and covered with Slatt, they, with their Servants and Dependants, exerting all their Power against it, and being relieved, as Occasion required, with a fresh Supply of Men, and the Wind ceasing, by the Blessing of God upon their Endeavours, put a stop to the Progress of it about Four a-Clock in the Morning.

165 *Journal*

28 *Nov.* 1785. We brew a hogshead of ale.

29 *Nov.* 1785. What is remarkable is, that in all places, I have been beloved by the inhabitants, when known, but at first, called mad, in Scotland, hated in England . . . owing entirely to my studying to be singular, in as much as can be so. My family consists of 4 people only, yet 4 different nations, *viz*: Scotch, Dutch, English, and American—who speak no less than 6 different languages. The people in Devonshire never swear, nor have I heard one speak ill of another during almost 9 months I have lived in it.

30 *Nov.* 1785. Mrs Stedman and I go completely drest to the assembly in Tiverton, and dance. I play and win 5 shils. We then lodge at Mr Dunsford, who shows us indeed every degree of politeness. I paraded with my *Saint Andrew's* Cross, this being *Saint Andrew's Day*. N.B. The parsons in this town are a number of puppies.

24 *Dec.* 1785. Christmas evening. All burn the ashen faggot, and Johnny Stedman most mortally drunk.

6 *April* 1786. My neighbour Cook complains on Sally, my maid, for throwing filth in his gutter, under his window, which is no more than a dog's t-rd.

7 *April* 1786. I tell Cook of his mistake, and that he ought to know a dog's t-rd from another, after getting so many . . . etc, and that this was but a s-t come off. He loses temper again and is enraged at me not being on his side against my own servant, whose part I take. He roars, damns my eyes, and him, us, blackguards, threatens, etc. when I step up to him in his own house, challenge him to fight . . . and that I would shoot him through the head if he only had offered to touch me. I then say he is a blackguard, and he may go again to Barton and tell his papa. Damn him. He has shot hares, cut off the roots of his landlord's trees, and amused his masons to catch rats, etc. At last I pity the bugger and call to him will he drink with me. Yes! and again we are once more reconciled, he treating me with ale and cider, and I ask his wife to drink tea. One, farmer Collard, loses his horse. This is the 2nd this winter, besides his fine boy, his dear son. His parlour fell down, and his crop of potatoes all spoilt. Poor man, how unlucky all this.

166 *A Great Invention*

I cannot withhold the tribute that is due to him [John Heathcoat] for originality and for ingenuity through all the various combinations he has brought into action for the purpose of accomplishing a textile which had been attempted before, but, to my knowledge, with no success.

Viewing the machine as invented by Mr Heathcoat and as represented in the Drawing and described in the Specification, it appears to me one of the most complete mechanical combinations, in which the author displays uncommon power of invention, for which he is entitled to the protection which the law affords to useful discoveries.

167 The Luddites' Anthem

The guilty may fear, but no vengeance he aims
At the honest man's life or estate,
His wrath is entirely confined to wide frames
And to those that old prices abate.

These engines of mischief were sentenced to die
By unanimous vote of the trade,
And Ludd who can all opposition defy
Was the grand executioner made.

And when on the work of destruction employed
He himself to no method confines,
By fire and by water he gets them destroyed,
For the elements aid his designs.

Whether guarded by soldiers along the highway,
Or closely secured in the room—
He shivers them up both by night and by day,
And nothing can soften their doom.

168 The Song of the Great Heathcoat Wheel

For I was born some years ago,
When George the Fourth was King;
It seems to me but yesterday,
For time is on the wing.
Am I not out of the olden time,
And may be thought too S—L—O—W!
But give to me the good old days—of fifty years ago!

169   Thank You

It will be within the recollection of many whom I [John Heathcoat] see here
that I came almost like a shipwrecked mariner cast away upon your shores.
From that day until the present I have only experienced one series of
kindnesses from you and of happiness among you [the people of Tiverton].
I am not aware that I have ever done anything to merit this kind compliment.
To contribute to the comfort of the town one lives in is but to secure one's
own, and to attribute merit to a man for so doing would be almost as in-
consistent as to be surprised at his endeavouring to make his own house
comfortable. Our happiness depends so much on the comfort of our neighbour as on our own. No individual can be happy unless his neighbour is
happy with him. . . .

170   Parson's Power

At this time [the General Election of 1837] the Congregational minister
[of Tiverton] was the Rev William Harvey Heudebourck, a zealous Radical
and an advocate for disestablishment. Lord Palmerston waited on and pressed
the rev. gentleman for his vote and (what was of more consequence) his
interest with his congregation and with other Dissenting bodies in the
town. No promise, however, was given, and on the day of polling the Liberal
Party began to be anxious in as much as at three o'clock in the afternoon the
returns showed only a bare majority in their favour. About half past three,
however, a shout went up from the crowd, and on looking down through
St Peter Street a long procession was seen approaching the hustings. In
front was Mr Heudebourck, arm-in-arm with Mr John Singleton, the
venerable Baptist Pastor. Next came two other Nonconformist ministers
followed two by two by some 30 or 40 electors, all of whom recorded their
votes for his lordship. This demonstration was conceived and acted on by
Mr Heudebourck, who took this method of showing Lord Palmerston that
his election or rejection was virtually in the power of the Nonconformist
voters. The lesson thus taught was never forgotten and many years after
the Rev. Henry Madgin succeeded Mr Heudebourck in the pastorate one
of the first calls his lordship made when visiting his constituents was at
the parsonage on Angel Hill.

171   'P.B.'

Other customs, no less worthy, abide in the school of Blundell, such as the
singeing of nightcaps; but though they have a pleasant savour, and refreshing
to think of, I may not stop to note them, unless it be that goodly one at the

incoming of a flood. The school-house stands beside a stream, not very large, called 'Lowman', which flows into the broad river of Exe, about a mile below. This Lowman stream, although it be not fond of brawl and violence (in the manner of our Lynn), yet is wont to flood into a mighty head of waters when the storms of rain provoke; and most of all when its little co-mate, called the 'Taunton brook'—where I have plucked the very best cresses that ever man put salt on—comes foaming down like a great roan horse, and rears at the leap of the hedgerows. Then are the grey stone walls of Blundell on every side encompassed, the vale is spread over with looping waters, and it is a hard thing for the day-boys to get home to their suppers.

And in that time, the porter, old Cop (so called because he hath copper boots to keep the wet from his stomach, and a nose of copper also in right of other waters), his place it is to stand at the gate, attending to the flood-boards grooved into one another, and so to watch the torrent's rise, and not be washed away, if it please God he may help it. But long ere the flood hath attained this height, and while it is only waxing, certain boys of deputy will watch at the stoop of the drain-holes, and be apt to look outside the walls when Cop is taking a cordial. And in the very front of the gate, just without the archway, where the ground is paved most handsomely, you may see in copy-letters done a great P.B. of white pebbles. Now, it is the custom and the law that when the invading waters, either fluxing along the wall from below the road-bridge, or pouring sharply across the meadows from a cut called 'Owen's ditch'—and I myself have seen it come both ways—upon the very instant when the waxing element lips though it be but a single pebble of the founder's letters, it is in the licence of any boy, soever small and undoctrined, to rush into the great school-rooms, where a score of masters sit heavily, and scream at the top of his voice 'P.B.'

Then, with a yell, the boys leap up, or break away from their standing; they toss their caps to the black-beamed roof, and haply the very books after them; and the great boys vex no more the small ones, and the small boys stick up to the great ones. One with another, hard they go, to see the gain of the waters, and the tribulation of Cop, and are prone to kick the day-boys out, with words of scanty compliment. Then the masters look at one another, having no class to look to, and (boys being no more left to watch) in a manner they put their mouths up. With a spirited bang they close their books, and make invitation the one to the other for pipes and foreign cordials, re-commending the chance of the time, and the comfort away from cold water.

172   Past Glory

Silferton, now Silverton; but whence it should take its later rich name we may doubt, unless from the fertility of the glebe; for the parish is large and fruitful. It was anciently the land of Beauchamp, lately of Wadham, and now of his heirs general. It hath a little market every Saturday, and two fairs, the one on Midsummer day, the other on Saint Bartholomew's.

173   The Trade Way

Exe on the right hand leaveth Thorverton, or rather Thorowford-ton, so called of a brook running through the town, where it yields good commodity by driving their mills and fattening their meadows and pastures; for which kindness it decks him with a fair bridge of stone, of much use, as being in the trade way from the Land's End in Cornwall, and all that country, to the city of London; and gives him also a continual tribute of the waters of her brook which spring in.

174   Sweet Water

One Dyrwood, Lord of the demesnes and manor (I think) of Dyrwood, (some half mile forth of the north gate of the city [of Exeter]) a man given altogether to gluttony and riot, and, as the sequel shows, of no great discretion, and less careful of his estate, passed away most of his possessions, and in fine had nothing left but only this large and spacious demesne, which he also offered to sell, and to have nothing else for it but only his diet for one whole year, but it must be of choice cheer; nothing else but the skins of roasted geese, which he called goose-vells. The agreement was made, and at the year's end he was to make *dedi et concessi*, which he denied to do, by making a question (by some wiser man's advice), whether they would swear he had eaten the skins of geese only, and none of ganders: and for that they would not swear that directly, he was cleared (as the tale saith), of the bargain. But not long after he convenanted with the magistrates of the city to pass it unto them for as much money as he could bear, or for as many pieces of silver (which we now call old groats), as would lie, one by one, in a lineal row, between Dyrwoodwell and the great conduit which stands in the umbril point of the city: he made choice of his burden of silver, which was paid him. But within a few years after he comes that way, having spent all and being in great want and penury, refreshed himself with a draught of the water of the well, and with many sighs and sobs woefully cried out, "O Dyrwood! Dyrwood! had I known thy water to be so sweet I would never have sold thee." I cannot aver this for a truth, neither perchance will you take it so, but it is a tale of great age and often reported, and not unfit to give a caveat to young men, that they draw not hastily manors and farms through their throat, lest such morsels choke them; or lay them too heavily on their backs and so break them.

175 *Esquire Athelstan's Donation*

Our river cometh now with a large extent to Stoke, surnamed of his ancient lords Canon, as belonging to the Canons of St Peter's of Exon, given, as some say, in *perpetuam elemosynam*, by King Athelstan; others say, by a gentleman of that name that lived in Athelstan's-Hall, in the South-hams; but we suppose, by a window in the church, that it was given by that puissant prince King Canutus, or Knott, in the way of expiation of the cruel slaughter which his father, Swayn, the Dane, made of the citizens and monks of Exeter; for in one of the windows he is portraited with this inscription,

Stock-Chanon, a place of residency for canons, and belonging to the canons of the cathedral church of Exon.

This is but a tradition: this window was not glazed in divers hundred of years after; nor in his age, nor long after were there any canons; and therefore I do rather consent to Esquire Athelstan's donation.

176 *Exe Musters Gloriously*

Here our river (though in his greatest strength and fullness), falls into a melancholy fit, and, as loath to be seen, creeps by the side of a high hill, under two bridges near together, and sinks deep into the earth, and, at Cowley, desperately drowns herself in Exe, where is the seat of Skinner.

Here Cowley-Bridge, built of fair square stone, takes name; where Exe musters gloriously, being bordered on each side with profitable mills, fat green marshes and meadows (enamelled with a variety of golden spangles of fragrant flowers, and bordered with silver swans), makes a deep show as if she would carry boats and barges hom to the city; but we are opposed by Exwick wear; and indeed wears have much impaired his lustre and portable ability, which else might have brought his denominated city rich merchandise home to the very gates, which hath endured (to their great damage), the want thereof many years: the occasion thus:

This river was navigable from Exmouth, where it falls into the sea, unto the city gate (being eight miles distant), until the time of Baldwin the 4th and Baldwin the 5th of that progeny Earls of Devon. After whose death Isabella (daughter of the first and sister and heir of the last) married to William de Fortibus, Earl of Albemale and Lord of Holderness, and of him named Isabella de Fortibus, having the two manors of Exminster and Topisham, one on the east and the other on the west side of the river, erected certain wears thwart the river for the benefit of her mills, which to this day bear the name of Countess-wears, leaving yet between the wears a convenient length of thirty feet for barks and other such vessels to pass to and from the city. This was about the year of our salvation 1250: and thus it continued unto the time of Hugh the second of that name, Earl of Devon, about the year 1313: who, taking displeasure of the city, stopped the main current of the stream, to the great and continual detriment of the city. Edward, his grandson proceeded yet farther, and made two other wears, at St James's and Lampreford, cross the river, building a quay or pier at his town of Toppisham (three miles from the city), for the landing of all merchandise, to the great gain of the inhabitants for portage and otherwise. There was no hope a long time to redress this inconvenience; until, in these later times, by an ingenious device, a new channel was cut and part of the river, by sluices, conveyed and kept for the more convenient and cheaper carriage of their wares from Exmouth.

It is plentifully stored with fish, as trout, peal, dace, and pickerel (in outlets and standing pools), but especially salmon, which is highest priced, for that it is reputed to excel, in that kind, those in other rivers, being never out of season; but these fishes are of the less esteem by means of the great variety and abundance of delicate sea fish brought hither from the south and west parts of this shire and Cornwall; wherein no city in Great Britain may equal it: but hereof sufficiently hath been already spoken.

177   A Golden Share

Cadberry, alias Caderbyr, the land of William de Campo Arnulphi, and after of Willoughby, Fursdon, and now Carew. The castle may be seen afar off, so they term a high upright topped hill, by nature and slight art anciently fortified, which in those Roman or Saxon wars might be of great strength, containing within the compass thereof near two acres. Hence you may see some five miles distant to the south-east, in the parish of Broad-clist, another down called Dolbury-Hill. Between these two hills (you may be pleased to hear a pretty tale), it is said (I set not down these words to lessen your belief of the truth of the matter, but to let you

> Take it on this condition,
> It holds credit by tradition),

that a fiery dragon (or some *ignis-fatuus* in such likeness) hath been often seen to fly between these hills, coming from the one to the other in the night season, whereby it is supposed there is great treasure hid in each of them, and that the dragon is the trusty treasurer and sure keeper thereof; (as he was of the golden fleece in Colchos, which Jason, by the help of Medæa, brought thence); for, as Ovid saith, he was very vigilant—

> A watchful dragon set
> The golden fleece to keep,
> Within whose careful open eyes
> Came never sink of sleep.

Dawlish—'The Strand'

Dartmouth—from the south

And these two relations may be as true, one as the other, for anything I know, for this is constantly believed of the credulous here, and some do aver to have seen it lately. And of this hidden treasure this rhyming proverb goes commonly and anciently,

> If Cadbury Castle and Dolbury Hill dolven were
> All England might plough with a golden share.

178 Rivalry

It [Bradninch] is very ancient, and so it must be to claim priority and antiquity of Exeter, and yet should seem to have some reason for it, if the proverbial speech be true which saith, that the mayor of Exeter is to hold the mayor of Bradninch's stirrup when they meet together, which is strange; and yet no stranger in some men's opinion than for the emperor to do the like service to the Pope, and that we read hath been done; but how the Pope holds this privilege and continueth it I know not; but Bradninch (they say) hath lost it, for which a pretty reason is alleged; but our journey is long, and the reason also, and therefore I cannot stay to deliver it: but howsoever lost, there be gentlemen yet (I thank God) living that have seen the recorder of Exeter hold the recorder of Bradninch's stirrup. You will think perchance it was in merriment; and to say the truth, so do I also.

179 Origins

Exeter was certainly in English hands before 700, since Boniface, the great West-Saxon missionary who was born c. 675, received his education in an English monastery there. Ine, king of Wessex 688–726, founded a bishopric at Sherborne in 705, to serve Wessex west of Selwood and he is also credited with the establishment of a town at Taunton. In 710 he fought against Geraint, king of Dumnonia, all that remained of British territory in the south-west, and in 722 he was as far west as the River Hayle in Cornwall, but the people of Cornwall continued to enjoy some degree of independence for another century. They were active against the English of Devon early in the ninth century, at the height of the Danish wars, and they did not suffer final defeat until the victory won by Egbert of Wessex in the battle of Hingstone Down near the Tamar in 838.

9

180 Malediction Against Book Thieves

Leofric, Bishop of the Church of Saint Peter the Apostle, in Exeter, gives this book to his cathedral church, for the relief of his soul and for the use of his successors. If, however, anyone shall take it away from thence, let him lie under perpetual malediction. Amen.

181 The Exeter Book

The Exeter Book was possibly written in the scriptorium at Glastonbury Abbey about the middle of the 10th century. In its present form it contains 131 leaves of strong vellum, but some of these are damaged; particularly— as one might expect—at the beginning and end of the volume, and several leaves are missing from the middle. It is written in darkish brown ink in a fine hand of great character. Dr Robin Flower describes the script in these terms:

"The Exeter Book in its best pages ... is written in what one may unhesitatingly describe as the noblest of Anglo-Saxon hands. The script achieves a liturgical, almost monumental, effect by the stern character of its design and the exact regularity of its execution."

The manuscript contains no colour, and little ornamentation of any kind except some rather rough decoration to a few initial letters. On the margins of six leaves, however, there are incised ornaments of a unique type, probably made with a stylus, and dating from the latter half of the 11th century.

How much of the manuscript is now lost, or when the losses occurred, is not known. It was described in Leofric's donations list as 'a great English book', but the description seems excessive for the manuscript as we now have it. No trace of the original binding now exists, though the calf binding of *c.* 1700 has been preserved. The manuscript must have been lying about unbound for centuries, exposed to all sorts of casual damage, and, as R. W. Chambers remarks, 'the wonder is that any part of it should have survived'. One of the preliminary leaves still bears the mark of the beer-pot which was once placed upon it, and some of the leaves at the end look as though they have been scorched; though the damage may possibly have been caused by damp. It is to be remembered that during some seven hundred years the book would have been completely unintelligible to anyone who chanced to look into it; and it could have had very little interest except as a curiosity. Even in this imperfect and mutilated state, however, its importance to the study of Old English poetry is almost incalculable. There are only three other codices of Anglo-Saxon poetry in existence: the manuscript of *Beowulf* in the British Museum, the 'Cædmon' poems in the Bodleian, and the manuscript now in the possession of the Cathedral Library of Vercelli in Piedmont which contains, among other fine things, *Andreas*, *Elene*, and *The Dream of the Rood.* Though it cannot fairly be maintained that any single poem in the Exeter Book rises quite to the artistic level of *Beowulf*, it is at any rate certain that the Exeter collection is at once the largest and the most varied of the four codices. The stately and heroic narratives of Guthlac and Julians; the echoes of the early days of our race in Widsith and Deor; the strange half-lyrical charm of the *Wanderer*, with its regret for happier days long past; the *Seafarer*, with its pictures of the hardships and fascinations of the sailor's life; the description of a dead Roman city—Bath perhaps—in the *Ruin*; the unique *Riddles*—all these make up an anthology of the very greatest interest and importance. Without it our knowledge of Anglo-Saxon poetry would be immeasurably the poorer.

Today the Exeter Book is happily in as fine state of preservation as modern resources can achieve. It was thoroughly repaired, strengthened and rebound at the British Museum some forty years ago, and given reasonably good fortune there is no reason why it should not continue to delight—and astound—a host of generations to come.

182   Seafarer

In my ears no sound	but the roar of the sea,
The icy combers,	the cry of the swan;
In place of the mead-hall	and laughter of men
My only singing	the sea-mew's call,
The scream of the gannet,	the shriek of the gull:
Through the wail of the wild gale	beating the bluffs . . .
Yet still, even now,	my spirit within me
Drives me seaward	to sail the deep,
To ride the long swell	of the salt sea-wave.

183   Riddle of the Song Thrush

I carol my song	in many a cadence,
With modulation	and change of note.
Clearly I call,	keeping the melody,
An old evening-singer	unceasing in song.
To earls in their houses	I bring great bliss;
When I chant my carols	in varying strains,
Men sit in their dwellings	silent and still.
Say what I'm called	who mimic so clearly
The songs of a jester,	and sing to the world
Many a melody	welcome to men.

184 Decent Burial

Of Griffeth Meredith emonge sundrie his good actions this one thinge is not to be forgotten: it was the manner yn those daies that suche prysoners as for theire offenses were exequuted at the forches [gallows] at Ryngeswelle place aboute some myle out of Exeter, that the bodies of suche as had no ffrendes otherwise to bury theym, they were verie irreventlye brought backe to the Citie upon a staff betwene two men to be buried yn the Churche-yard, and there yn theire clothes for the most parte were caste yn to the grave. This man piteinge so inhuman and Lothesome manner of theire buryall dyd for redresse thereof geve infeoffe certeyn landes which he had at Sidfford of the yerely (value) of about XXXVIIIs for the buyenge of schrowdes for all suche as had neede; . . . which his good example so moved a godly matrone Jone Tuckeffelde that she, lothinge the lothesome manner of the caridge of the dedd prisoners to the Citie, dyd purchase a pece of land neere adioyninge to the said forches and dyd inclose the same with a stone wall for a buryall place, and hathe geven certeyn landes for the meanetennance of the same.

185 A Fair Walled City

The Town of Excester is a good Mile and more in Cumpace, and is right strongly waullid and mainteinid. Ther be diverse fair Towers in the Toun Waul bytwixt the South and the West Gate; as the Waulles have been newly made, so have the old Towers decayed. The Castelle of Excester standith stately on a high Ground bytwixt the Est Gate and the North. Ther be 4 Gates in the Toune by the names of Est, West, North, and South; the Est and the West Gates be now the fairest and of one fascion of Building, (but) the South Gate hath beene the strongest.

186 Built on Cloth

Exeter is a town very well built, the streets are well pitched, spacious noble streets, and a vast trade is carried on. As Norwitch is for "coapes, callamanco, and damaske," so this is for serges. There is an incredible quantity of them made and sold in the town. Their market day is Friday, which supplies with all things like a fair almost; their markets for meat, fowl, fish, garden things, and the dairy produce take up three whole streets besides the large market house set on stone pillars, which runs a great length, on which they lay their packs of serges. Just by it is another walk within pillars, which is for the yarn. The whole town and country is employed for at least twenty miles round in spinning, weaving, dressing and scouring, fulling, and drying of the serges. It turns the most money in a week of any thing in England. One week with another there is £10,000 paid in ready money, sometimes £15,000. The weavers bring in their serges, and must have their money, which they employ to provide them yarn to go to work again. There is also a square court with pent-houses round, where the malters are with malt and oatmeal, but the serge is the chief manufacture. There is a prodigious quantity of their serges they never bring into the market, but are in hired rooms which are noted for it, for it would be impossible to have it all together. The carriers I met going with it, as thick, all entering into town with their loaded horses; they bring them all just from the loom, and so they are put into the fulling-mills, but first they will clean and scour their rooms with them, which, by the way, gives no pleasing perfume to a room, the oil and grease, and I should think it would rather foul a room than cleanse it, because of the oils, but I perceive it is otherwise esteemed by them, which will send to their acquaintances that are tuckers the days the serges come in for a roll to clean their house—this I was an eye-witness of. Then they lay them in soak in urine, then they soap them and so put them into the fulling-mills, and so work them in the mills dry till they are thick enough; then they turn water into them, and so scour them. The mill does draw out and gather in the serges. It is a pretty diversion to see it—a sort of huge notched timbers like great teeth. One would think it should injure the serges, but it does not. The mills draw in with such a great violence that, if one stands near it and it catch a bit of your garments, it would be ready to draw in the person even in a trice. When they are thus scoured, they dry them in racks strained out, which are as thick set one by another as will permit the dressers to pass between, and huge large fields occupied this way almost all round the town, which is to the river side; then, when dry, they pick out all knots, then fold them with a paper between every fold, and so set them on an iron plate and screw down the press on them, which has another iron plate on the top, under which is a furnace of fire of coals—this is the hot press. Then they fold them exceedingly exact, and then press them in a cold press. Some they dye, but the most are sent up for London white.

I saw the several vats they were a-dyeing in of black, yellow, blue, and green, which two last colours are dipped in the same vat—that which makes it differ is what they were dipped in before, which makes them either green or blue. They hang the serges on a great beam or great pole on the top of the vat, and so keep turning it from one to another—as one turns it off into the vat, the other rolls it out of it; so they do it backwards and forwards till it is tinged deep enough of the colour. Their furnace that keeps their dye-pans boiling is all under that room made of coal fires. There was in a room by itself a vat for the scarlet, that being a very changeable dye, no waste must be allowed in that; indeed, I think they make as fine a colour as their 'bowdies' are in London. These rollers I spake of, two men do continually roll on and off the pieces of serge till dipped enough. The length of these pieces is or should hold out 26 yards.

This city does exceedingly resemble London, for besides these buildings

I mentioned for the several markets, there is an Exchange full of shops like
our Exchanges are, only it is but one walk along as was the Exchange at
Salisbury House in the Strand; there is also a very large space railed in by the
Cathedral with walks round it, which is called the Exchange for Merchants,
that constantly meet twice a day, just as they do in London. There are
seventeen churches in the city, and four in the suburbs. There is some
remains of the Castle walls: they make use of the rooms which are inside
for the Assizes; there are the two bars, besides being large rooms with seats
and places convenient and jury room. Here is a large walk at the entrance
between rows of pillars. There is, besides this, just at the market-place a
Guildhall, the entrance of which is a large place set on stone pillars, beyond
which are the rooms for the session or any town affairs to be adjusted. Behind
this building there is a vast cistern, which holds upwards of 600 hogsheads
of water, which supplies by pipes the whole city; this cistern is replenished
from the river, which is on purpose turned into a little channel by itself to
turn a mill, and fills the engine that casts the water into the trunks which
convey it to this cistern. The water engine is like those at Islington and
Darby, as I have seen, and is what now they make use of in divers places
either to supply them with water or to drain a marsh or overplus of water.

187   A Hard Condition

Your Majesty commands our obedience to the commission of array, whilst
both houses of Parliament adjudge us to be betrayers of our liberty and
property if we do so. They persuade submission to the militia, whilst your
majesty proclaims it unlawful and derogatory to your prerogative; how
unhappily are we here made judges in apparent contraries; in how hard a
condition are we whilst a two-fold obedience, like twins in the womb strive
to be born, to both we cannot chose but look upon the privileges of Parliament
with a natural affection; from our fathers' loins we derive a touch that leads
us thither as the needle to the loadstone. We desire to preserve them because
the death of liberty without that support is inevitable.

188   We, Your Humble Petitioners

That the true Protestant Religion may be still preserved, the Rights and
Privileges of Parliament maintained, and the just Liberties of the subject
supported; and that the Popish party may be disarmed, which (notwithstanding the former Laws and Orders) have been neglected; and that the
Kingdom may be put into a posture of defence, and the Forts and places of
strength may be committed to the hands of trusty persons; and that the

power of voting in Parliament may be taken from the Bishops and Popish Lords, and also the said distresses of our afflicted Brethren in Ireland may thoroughly be taken to heart, and speedily remedied.

189 Great Bell, High Seat, Fair Pipes

The first thing I view'd after my weary p'ceeding dayes Journey was the Cathedrall Church, the which was built, and finish'd (some yeeres after the first foundation thereof lay'd) by a Saxon King: At her west entrance, I found a fayre Frontispice, which rep'sented to the eye, a lively Prospect, Rowes of goodly great Statues, artificially cut in Freestone (much like the Cathedrall at Wells), the highest whereof are the Prophets, Apostles, & Fathers, the other two of the Saxon & Roman Kinges. And on the top aboue them all, is K. Edward the Confessor, & Leofricus the 1. Bishop, receiving his Congee desleere in an humble Posture on his Knee.

Although the Cathedrall be not exceeding long, yet itt is very wide, fayre, & lofty, & hath standing on either side of her Crosse Isle 2. Towers, in one of them hangs a braue Ring of 8. Bells; In the other but one onely, but it is a goodly one, brother to Tim of Lincolne, sure one of the breed of Osney w^{ch} (as they say) weighs aboue 10000. Weight, and is in Compasse 18. Foote.

For 2. things in her besides that great Bell, she may compare Wth any of her Sisters in England; one is a stately, rich, high Seat for the Bishop; and the other is a delicate, rich, & lofty Organ wch has more additions then any other, as fayre Pipes of an extraordinary length, & of the bignesse of a man's Thigh, which wth their Vialls, & other sweet Instruments, the tunable voyces, and the rare Organist, togeather, makes a melodious & heauenly Harmony, able to rauish the Hearers Eares.

190 Verdi's Requiem
(In Exeter Cathedral)

Nothing very discreet about Verdi:
After the crescendo
The breathless hush,
The quivering strings,
The predictable repeat of 'the good bit'
(Starting each tune on a different stair),
Plenty of bim–bam–boom
And through and under and over
The big, fat, warm tune.

It needs a film really,
With lots of very clean nuns,
Flickering candles
And great spaces.

It's a funeral all right,
A tremendous, rumbling funeral,
The gun-carriage halting at intervals
To allow for the poignant solo.

Nice to go down with all that pomp;
Good curtain music—
For, after all, we all know
What whoever-it-was has done.
But supposing we worked at the other end
And wrote a thumping great
Birth Music,
Heralding the poor little chap
With enormous choirs
And massed bands
And said—
Now, mate, live up to *that*!

191   A Salubrious Air

This city of Exeter is seated in a salubrious air, exceeding pleasantly for the inhabitants, and commodiously likewise for the whole country for their convenient assemblies. For though I cannot say it stands equally in the midst thereof, as the yolk in the egg, or centre in a circle, yet opportunely and convenable for the farthest remoted, in a day's travel, for general meetings. It stands on a hill among many, the whole country being mountainous and full of little hills about it; towards the sea, at the mouth of Exe, only excepted. In form, rather circular than square; and in circumference near 1,600 paces (allowing five feet to the pace) which is somewhat above a mile and half: and though it be highly placed, yet is it well supplied with water both in itself and neighbouring springs conveyed in leaden pipes.

The four principal streets are from the four great gates, which take name from the four quarters of the heavens, west, east, north, and south, and meet in the umbril of the city, where standeth a great water-conduit, and the place called Carfoix, which I think more properly Quatrevois; and divides the whole into four quarters, or several parts.

In the north-east, in the most high and eminent part thereof (as commanding the whole) stands I may yet say so, an old ruinous castle called Rugemount, whose gaping chinks and aged countenance presageth a downfall ere long; yet hath it not any occasion to complain either of battery, undermining, or fire, but rather of age, storms, and neglect. (The ruin of most edifices.)

192 *The Spirit of Christmas Past*

The choirs of various churches would go around the parishes on Christmas Eve, stopping at the principal houses to sing an appropriate anthem or a Christmas carol; this over, the loudest tenor voice would call out the names of the nearest residents, such as "Good morning, Mr Snugg, good morning, Mrs Snugg, and all the young Snuggs, past three o'clock; a very cold and frosty morning"; or "the snow is falling fast". The young reader must understand, in those days, the winters were much more severe than now; skating almost a certainty, and snow falling at various times for two or three days, and remaining on the ground for several weeks. I have seen birds lying dead on the ground for want of food. My father informed me that the snow had been so high on Haldon that men were sent from Exeter to cut a passage through it, to allow the mails to pass. Returning to the perambulation, the choir consisted of singers, accompanied by a fiddle or two, bass viol, a clarinet or flute. The above-named instruments were used in churches that had no organ. On the rounds some parties were waiting the arrival of the choir with a cup of tea, coffee, or soup, which was very acceptable. A good efficient choir would be accompanied by a lot of 'camp followers,' who rendered assistance by carrying chairs, lanterns, &c., also by holding the music in front of the performers. About six o'clock the various rounds were finished; at half past six the Cathedral bell tolled out, the front doors were opened, and then there was a great rush of people, about half filling the nave, many in a state which indicated they were not members of the temperance society, being very noisy, and smoking. This conduct not meeting the approval of the Dean and Chapter they ceased to have the nave opened some years since. At seven o'clock the organist played the Old Hundredth Psalm on the 'Great Organ', the chorister boys singing from the 'Minstrels' Gallery', which was lit up with candles. The morning and afternoon services were thinly attended, but a great many outsiders went to hear the anthem. The parish churches were well attended in the morning, afternoon scarcely any one present, evening three or four churches open, and these very thinly attended. So universal was the social and family gathering, that the High street in the evening had the appearance of a deserted town, with respect to people moving about.

Now for family meetings on Christmas days. 'Grandfather' would, if possible, invite the whole of his family descendants, including grandchildren, to partake of what the festive table produced, which generally speaking, consisted of a goose, beef, and a large smoked ham, &c., followed by a huge fig pudding, covered with white sugar to correspond with the snow clad roofs. Beer was not forgotten, good home-brewed October twelve months was tapped by the landlords for their customers. Dinner over, chairs were placed in a semicircle around the blazing fire, children sitting in front or on the knee, and the topic of conversation would be old family times, absent friends, and passing events, until about five o'clock, when the old ladies' delight, a good cup of tea with a little bit of green in it, was announced. After this ceremony, which occupied about an hour, cards were introduced; the family game, twopence halfpenny loo was played until supper-time, nine o'clock. The coin was put in the snuffer-tray; a cup or small basin called the 'pitcher' was also placed in the centre of the table, the holder of the ace of trumps depositing a halfpenny in it, the amount being divided amongst the younger branches. After supper, again sitting round the ashen faggot fire, healths and toasts were proposed, and good old seasonable and patriotic songs sung until about midnight. Then came the trying time of departure, with respect to children, some sleepy, others crying. Before leaving, a hint was given that the ham would be nice and solid about eleven the following day. "Oh yes, I understand, you are all welcome. Now mind I shall expect you." This led to another family day's enjoyment.

There was another prominent incident in these parties, the maternal headdress, net caps, the polls about three inches high, lace trimmings, interspersed with various coloured ribbons. This piece of gear having to last the season, the different milliners' tastes were well scrutinized. Hair fronts, too, were worn across the forehead, according to taste either plain or dangling curls, nicely put out of hand by the barber. This paraphernalia was pinned up in a white handerchief and carried with great care through the streets which was an intimation that "I am going to a party." No doubt the reader will think why this show off, but the people had not the convenience of cabs then as now. Sedan chairs were the only conveyances available. In 1823, Humphrey Stark started four pair-horse hackney coaches; now we have about one hundred cabs and flies. That assistants in shops might have an opportunity of spending a few hours with their friends on Christmas Eve, shutters were put up about six o'clock, continuing a little later each evening until New Year's Eve.

Another event not noticed now was Old Christmas Eve, on 5th January, when confectioners tried to excel each other in their art. The streets were crowded with parents and children visiting the various shops; the outsiders were more numerous by hundreds than buyers. Another Christmas pastime, but one scarcely known to the present generation, was the 'mummers', who would visit private houses, and ask permissions to perform before the assembled company. The different characters were generally well got up, and the parts very creditably performed. For this a liberal collection was made, and some of the good things on the table presented to the players. It was customary at some of the inns at this season to invite the 'landlord's' customers and friends to supper, and have a bowl of punch, &c. I will give one instance of it which was at the Barnstaple Inn, North Street, kept by Mr Ireland. After supper the guests, numbering from thirty to forty, would, if convenient, adjourn to the large kitchen, which was nicely decorated. The chairman and vice with their yards of clay occupied seats on each side of the fireplace, with a huge ashen faggot burning; on this occasion they were named "Gogg and Magog," it being in the "pattern parish" of St David's. Mr Carpenter, the organist, with the elder portion of the choir, added to the musical department by singing glees, catches, duets, and songs; other parties filling up the interval with toasts, songs, or recitations, and a very pleasant enjoyable evening was spent. Those who had no domestic ties would remain until the small hours, when the kind host and hostess would bring around tea or coffee. Such were the incidents of bygone days, and to those whose memory goes back to that old time, no doubt the foregoing remarks will bring to mind many happy hours spent, many sincere friends, and many a good old citizen.

193 A German Tree

My sister writes to my grandmother, 29 January 1851, "Brother Henry and I went to a party on Tuesday evening. We danced and saw a magic lantern, and there was a German tree, and many nice things to eat. We enjoyed it all very much, and did not get ill after it." At that date a Christmas tree was still a novelty, and was called a German tree, as the fashion came from Germany.

194 Junket or Jonquil

I am Victorian enough myself to think it rather vulgar to call an omnibus a 'bus, but never had qualms in saying 'van for caravan or 'wig for periwig, that is, peruke. People habitually say You for Ye, yet snigger at our saying Us for We. What they call 'a chapter of accidents' is 'a proper old pedigree' here. That is etymologically right, as a pedigree is a thing that goes on step by step. Etymologically there is not much difference between a junket and a jonquill, or porcelain and pigs, or venerable and venereal; but a Venerable Archdeacon got quite cross when I applied the other adjective to him. Down here we soften 'immodest' into 'vulgar' and 'immoral' into 'rough'; and a stranger may give great offence, when only meaning 'rough' and 'vulgar' in the usual sense.

195 Broad Gauge and Narrow

A friend writes to him [Torr's father] from Exeter, 8 April 1844—"Our railway will be sufficiently complete for an engine to travel here to-morrow, and I suppose will be completed about the first week in May." It was opened on 1 May, and another friend writes on 17 September—"From Bristol to Exeter we experienced the shaking of the carriages exceedingly, and were really obliged, as I have before said, to hold by the side of the carriage to endeavour to steady ourselves." Yet this line was on the broad gauge, and that was much less jerky than the narrow. I remember people saying that they would never go up by the South Western, as the Great Western shook them less.

196   A Burst of Bells

I arrived at Exeter late on a beautiful, clear Sunday evening; too late, alas, to hear the bells of the cathedral that I had been hoping, on the way, to be in time for. For I have always heard of them as one of the loveliest peals of bells in all England; and I have a passion for church bells. It is perhaps the thing that I miss most subtly in leaving England; there are all sorts of church bells abroad in their place—the curious chimes in the towers of old German cities, the unlovely nostalgic jangle of the bells ringing out over flat and woodland of the North German plain, the sweet tinkling from little belfries in the Tyrol, the low and exciting boom of the bells from the great Paris churches reminiscent of such dangers and past excitements. But there is something distinctive of England that I miss when out of the range of our church bells: a sweet melancholy, charged with memories, and yet bordering always upon a subdued joy in life.

And this Sunday evening, as I drew near to Exeter in the train, there was a rousing burst of bells ringing to service from the church-tower at Whimple across the cider orchards and blowing in a gust straight into the compartment of the window as the train drew away again from the station.

Exeter is a city that any county, or rather, any country, might be proud of. And yet it may not strike you all at once: you have to put in the sort of apprenticeship I did, wandering around its streets at all hours of the day, keeping your eye open for the old and curious houses that may pop up anywhere, tracing out the lines of the medieval city that subsist unchanged if you follow out the line of streets where formerly the walls went; and there are all kinds of pleasant surprises you may come upon, here a stretch of the city wall running along behind a row of houses, there a diminutive church that runs into a backyard, or is so cramped by houses on every side that it is forced to take the oddest shape, or again a dark passage that leads to something straight out of the Middle Ages like the Hall of the Vicars-Choral of the Cathedral, or just a ring in the wall where they attached the chains at night to keep people out of the precincts of the Close.

You may be disappointed until you have done all this, and got an inner feeling for the distinctive character that the city has. Coming straight from the green spaciousness of Salisbury Close, with its acres of wide lawns and gardens and the perfection of the houses there, I felt a little apologetic for the Close at Exeter, which is altogether smaller and less beautiful. But the longer I stayed there, the more I saw what a remarkable character of its own the city has, just as remarkable in its way as Salisbury, or Münster, or Bourges.

It may be fanciful, or it may come from dwelling too much upon old times—until in fact I sometimes feel I know what was going on in a place three hundred years ago better than what is happening there today—but the predominant impression of Exeter upon my mind was that of a frontier town. It was unmistakably of the West; Sherborne had been an approach to the West, but this was really the key to it. This position has given it its character throughout the ages; and not all the changes and the indignities that the modern world has brought upon it can altogether overlay the spirit of the place or prevent its genius from appearing. One night, fairly late, I went down the High Street to the bridge across the Exe, and turned back to get a view of the figure the city made. It was like a fortress. At night you could see the bold lines of it standing out as it had always been through the centuries, undistracted by the sights and the disturbing detail of the day. There was the main artery of the city, the long High Street coming bold and straight downhill to where the river was bridgeable; the bridge carrying the thoroughfare across river and island to the west; and here at the gate, the danger-point in the city's defences, so often assaulted and so faithfully guarded, the houses on either side crowd together to narrow the entry; and at night, seeing only the essential lines, I thought how like great bastions they were, with the city wall running up from the river on either side.

197   Seated General
(The Buller Statue in Exeter)

'He saved Natal'—
In a plumed hat
And well-cut khaki,
Savage only on top of his head,
Civilized below.

I knew once a relative of his,
Also well turned-out,
But given to rages
(Mostly, it is true,
In the cause of uprightness
Hard work
And similar good ends)

And you cannot perhaps build an Empire
Without such bouts of savagery.

In retirement
The power is muted from the J.P.'s Bench,
Urbane almost on the hospital board,
Nearly reverential at the lectern.

Only at speed, close to,
In the fury of the chase,
Pounds of flesh and muscle
Held between the legs,
The face purple
Over the pink,
Will you see the former glory.

198   And Did Those Feet?

Somewhat above this village [of Kenford] as you descend from the great hill
Haldown towards Exeter, at the foot thereof stood a long time (I cannot say
now stand) two stones pitched in the ends, which to strange travellers seemed
to be there placed for passengers with the more ease (especially women
which there perchance were not used to be lifted up, and in that age went
not in coaches) to take their horses; for commonly all men walk down that
steep descent. But from the neighbours and those that anciently dwelled
near it you have another and strange relation, thus:

They first name them the giant's stones: and they say, by an ancient
tradition, that a giant (so men of an extraordinary stature are called, and
some such are seen in every age) was there buried; who, not only for his
large bulk and length, but for his strength and valour, surpassed (by far) all
men of his time. And that I spin not out the thread of this tale to a farther
length, how he fell here suddenly down dead, and the cause of his death,
worth (I can tell you) good fire in a winter's cold night, that he was buried
in this place; and these two stones were placed, one at his head and the other
at his feet, which expressed him to be no pigmy but of the longest size; yet
not peradventure so large as he whom the noble poet (by an hyperbolical
licence) describeth thus:

> His legs, two pillars; and to see him go
> He seem'd some steeple reeling to and fro.

But the wonder was, that albeit the placing of these two stones showed where
his head and feet lay, yet the true length of his stature could never be directly
known; for measure the distance between them as often as you would, yet

should you not take it twice together alike equal, but at every several time there would be some difference, longer or shorter. What fallacy there was I cannot conceive, but this report was general, yea, and by such whose credit was not to be questioned, that either themselves had found it so by trial, or heard by those affirmed, of the truth of whose relation no doubt or mistrust was to be made; yet to call them now to witness is needless; yet would I not persuade you to believe more of this than of other self-like nature: as Mayn-Amberstone in Cornwall, yet to be proved, a huge rock sensibly moving to and fro (as tis verified), by power of a finger, but not to be removed by the strength of many shoulders; as these verses say:

> Be thou thy mother-nature's work,
>   Or proof of giants' might;
> Worthless and ragged though thou show,
>   Yet art thou worth the sight.
> This hugy rock one finger's force
>   Apparently will move;
> But to remove it many strengths
>   Shall all too feeble prove.

Some years since the stones, secretly in the night, were undermined and taken up, but by whom and for what cause is not vulgarly known, neither is it discovered what was found under them. Some suppose they made search for treasure, conceived there to be hidden; others again imagine to seek out the certainty whether there were any bones there to be seen as the remainder of that large corpse, if so, thereby to confirm the belief (of divers incredulous persons) that there were such tall men in fore-past ages.

199 Weather Again

When Haldon hath a Hatt
Let Kenton beware a Squatt.

200 A Fishing Town

On the Est side of Exmouth Haven (is) Exmouth, a Fisschar Tounlet, a little withyn the Haven Mouth. Apsham, a praty Tounlet on the Shore, (is) a 4 Miles upper in the Haven; heere is the great Trade and Rode for Shippes that usith this Haven, and especially for the Shippes and Marchant Menne's Goodes of Excester. Men of Excester contende to make the Haven to cum up to Excester self, (but) at this Tyme Shippes cum not farther up but to Apsham.

201   Powderham's Place

Where Exe meets curlèd Kenne with Kind Embrace
In crystal Arms they clip fair Powderham's Place.

202   Estuary Scenes

Exmouth, lying three miles to the eastward of Dawlish, on that side of the
river Ex, is by no means liable to the criticism which I have just ventured
to throw out on the latter place. It is a town of some extent; and, therefore,
neither simplicity, nor picturesque beauty, is expected in it. The houses
may be grouped into any forms that fancy suggests, without the builder
incurring the censure of having spoiled the scene by incongruous architecture.

The variety and grandeur of the view which the houses near the shore
command, is seldom equalled. Old Ocean opens his heaving bosom to
the south, and the Ex comes sweeping down in a broad sheet of water, from
the opposite point. This estuary, sprinkled with shipping, inclosed between
hills, which are ornamented with groves and mansions, castles and cities,
presents, at full tide, and under a calm sky, the picture of an Italian lake.
Limited in time, I could only visit, by a distant view, scenes which promise
much gratification on a closer inspection—Topsham, and the beautiful
country around it; Exeter and its venerable cathedral; the bold, broad,
commanding summit of Hall-Down; and the magnificent seat and grounds
of Manhead, which ornament its eastern declivity. Powderham-castle is
immediately opposite to me, but I do not regret my inability to visit it, since
its situation is low, and the grounds about it are uninteresting. Besides, I
have no passion for magnificence, unless it be united with a little taste; and
should therefore receive no sort of pleasure in contemplating such gew-gaws
as a silver grate plaistered over with gold, and three window-curtains, on
each of which has been lavished the enormous sum of seven hundred
guineas!!!

203   Chick-Stones

Somewhat lower upon the mouth of the river stands Exmouth, that is,
the mouth of Exe; anciently Exanmouth; but then only known by the name,
as being but a poor fisher-town, yet it should seem it had a castle for its
defence above 600 years since; for Mr Hollinshed saith about the year 1001
the Danes with their navy returned out of Normandy, came to Exmouth and
there assaulted the castle, but were valiantly repelled by the guarders
thereof. It hath no castle now, but of far better worth than in that age, and
in more respect, as graced of late with the presence of our royal sovereign

Penzance—from the sea

Fowey

King Charles I. Here our river, like the great Sultans and Khans of that powerful monarch, the Great Mogul, pays to her sovereign, the mighty ocean, whatever treasure of waters she hath collected from every those rills, brooks, riverets, streams and rivers whatsoever fore-spoken of; as they at their decease to the emperor what so they have by any means whatsoever wrung, wrested, or exacted from their inferiors.

It is a barred haven, and before the mouth thereof stand two huge stones or rocks (a great and a less), called Chick-stones (it may be rather, chuck-stones, as choaking the haven); of which is grown a usual proverb in these parts: for if anything stumble us or be a rub in our way, when we are hasty, if anything hinder our purpose, or if we desire to be rid of any thing, we forthwith wish it to be on Chick-stone.

We have this far proceeded in our discovery without danger or obstacle; the weather continues fair, the wind calm, the coasts clear, the sea smooth, a trim tide, be pleased to take a boat and view the eastern coasts as far as Lyme (the limits or marches of our shire); the law and necessity of our journey and talk exacteth no less. I am enforced to say with the good old knight—

> Whate're bety'd, for sithe I have begonne,
> My journey will I follow as I kone.

If your stomach wamble (as mine hath often done at first setting forth), your health may be better by evacuating choler, which once well purged, (I may perchance escape the clearer from censure, taxations, and aspersions), we will land at every river's mouth, where and when you please: the steersman at helm is at your command.

204 *Sympathetic Moisture*

Being agog to see some Devonshire, I would have taken a walk the first day, but the rain would not let me; and the second, but the rain would not let me; and the third, but the rain forbade it. Ditto 4—ditto 5—ditto—so I made up my mind to stop in-doors, and catch a sight flying between the showers: and, behold I saw a pretty valley—pretty cliffs, pretty Brooks, pretty Meadows, pretty trees, both standing as they were created, and blown down as they are uncreated. The green is beautiful, as they say, and pity it is that it is amphibious—*mais*! but alas! the flowers here wait as naturally for the rain twice a day as the Mussels do for the Tide; so we look upon a brook in these parts as you look upon a splash in your Country. There must be something to support this—aye, fog, hail, snow, rain, Mist blanketing up three parts of the year. This Devonshire is like Lydia Languish, very entertaining when it smiles, but cursedly subject to sympathetic moisture.

205   *Excepting Exeter Town*

My grandmother writes to my father, 13 September 1845—"When in Exeter four weeks since, I went to see the trains go off for London: the first time of my seeing anything of the kind." My grandfather writes to him, 16 May 1852—"I hope we shall have a fine day, as your mother never was at Torquay, and I not for near thirty years." He was sixty-three then, and she was seventy. Torquay is fifteen miles from here, and neither of them had ever lived more than thirty miles away.

Such immobility seemed strange to me not many years ago, but now I have come down to it myself. I have not been out of Devon since 1914, or rather, I have not been out of Devon 'ceptin' Axter town, as people used to say. Henry the Eighth took Exeter out of Devon and made it a county by itself. In old conveyances of land in Devon, e.g. of part of Lower Wreyland in 1728, the covenant for Further Assurance often has the words "so as for the doing thereof the persons comprehended within this covenant be not compelled or compellable to travel out of the county of Devon unless it be to the citie of Exon."

206   *The Devon Maid*

Where be ye going, you Devon Maid?
   And what have ye there in the Basket?
Ye tight little fairy just fresh from the dairy,
   Will ye give me some cream if I ask it?

I love your Meads, and I love your flowers,
   And I love your junkets mainly,
But 'hind the door I love kissing more,
   O look not so disdainly.

I love your hills, and I love your dales,
   And I love your flocks a-bleating—
But O, on the heather to lie together,
   With both our hearts a-beating!

I'll put your Basket all safe in a nook,
   Your shawl I hang up on the willow,
And we will sigh in the daisy's eye
   And kiss on a grass-green pillow.

207 Dawlish Fair

Over the Hill and over the Dale,
  And over the Bourne to Dawlish,
Where ginger-bread wives have a scanty sale,
  And ginger-bread nuts are smallish.

208 The Man They Couldn't Hang

Pop fans possibly know more about John Lee than most students of social history.

If this is so, credit must go to the folk-rock group Fairport Convention and their LP "John Babbacombe Lee", rather than to his own story: "The man they could not hang" which for years gathered dust on the shelves of Exeter and Plymouth City Libraries.

This unfortunate fellow was only 20 when he beat the gallows and, convicted murderer though he was, it is only fair to say that he had very little happiness on which to look back.

From a poor home he had joined the Navy at Devonport as a boy seaman but was soon invalided out. At 19 he got his first job as 'boots' at the Yacht Club Hotel, Kingswear; then he went into service as a footman, soon however getting into trouble for pawning his employer's silver.

While Lee was serving six months' hard labour in Exeter Gaol perhaps for the first time somebody was kind to him, although in a somewhat bent way, that was to sow the seed of his eventual downfall.

His benefactor was Miss Keyse of Babbacombe, a distinguished old lady who had been a Maid of Honour to Queen Victoria. She had known his mother and given odd jobs to John as a lad, and his step-sister was her cook. Now she asked for him on release, for employment at a nominal wage, to give him the chance to earn a testimonial for good conduct.

Young Lee was less grateful for this than he was expected to be, and made no secret of his dissatisfaction. In fact he had been overheard threatening Miss Keyse when she had occasion to reduce his wages and this told against him in the terrible events that were to follow on November 15, 1884.

That morning the servants at "The Glen" were awakened by the smell of burning and rushing downstairs they found their mistress lying in a pool of blood, her head battered in, the room on fire.

Suspicion immediately fell on Lee who was speedily apprehended on strong circumstantial evidence. Quite apart from his known feelings towards his employer, there was blood on his clothes and a knife and oil-can were found in his room.

His case came up at Exeter Assize in February, with Mr St Aubyn, M.P. in charge of the defence. Counsel's case was based on the fact that Lee's half-sister, Harris, the cook, was pregnant, and the supposition that the perpetrator of the deed was her lover, who had been discovered in the house by the deceased on one of her nocturnal walks. The blood on the accused could have come from cuts when opening a window to let out the smoke and from helping to carry the corpse.

But judge and jury were unimpressed, either by legal eloquence or by the calm, almost unconcerned demeanour of the prisoner. Mr Justice Manisty took two hours to sum up, which did not prevent the jury from returning their verdict of guilty after only half an hour.

As John Lee heard his sentence of death by hanging, he remained apparently unmoved and, according to the local paper, when invited to speak addressed the judge thus, in a firm, clear voice: "Please, my lord, to allow me to say that I am so calm, because I trust in the Lord and He knows I am innocent!" No reprieve was sought and Lee was taken to Exeter Gaol to await execution, fixed for February 23.

On the morning that should have been his last on earth, he was awakened by the chaplain to pray with him. Invited to make his confession, Lee replied, according to his own story, "Confess! I have nothing to confess. I have finished with this world. I want to think about the things of the next."

At a few minutes before eight, as the prison bell tolled, the solemn funereal procession formed up for the short walk to the gallows, past the assembled reporters. The chief warder led, followed by the chaplain reading the burial service; then, rather surprisingly, the schoolmaster, behind whom came the condemned man ringed round by warders with Berry, the executioner, close at his heels, and the cortege was completed by under-sheriff and governor.

The eye-witness accounts next day in the *Western Daily Mercury* and the *Plymouth and Exeter Gazette* confirm that Lee was still incredibly calm and even helped the executioner fix the noose after his legs had been belted together above the trap and the grisly bag placed over his head.

As he hitched the rope into its exact position, Berry duly asked the condemned man whether he wished to say anything.

"No," was his reply, "drop away!" Then, as Lee recalled in his own story, he held his breath and clenched his teeth.

He heard the chaplain's voice droning on, the peal of the bell, the grinding wrench as the bolt was drawn and—"My heart beat! Was this death? Or was it only a dream? A nightmare? What was this stamping going on?"

A watching reporter takes up the story: ". . . a thrill of horror ran through the assembled spectators, for it was evident that something was wrong . . . the stamping of the executioner and warders showing that the trap would not work."

It had only shifted about two inches and the jumping around on the platform lasted several minutes while the unfortunate victim was left standing there.

Lee, not surprisingly, remembered clearly that he was in fact literally resting on his toes as the trap shook and the bolt was pulled, his neck jerked in an agonising fashion, but not enough to end his torment.

At last he was led away a few yards while the mechanism was overhauled and the drop was tested, with an officer hanging on the rope. Lee, still blindfold, could hear all this—the working of the lever, the thud of the trap being released and falling inwards. To the unfortunate man, this must have seemed an æon but it was, in fact, four minutes before he was repositioned under the rope and the noose secured.

No ritual question this time; the bolt, already in Berry's grasp, was quickly pulled. There was a jerk, but nothing more. Again there was a great stamping around and pulling at the lever, but still the trap stood firm and at last the prisoner was taken down. According to an eye-witness the prisoner's features were corpse-like as his hood was removed, and he walked mechanically.

As for the governor and under-sheriff they were almost frantic, and Lee recalled that the chaplain was so distressed as to be near collapse and the warders were as white as ghosts. Meanwhile Berry was heard protesting that he had tested the mechanism twice the day before.

At about 8.10 the whole ghastly procedure was repeated, but with no more success than before, and this time Lee was taken away. Tools were brought and a portion of the trap cut away, yet even then it would not work so finally, at 8.30, it was decided the execution would have to be postponed.

The reporters were summoned to the committee room where Mr James, under-sheriff, told them that as "... the wretched convict had suffered agonies of death over and over again, he was postponing the execution and going to London to see the Home Secretary."

Meanwhile, outside the prison gate there was great excitement, with the large crowd all agog at the inexplicable delay in hoisting the black flag.

Much later that day the governor came to Lee's cell to tell him that a respite had been granted and his sentence commuted to life imprisonment.

Various explanations and theories were forthcoming, ranging from Lee's own story of a dream that he would survive three attempts at hanging, to the eye-witness who swore he had seen a white dove hovering over the condemned man's head and then settle on the scaffold.

Then, years afterwards, came the story of a death-bed confession by an old lag who, as prison carpenter, had had the job of erecting the scaffold and said that he had doctored the trap-door so that it would jam.

More convincing was the theory that several days of heavy rain had caused the new woodwork to swell. This may certainly have contributed to the malfunctioning but it was believed by contemporary students of the event that most probably the newly japanned bolts and hinges needed greasing.

Lee was finally released from Portland Prison on December 18, 1907, and then earned a living by touring music halls. Little is known of his later years, but he is believed to have married, kept a pub at Abbotskerwell, then emigrated to America where he died at the age of 69.

The professional career of Berry, the executioner, was terminated after his next engagement, when at Norwich Gaol he succeeded in pulling the unfortunate victim's head clean off. He then retired and did the rounds as a magic-lantern entertainer—a set of his slides and notes only recently came up for auction. He combined this activity with evangelism and he certainly came to Plymouth preaching on "How I became converted."

A correspondent in this newspaper *(The Western Morning News)* in 1935 recalled his attendance at one such function when Berry claimed that the Holy Spirit had descended on him, but the writer went on to comment that on this occasion the spirit was clearly not of the holy kind!

Happily there was never again to be such a gruesome farce, but in a small way it may have contributed towards the eventual end of capital punishment.

This, anyway, was the opinion of a commentator in the *London Echo* who wrote: "The executioners are agitating with more success against capital punishment than it would be possible for the little band of political philanthropists in Parliament to do."

And at least John Lee received the accolade of a place in the *Guinness Book of Records*.

209   Ninepence for Joy

The bishop's triennial visitation together with the archdeacon's and the rural dean's annual visitations formed the keystone of ecclesiastical administration. Months before the visitation began the clergy had been obliged to answer a series of written questions which gave the bishop detailed information of each parish. Furthermore, he had already received the rural dean's report on each incumbent's church and parsonage. In his visitation the bishop progressed from centre to centre, to which the clergy and church-wardens from neighbouring rural deaneries were summoned by citation. This meant that non-attendance, except through sickness, called for discipline in the bishop's consistorial court. It is not surprising that the Call Books, which recorded attendances, give convincing proof that throughout the eighteenth century the Devon clergy were diligent in their attendance. Churchwardens, who had been reported for neglect of church fabric or furnishings, were ordered to send a certificate of completed repairs to the bishop's consistorial court by a specified date. Failure to do this was followed by prosecution or 'presentment' of the negligent churchwarden in the bishop's court. The visitation was also the occasion for the bishop's charge, in which he drew the attention of clergy and churchwardens to important matters. It is a great misfortune that none of these charges has survived. At each visitation centre the bishop administered confirmation to candidates from neighbouring parishes. Lastly came the visitation dinner when bishop and clergy relaxed together in good fellowship. The visitation dinner was chargeable to each incumbent's parish, and was enjoyed at the principal inn at the centre, the White Hart at Okehampton, The Half Moon at Exeter, the

Three Cranes at Liskeard, or the King's Head at Truro. Some receipted bills from these hotels survive showing that the ladies in the bishop's party drank a spiced wine called Negus. The gentlemen drank Port and March beer both at 2s. 6d. a bottle, while the servants had to make do with Brandy at 1s. 11d. a bottle. A bill from the White Hart at Okehampton ends with the delightful entry '9d. for Joy.' One presumes that Joy was a serving maid.

210 *On Jane Gee*

O that in Hymenæus' books
  I ne'er had been enrolled:
O worth, alas! my light, my Jane,
  Lies here yclad in mould.

Scarce two years had we lived in bliss,
  But death took Jane away;
Envious death! woe worth my light,
  My Jane lies here in clay.

Here, Jane, thou liest, to whom
  Admetus' wife unequal was;
In faithfulness Penelope
  Thou diddest far surpass.

Never was woman to her spouse,
  Or to her imps, more kind;
A more godly and a modest one
  Than thee no man could find.

Therefore, O happy soul, in peace
  Eternally remain,
In heavens high, where thou dost
  In blessed kingdom reign.

Yet shall thy features, O my Jane,
  Out of my heart then slide,
When beasts from fields, and fishes all
  Out of the sea, shall glide.

Henceforth I will no more alight
  Upon a fair green tree;
But as a turtle which hath lost
  His dear mate, will I be.

211   Crying the Neck

Mrs Bray, in her *Borders of the Tamar and Tavy*, thus describes it in 1832:
"One evening, about the end of harvest, I was riding out on my pony,
attended by a servant who was born and bred a Devonian. We were passing
near a field on the borders of Dartmoor, where the reapers were assembled.
In a moment the pony started nearly from one side of the way to the other,
so sudden came a shout from the field which gave him this alarm. On my
stopping to ask my servant what all that noise was about, he seemed surprised by the question, and said: "It was only the people making their
games, as they always did, to the spirit of the harvest." Such a reply was
quite sufficient to induce me to stop immediately, as I felt certain here was
to be observed some curious vestige of a most ancient superstition; and I
soon gained all the information I could wish to obtain upon the subject. The
offering to the 'spirit of the harvest' is thus made:
"When the reaping is finished, towards evening, the labourers select
some of the best ears of corn from the sheaves; these they tie together, and
it is called the *nack*. Sometimes, as it was when I witnessed the custom,
the nack is decorated with flowers, twisted in with the seed, which gives it
a gay and fantastic appearance. The reapers then proceed to a high place
(such, in fact, was the field on the side of a steep hill where I saw them),
and there they go, to use their own words, to 'holla the nack'. The man who
bears the offering stands in the midst and elevates it, whilst all the other
labourers form themselves into a circle about him; each holds aloft his
hook, and in a moment they all shout as loud as they can these words,
which I spell as I heard then pronounced, and I presume they are not to be
found in any written record. 'Arnack, arnack, arnack, wehaven, wehaven,
wehaven.' This is repeated several times; and the firkin is handed round
between each shout, by way, I conclude of libation. When the weather
is fine, different parties of reapers, each stationed on some height,
may be heard for miles round, shouting, as it were, in answer to each
other.
"The evening I witnessed this ceremony, many women and children,
some carrying boughs, and others having flowers in their caps or in their
hands or in their bonnets, were seen, some dancing, others singing, whilst
the men (whose exclamations so startled my pony) practised the above rites
in a ring."
Mrs Bray goes on to add a good deal of antiquated archæological nonsense
about Druids, Phoenicians, and derivations. She makes 'wehaven' to be
a corruption of 'we ane,' 'a little one,' which is rubbish. 'Wehaven' is 'we
have 'n,' or 'us have 'n,' 'we have got him.' As I remember the crying of the
neck at Lew-Trenchard, there was a slight difference in the procedure to
that described by Mrs Bray. The field was reaped till a portion was left
where was the best wheat, and then the circle was formed, the men shouted,
'A neck! A neck! We have 'n!' and proceeded to reap it. Then it was hastily
bound in a bundle, the ears were plaited together with flowers at the top

of the sheaf, and this was heaved up, with the sickles raised, and a great shout of "A neck! A neck!" &c., again, and the drink, of course.

The wheat of the last sheaf was preserved apart through the winter, and was mixed with the seed corn next year.

212 *The Reverend Sabine Baring-Gould*

The Reverend Sabine Baring-Gould
　Rector (sometime) at Lew,
Once at a Christmas party asked,
　'Whose pretty child are you?'

(The Rector's family was long,
　His memory was poor,
And as to who was who had grown
　Increasingly unsure).

At this, the infant on the stair
　Most sorrowfully sighed.
'Whose pretty little girl am I?
　Why, *yours*, papa!' she cried.

213 *The World As It Was*

And it is its solitude that those who would preserve Dartmoor should particularly guard from invasion. While they remain Devon will be able to show that which can be seen in no other part of the kingdom—uncultured Nature without a sign that man has ever intruded upon her domain. The central part of the Forest—the district lying between Princetown and Meripit Hill—has ceased to be as it once was, but the great stretches of moor to the north and to the south are still as ever they were. If these solitudes should be invaded, nowhere in England will the eye be able to look upon a scene in which there is nothing but the handiwork of Nature. No amount of profit, even supposing they could be made to yield such, would compensate for the loss of their primeval character, and it behoves those who believe there is something of more value to a nation than money to aid in the preservation of these stretches of wild moorland, which have come down to us untouched, and in which we have a glimpse of the world as it was.

214 The Forest of Tin

The chiefest place where tin is found is in the forest of Dartmoor and the purlieus thereof, and places near adjoining thereunto. This forest swelleth up with many mountains, hills, and tors of large vastness, especially the moorland, which is very spacious. It is called moor, not only because it is mountainous, but withall less fruitful and full of bogs (which kind of soil we call, in our common speech, moors) and in the winter season hard and comfortless, bare and cold: keeping his white winter livery lying upon it long time, if not washed away with rain. Yet hath bountiful and prudent nature, for such defects, supplied it with another necessary commodity, and made amends for the want of corn and fruitful herbage in the moor, furnishing it with metals—

> And as each one is prais'd for her peculiar things,
> So only she is rich in mountains, moors, and springs,
> And holds herself as great in her superfluous waste,
> As others in their towns and fruitful tillage grac'd,
> And chiefly for her mines.

215 Spadiards and Others

There are also Labourers, which serve for daily Wages, whereof be two Sorts; the one is called a Spadiard, a daily Labourer in Tin-Works, with which there is no Labourer in Hardness of Life to be compared; the other is also a daily Labourer at Husbandry, and other servlie Works for his Hire, but he worketh at more Ease; notwithstanding they be both of a strong Body, able to endure all Labours and Pains.

216 How Now, old Mole!

I speak of them that work by week or day in husbandry labour, or thereunto belonging, or in tin-works. Of the last are two sorts; one named a spador or searcher for tin, than whom (as it seems to me) no labourer whatsoever undergoes greater hazard of peril or danger, nor in hard or coarse fare and diet doth equal him: bread, the brownest; cheese, the hardest; drink, the thinnest; yea, commonly the dew of heaven; which he taketh either from his shovel, or spade, or in the hollow of his hand; as Diogenes, the cynic, was taught by a boy. He spends all day (or the major part thereof) like a mole or earth-worm underground, mining in deep vaults or pits, as though he intended (with noble Sir Francis Drake) to find a way to the antipodes; yea, a nearer, and so to surpass him: for it is some time of that profundity, that notwithstanding the country (so they term the earth over their heads) is propped, posted, crossed, traversed, and supported with divers great beams of timber to keep them in security, yet all is sometimes too little; they perish with the fall thereof notwithstanding.

217   Tinners' Law

This last [the Stannary Laws] is severed from all the rest, and only peculiar to this county and Cornwall, appropriated to tinners, tin-works, and tin causes only, and appertaineth to the honour of the Duchy of Cornwall, and is hereditary primogenito Domini Regis, whereof he is born duke, by virtue of an especial Act of Parliament, and the very day of his birth he is holden of full and perfect age, but is created Prince of Wales. His deputy, or chief officer, in Latin is named senescallus; in English, warden of the stannaries, of stannum; in English, tin: or high seneschal, or steward of the duchy: whose authority is very large, being both chief justice and chancellor; giving sentence both for law and equity: for whom there is no appeal but to the duke himself, and from him to the sovereign.

218   The Bowed Figure of Solitary Man

As the tin could only be stamped twice a year at the coinage towns and could not be sold before being stamped, the smaller tin workers inevitably fell into the hands of capitalist 'adventurers' and tin dealers. As early as the 13th century we hear of wage-earners in the trade, working for others. By the early 16th century, indeed, the Devon tin trade had attracted a remarkable variety of investors from all ranks of society. The coinage roll of 1523 has 1,177 entries on it, possibly seven or eight hundred different names. The Earl of Devon himself had three hundredweight of tin coined at Plympton. The names of many well-known landed families appear—Copplestone, Prideaux, Cole, Edgecumbe—together with those of great town merchants like John Giles of Totnes, William Periam of Exeter, and William Hawkins of Plymouth. Bakers, tanners, and tuckers also figure in the list. But fewer than 10 per cent of the entries record the coinage of a thousandweight or more at a time: the largest producer was Elis Elforde, who had rather more than $3\frac{1}{2}$ tons coined in two instalments at Tavistock.

It was still mainly a small man's trade. 'The big capitalist has already appeared on the scene . . . but there is still ample room for small working partnerships, and even for the lone adventurer toiling with pick and shovel at his own claim': the immemorial bowed figure of solitary man, working in the vast silence of the Moor as his ancestors had done in the Cornish wastes three thousand years before.

219   Warreners

It is a cheerless evening, and as you leave the warren house and feel the cold breath of air that sweeps down from the naked hills, you think what a pity it is they do not catch rabbits in the summer and during the daytime. But the warrener takes no notice of it. Carrying a huge bundle of nets he plods onward, followed by his assistant, who is laden in a similar manner. By-and-by you reach the beginning of a row of sticks, which have been stuck into the ground during the day, and the work of hanging up the nets commences. On one side of the row are some burrows, on the other are the rabbits. They have left their snug habitations to feed in quietness at night, and the warrener's first work is to take care that they shall not get back again.

The nets being hung the warrener returns to the house, which you do not feel particularly sorry for. When he calls you very early on the following morning you cannot help regretting that you have been so rash as to express a desire to go with him. But it is too late to retreat, and you rise and dress to the accompaniment of chattering teeth. Once more you make your way towards where the rabbits are feeding, and getting behind them drive them into the nets, being assisted in your work by spaniels. The warrener seizes the rabbits as they vainly endeavour to pass the nets, and kills them instantly by twisting their necks. When you look upon the heap of slain you are astonished.

The burrows, or burys, as the warrener calls them, are formed by first digging a narrow trench, with small ones branching from it on each side, but not opposite to each other. Large slabs of turf are then cut, and with these the little trenches are covered. Over this is heaped a mound of earth, and the burrow is finished. A few holes are made for the rabbits to enter, and they quickly take possession of their new abode.

During hard winters when food is scarce, the rabbits have to be fed, or they will leave the warren. This is a part of the warrener's work that has to be carefully attended to. Any neglect may result in considerable loss. The rabbits are usually fed on furze and hay.

The trapping season usually commences at the end of August or beginning of September, and lasts until the end of February or beginning of March. The warrens in the Plym valley find a market for their rabbits in Plymouth and Devonport, though from Ditsworthy many are sent to Birmingham. Birmingham and Sheffield are also markets for those caught in the warrens on the east side of the moor, the rabbits being dispatched from Moretonhampstead.

But the warrener's profits are declining. There are no such times now as those when the skin-packing at Ditsworthy was as important a matter as the wool-packing of an in-country farmer—when as much as £110 was received for skins in one year. Now that is over; the rabbits have to be sold in their skins, and much that once belonged to the warrener is lost to him. Prices are lower, too, than they were. Farmers take a great many rabbits to market now, and the warrener feels the competition. But what he has chiefly suffered from during late years is the scarcity of rabbits on the moor. In the great blizzard of 1891 thousands of rabbits died on Dartmoor, and the effect of the partial depopulation of the warrens in that year is still felt.

220 Wheels and Sledges

The first time that a motor-car was seen here (which was not so very long ago) it stopped just opposite the cottage of an invalid old man. He heard somethin' there a-buzzin' like a swarm o' bees, and he went out to look, although he had not been outside his door since Martinmas. It was a big car, and he said that it was like a railway-carriage on wheels. I can myself remember the first railway-train that came here—that was in 1866—and I knew old people who said that they remembered the first cart. Before the days of carts, they carried things on horses with pack-saddles.

These old people's recollections are confirmed by Moore. His *History of Devonshire* came out in 1829, and he says there, vol. 1, page 426—"Fifty years ago a pair of wheels was scarcely to be seen on a farm in the county, and at present the use of pack-horses still prevails, though on the decline. . . . Hay, corn, fuel, stones, dung, lime, etc., and the produce of the fields, are all conveyed on horseback: sledges, or sledge-carts, are also used in harvest time, drawn chiefly by oxen". The pack-saddles have vanished now, and the oxen also; but sledges may still be seen at work on very steep fields.

221 John Bishop's Walls

The newtake walls are formed of stones piled to a height of about four or five feet, and in some cases more, no mortar, not even turf, being used. The material lay ready to the builder's hand; all he had to do was to collect the stones, and upon the size of those, of course, depended the character of his wall. They are sometimes seen to be so small that the wall has little stability, and in some cases the spaces between them are such as to cause the latter to present almost the appearance of a network of stones. In the moorman's language: one can see daylight through them. When the stones lying around him were large, a solid wall was the result, but the earlier builder never went out of his way to obtain his material, nor did he ever break any stones or attempt to shape them. In later years, however, a different plan was adopted.

Small stones were generally discarded, and the larger ones that were employed were roughly squared. One of the first to introduce this style of newtake wall building on Dartmoor was John Bishop, of Swincombe, whose work, as he would tell you, was 'ordained to stand'.

Examples of the old and the new styles may be seen on the road between Two Bridges and Cherrybrook Bridge, below Smith Hill. On one side are the enclosures belonging to Prince Hall, the wall of which was built many years ago, the stones composing it being comparatively small, particularly in places. On the other side is Muddy Lakes, a modern enclosure, and the wall—one of John Bishop's building—is formed of huge blocks of granite fitted closely together. Bishop had great faith in the powers of the crowbar, or "bar ire" as he called it. Asked on one occasion how he contrived to get such immense stones in their places, he replied, "Aw, 'tis surprisin' what you can do with a laiver or two." As a means of conveying stones to any required spot there was nothing in his estimation equal to the sled, or sledge. He was very fond of praising the performances of a certain pony with one of these carriages. "He belonged to my vayther," he used to say, "an' wudden no more'n vourteen, or vourteen an' a half, an' I've a zeed'n shift a stone up dree tin wight 'pon a sledge." When asked if he really meant to say that a pony of such a size could draw so heavy a weight, he would answer, "Ees; 'pon a sledge, I tell you."

222 Moorland Roads

The great roads over Dartmoor were not completed until about 150 years ago. One of them runs north-eastward from Plymouth to Moreton, and so to Exeter and London, and the other runs south-eastward from Tavistock to Ashburton. They cross each other at Two Bridges in the middle of the moor, and at some points they are nearly 1,500 feet above the level of the sea. About three miles out from Moreton on the Plymouth road there is a road from Ashburton to Chagford; and at the crossing of these roads the highwaymen were hanged in chains, when caught. At least, my father and my grandfather both told me so; and such things might have happened even in my father's time, as hanging in chains was not abolished until 1834.

223 Memorials

When a War Memorial was projected here, I thought that the names of the dead might be carved on one of the great rocks on Lustleigh Cleave, with the date and nothing more. As it is, they have been carved on a neat little wooden tablet with an inscription of the usual kind, and put up in the church.

I fancy our memorial might have been more worthy of them, had their names been on the granite in the solitude up there with that wild ravine below.

We have another memorial here, of which we all are proud. It is at the railway station. "Beneath this slab, and stretched out flat, lies Jumbo, once our station cat." That cat had many lives; jumped in and out between the wheels of trains, and yet died in its bed.

A tombstone is primarily a label for identifying what is down below; but survivors will not always face that brutal fact. They merely give the name and age; and in after years this may not be enough. I had to find the next-of-kin to an old servant of ours who was over ninety when she died. (She had always kept them at a distance, as they often wished to borrow money that she did not wish to lend). There was an entry in a Family Bible, say, A.B. born 1 January 1820; and there were tombstones of three persons named A.B. who died at ages answering to that. They ought to give the birthday and the parents' Christian names, to show exactly who is there. Instead of that, they usually give texts and verses out of hymns.

This has always been a healthy district, and so very quiet that people had no worries; and they usually lived on till a great age. I have heard it said regretfully, "Ah, her died young," and then heard it explained, "Her ne'er saw sixty." Times are changing now. Looking at the tombstones of some kindred of my own, I was observing how the ages fell from nineties and eighties to seventies and sixties. I said nothing aloud, but the sexton read my thoughts and put them into words, "Aye, zir, they do say as each generation be weaker and wiser than the last."

224 *Prison Life*

On the whole the prison officer speaks well of life at Dartmoor; what the convict thinks of it is quite another thing. "Crutchy Quin, 10 and ticket" has very kindly left us his opinion on the matter, and has also let us know what he thought of other similar establishments. Not being provided with a notebook and pencil, he inscribed his impressions with a nail on the bottom of a dinner can, where they were discovered by Mr Michael Davitt during his incarceration in the prison.

> Millbank for thick skins and graft at the pump;
> Broadmoor for all lags as go off their chump;
> Brixton's for good toke and cocoa with fat;
> Dartmoor for bad grub, but plenty of chat;
> Portsmouth's a blooming bad place for hard work;
> Chatham on Sunday gives four ounces of pork;
> Portland is worth all the lot for to joke in—
> For fetching a lagging there is no place like Woking.

225   *Instant Archaeology*

In the eyes of the Dartmoor man, by which we mean the moor farmer and
the labourer, the pursuit of the antiquary is regarded as a craze, and the
archæologist as one almost to be pitied that he has not something better to
do than to trouble himself about 'a passel ov ole stones', though a few of the
more intelligent view the matter in another light. But I have nevertheless
invariably found that they will take some sort of an interest in what you may
tell them respecting these remains, and they are always ready to let you know
what they have heard concerning them. I know of a case in which some
labourers were so desirous of helping the investigators that they actually
took the trouble to build a kist they were ordered to search for but could not
find. It happened some five or six years ago. A belief was expressed by a
couple of antiquaries that a kist would be found in a certain spot, and in
their absence the men employed in the work of exploration, having previously
inquired as to the kind of object they would be likely to come upon in their
digging, constructed a kist of their own, not wishing, so I was informed,
"that the gen'elmen should be disappointed". They proved themselves to
be quite as good kistvæn builders as the men of prehistoric times, for their
erection passed muster, one of the antiquaries observing that he was certain
such an object would be discovered on the spot he had indicated.

226   *Man's Days*

A sudden wakin', a sudden weepin';
A li'l suckin', a li'l sleepin';
A cheel's full joys an' a cheel's short sorrows,
Wi' a power o' faith in gert to-morrows.

Young blood red hot an' the love o' a maid;
Wan glorious day as'll never fade;
Some shadows, some sunshine, some triumphs, some tears,
Wi' a gatherin' weight o' the flyin' years.

Then auld man's talk o' the days behind 'e;
Your darter's youngest darter to mind 'e;
A li'l dreamin', a li'l dyin',
A li'l lew corner o' airth to lie in.

227   *Four Horseshoes Equal One Duck*

Within the last twenty years I have seen an account set out between a blacksmith and a farmer without any reference at all to money. On one side there were horseshoes, ploughshares, etc., and on the other side, pork, butter, geese, etc. And both parties reckoned the items up, and saw that the totals balanced. They seemed to have some weights and measures in their mind that are not found in books, say, 4 horseshoes make 1 duck.

228   Words and Phrases

My grandfather's letters have all sorts of words and phrases. After some heavy rains, 9 January 1860, "The waters have been very stiff, but not landed yet," meaning that the Wrey was high, but had not overflowed its banks. Whilst the railway was being made here, 30 April 1865, "There is a stagnation among the navvies about wages." He says that my brother "has a little hoarse", 12 June 1854, and habitually speaks of "having a hoarse" like "having a cough". He says that one of his neighbours "is confined in the chest", 18 February 1859, that is, confined to his house by a cold in his chest, and another one "is confined in the same complaint". Another neighbour was unsystematic in her housekeeping, and he says that "she keeps a disorderly house", 14 January 1848. Somebody left a letter of his unanswered, 2 February 1859, and he calls this "a very unhandsome thing".

229   'Urting

Although by the majority of the villagers a day on the moor for this purpose is regarded more in the light of a holiday than anything else, there are some with whom gain is the sole motive for going there. These go out perhaps two or three times a week throughout the season, and the quantities they gather are often very large. One family in the parish of Mary Tavy, consisting of father, mother, and daughter, and who have been regularly to the moor for whortleberries for many years, have during the past season gathered sufficient to give them a return of £9. The berries were mostly sold at Tavistock, and fetched 6d. and 7d. a quart. One lot was sold at 5d. and some few lots made as much as 8d. but the average was as stated. On one day the two women gathered 26 quarts between them, and on another occasion the father gathered a like quantity unassisted, and this he did within twelve hours, including a walk of about a dozen miles. On Omen Beam this season a man and his wife and child gathered 38 quarts in one day, and other large gatherings have also come to our notice.

It is said that a drink made from the whortleberry is sold in the streets of St Petersburg. The fruit is also sometimes used for making a kind of cordial here. This is known as 'hurt gin', and the mode of preparing it is similar to that followed in making sloe gin. But it is not considered to be equal to the latter. A dish of stewed whortleberries, however, or a tart made from them, nobody can find fault with, and it is in such a manner that they are generally used.

It is rather curious to note the different customs observed in the villages round the moor by the gatherers. In the southern part it is quite the usual thing for each to carry a small can—often one that holds exactly a quart—as well as a basket. As the berries are picked they are put into the can, and when it will hold no more it is emptied into the basket. By this means the gatherer can tell if he chooses what quantity of fruit he has, and he also finds it easier to move about, especially if the ground be thickly strewn with rocks, with only a small can than with a good-sized basket. But in the northern part of the moor the can is very seldom seen. The berries are thrown into the basket as they are gathered, and the quantity is measured on the gatherer's arrival at home.

The words, too, formerly uttered by the whortleberry picker in southern Dartmoor, when commencing to gather, and considered so essential to the success of his endeavours to fill his basket, we have never been able to meet with elsewhere. Readers of *The River* will remember how Hannah Bradridge, when she went whortleberry gathering with Mary Merle, did not forget to speak them,

> The first I pick, I eat;
> The second I pick, I throw away;
> The third I pick, I put in my can—

and how she followed this up with the observation:

"There, Molly, now us shall have good hurting." We first heard these lines about thirty years ago, but even then those who used them did not appear to place too much reliance upon the charm.

230   Ups and Downs

A friend at Moreton writes to him [Torr's grandfather], 11 January 1846, "The poor will suffer much from the high price of corn and no potatoes. The farmers never had such times. Cattle and sheep are at enormous prices —a farmer told me his stock was worth £1300 more than last year." He writes again, 30 September 1849, "Farmers are down in the mouth: cattle selling very low, and there is a complete panic. All the little farmers will be ruined."

231   Peat Digging

The turf-iron is then brought into requisition. This is semi-circular in shape, one of the horns being turned up at right angles, and is about seven inches wide. A flat socket of iron receives the wooden handle, in which is a 'shoulder', where the foot may be placed when an extra pressure is required to drive the tool into the peat. Standing on the uncovered strip at one end of the tie, with his face turned from it, and having it on his left hand, our companion, holding his iron at right angles to the edge, presses it into the peat, and brings away a small portion. This is repeated, the cutter moving backward, until he has got to the required depth of twenty inches. Again he thrusts it downward, not quite perpendicularly, and with a motion somewhat similar to that made in turning up ground with a spade, lifts out a slab of peat twenty inches long, seven inches wide, and two inches thick. The turned up end of his semi-circular blade really enables the cutter to make two cuts at right angles to each other at once, one being the width and the other the thickness of the slab. Our companion throws his first turf into the tie, and then cuts another from the inner half of his fourteen-inch strip, which is thrown on the ground on his right. This operation the labourer continues, half the slabs that he cuts going into the tie in rows three or four deep, and the other half being similarly disposed on the heather. They are of the average thickness of two inches, but in this the cutter has only his eye to guide him. When the forty yards forming the length of the tie have been gone over in this way our companion has completed a journey. No less than 1,440 slabs of peat have been cut, which cannot be called a bad half-day's work.

232 Wart Charming

One of the best wart-counting stories I have heard was told me by the daughter of an old-time squire. Both his hands had been peppered with persistent warts for years, every possible remedy having been tried unavailingly. Walking home from church one Sunday, he overtook an old village neighbour with whom he joined company. Presently, with characteristic directness, the old man commented on the squire's disfigurement. "How many warts have 'ee got then, zur?" he asked. The squire counted, "Twenty-seven." "They'll go," was the response, and no more was said on the subject. At home relating this incident to his wife, she exclaimed, "You haven't as many warts as that, surely!" He counted again, "Actually I've got one more," he said, "I told old Charlie twenty-seven, but it's twenty-eight."

Very shortly, twenty-seven warts had disappeared without trace. One remained.

233 *The Widecombe Storm*

Upon Sunday the 21 of October last, In the Parish Church of Withycombe in Devonshire neare Dartmoores, there fell in time of Divine Service a strange darknesse, increasing more and more, so that the people there assembled could not see to reade in any booke, and suddenly in a fearefull and lamentable manner, a mighty thundering was heard, the ratling whereof did answer much like unto the sound and report of many great Cannons, and terrible strange lightening therewith, greatly amazing and astonishing those that heard and saw it, the darkenesse increasing yet more, till they could not (in the interim) see one another; the extraordinarie lightning came into the Church so slaming, that the whole Church was presently filled with fire and smoke, the smell whereof was very loathsome, much like unto the sent of brimstone, some said they saw at first a great ball of fire come in at the window and passe thorough the Church, which so much affrighted the whole Congregation that the most part of them fell downe into their seates, and some upon their knees, some on their faces, and some one upon another, with a great cry of burning and scalding, they all giving up themselves for dead.

The Minister of the Parish, Master George Lyde, being in the Pulpit or seate where prayers are read, however hee might bee much astonished hereat, yet through GOD's mercy had no other hurt at all in his body; but to his much griefe and amazement heard, and afterward beheld the lamentable accident; and although himselfe was not touched, yet the lightening seized upon his poore Wife, fired her ruffe and linnen next to her body, and her cloathes; to the burning of many parts of her body in a very pitifull manner. And one Mistresse Ditford, sitting in the pew with the Minister's wife, was also much scalded, but the maid and childe sitting at the pew dore had no harme. Beside, another woman adventuring to run out of the Church, had her cloathes set on fire, and was not only strangely burnt and scorched, but had her flesh torne about her back almost to the very bones. And another woman had her flesh so torne and her body so grievously burnt, that she died the same night.

Also one Master Hill a Gentleman of good account in the Parish, sitting in his seate by the Chancell, had his head suddenly smitten against the wall, through the violence whereof he died that night, no other hurt being found about his body; but his sonne sitting in the same seate had no harme. There was also one man more, at the same instant, of whom it is particularly related, who was Warriner unto Sir Richard Reynolds, his head was cloven, his skull rent into three peeces, and his braines throwne upon the ground whole, and the haire of his head, through the violence of the blow at first given him, did sticke fast unto the pillar or wall of the Church; so that hee perished there most lamentably.

Some other persons were then blasted and burnt, and so grievously scalded and wounded, that since that time they have died thereof; and many other not like to recover, notwithstanding all the meanes that can bee procured to helpe them. Some had their cloaths burnt and their bodies had no hurt, and some on the contrary, had their bodies burnt, and their cloathes not touched. But it pleased GOD yet in the midst of judgement to remember mercy, sparing some and not destroying all.

Also there were some Seats in the Body of the Church turned upside downe, and yet they which sate in them had little or no hurt. And one man going out at the Chancell doore, his Dogg running out before him, was whirled about towards the doore and fell downe starke dead: at the sight whereof his Master stepped backe within the doore, and GOD preserved him alive. Moreover the Church it selfe was much torne and defaced by the thunder and lightning; and thereby also a beame was burst in midst, and fell downe betweene the Minister and Clarke and hurt neither; and a weighty great stone, neare the Foundation of the Church is torne out and removed, and the steeple it selfe is much rent, and there where the Church was most rent there was least hurt done, and not any one was hurt either with the wood or stone, but only a maid of Manaton, which came thither that afternoone to see some friends, Master Frind the Coroner by circumstances, supposed she was killed by a stone. There were also stones throwne from the Tower as thick as if an hundred men had beene there throwing. Also a Pinacle of the Tower torne downe and beate through into the Church.

Also the Pillar against which the Pulpit standeth, being but newly whited, is now by this meanes turned blacke and sulphry. Furthermore, one man that stood in the Chancell, with his face towards the Bellfrey, observed the rising as it were of dust or lime, in the lower end of the Church, which suddenly (as with a puffe of winde) was whirled up and cast into his eyes, so that hee could not see in twelve houres after; but now his sight is restored, and hee hath no other hurt. The terrible lightening being past, and all the people being in a wonderfull maze, so that they spake not one word, by and by one Master Raph Rouse, Vintener in the Towne, stood up, saying, Neighbours, in the name of GOD shall we venture out of the Church, to which Master Lyde answering, said, it is best to make an end of prayers, for it is better to die here then in another place, but they looking about them, and seeing the Church so terribly rent and torne over their heads, durst not proceed in their publike devotions, but went forth of the Church.

234 *Britannia's Pastorals*

I that whileare neere *Tavies* straggling spring,
Unto my seely Sheepe did use to sing,
And plaid to please my self, on rustick Reede,
Nor sought for *Baye*, (the learned Shepheards meede,)
But as a Swaine unkent fed on the plaines,
And made the *Eccho* umpire of my straines:

Am drawne by time (although the weak'st of many)
To sing those lays as yet unsung by any.
What neede I tune the Swaines of *Thessalie*?
Or, bootlesse, adde to them of *Arcadie*?
No: faire Arcadie cannot be compleater,
My praise may lessen, but not make thee greater.
My *Muse* for loftie pitches shall not rome,
But onely pipen of her native home:
And to the Swaines, Love's rurall Minstralsie,
Thus, deare *Britannia* will I sing of thee.

235   *A Recipe for Killing Ratts*

One Quart of Oatmeal, four drops of Rhodium, one Grain of Musk, two Nutts of Nux Vomica finely rasp'd, the whole reduced very fine, and to be continued while they eat it.

236   *A Cure for the Bite of a Mad Dog*

Rue, Sage, Wormwood a large handful, three large handfulls of Garlick, bruise them all together in a Mortar, half a pd. of Stone Brimstone pounded, one pound of scrap'd Pewter, two ounces of Assafoetida, one pound of Treacle, boyl the Ingredients over a gentle fire in Eight Quarts of Strong Beer till half is consum'd, close stop'd in an earthen vessel. To a man, half a Qtr of a pint 3 mornings immediately after ye Bite if long before ye full moon and same Quantity 3 days before and after full moon in ye morning fasting. For Horse or Bullock a Qter of a Pint. To a Dog 3 spoonfulls.

237   *A Matchless Child*

This infant fled from our admiring sight
His stay so short, so sudden was his flight
That he has taught us by his hasting hence
That th' earth's too vile for so much innocence
Reader relent since thou noe more shall see
This matchless child but in his effigie.

238   Ringers' Rules

If any ringer shall curse, swear or profane the name of the Lord Almighty, or promote gaming, or debauch in the Society room, at any meeting of the ringers, he shall pay twopence for any such offence or be excluded.

If any person, at time of meeting, abuse either the Lord Chief, or the Crier, or any other ringer he shall pay twopence; and if any ringer strike another he shall pay 6*d*. for the first offence, one shilling for the second, and be excluded for the third.

That when any ringer is chosen Lord Chief or Crier, every ringer shall behave in a sober and decent manner, penalty for breaking this rule 6*d*.

If any ringer talks in the Society in a ridiculous manner, penalty 6*d*.

239   The Best Art

If thou be serious (Friend) peruse this Stone;
If thou be not soe: pray: let it alone.
Against Deaths Poison, Vetues the best Art:
When Good Men seem to die they but depart.
Live well: then at the last with us thoult feele
Bare dying makes not Death but dying ill.

240   The Seaman's Dial

And at Brent a mine, rather quarry if you please, of load-stones: in Latin, magnes, a precious gem, and of admirable use, the quality whereof is generally known, but in most especial use with the navigators, directing the needle of their compass (being but slightly touched therewith) to the north pole: a jewel far excelling all other precious stones, were they not so plentiful to be sold and bought. Great difference there is of opinions among writers concerning the invention or first knowledge of the virtues and use of these stones. Some think it to be as ancient as Solomon's time, and that by the help thereof his fleet performed the Ophirian voyages: to which others reply, that then he might have performed that course in far shorter time than three years: whereby it is supposed that the virtue hereof hath been unknown until these latter ages, and then discovered by one named, as they say, Flavio, of Malfi, not far from Naples (1013); before which time the exact and perfect skill of navigation was unknown. But whether by him, or brought us from China by Marcus Paulus Venetus, it is yet uncertain; and not much material, said one, when such a matter was in question, for he said:

As for my part I care not a jot
Whether I know him or know him not.

Yet I am of another mind, wishing the man (to whom God hath given so rare a judgment and knowledge to seek out those hidden secrets of nature, in any age, of what quality soever, so much for the benefit of mankind) perpetual remembrance with deserved honour; for so hath divine Du Bartas thought fit to give him in those eloquent and excellent verses of his concerning him and his invention,

W' are to Ceres not so much bound for bread,
Neither to Bacchus for his clusters red,
As Signior Flavio, to thy witty trial,
For first inventing of the seaman's dial:

The use of the needle turning in the same
Divine device; O! admirable frame;
Whereby through the ocean in the darkest night
Our highest carracks are conducted right.

These stones were said (upon what reason or assurance I know not) to be male and female, differing both in virtue and colour.

241   Count Your Time

Here lies in Horizontal position
The outside case of
George Routleigh, Watchmaker,
Whose abilities in that line were an honour
To his profession:
Integrity was the main-spring,
and Prudence the Regulator
Of all the actions of his life:
Humane, generous, and liberal,
His hand never stopped
Till he had relieved distress;
So nicely regulated were all his movements
That he never went wrong
Except when set-a-going
By People
Who did not know
His Key:
Even then, he was easily
Set right again:
He had the art of disposing of his Time
So well,

That his Hours glided away
In one continual round
Of Pleasure and Delight,
Till an unlucky Moment put a period to
His existence;
He departed this Life
November 14, 1802.
Aged 57,
Wound up,
In hopes of being taken in Hand
By his Maker
And of being
Thoroughly cleaned, repaired, and set-a-going
In the World to come.

242   Two Moors Way

Without danger, at length, though not void of tedious and wearisome travel, are we freed out of the liberty of tin-warrants; and a simple and unskilful pilot though I be (so you find, and so I frankly confess myself, and would never have so boldly undertaken to be your guide had not the more sufficient slid back or fainted), you are disembogued of the large gulf of land, the forest of Dartmoor; and under my conduct safely and securely excaped the peril of deep tin-works, steep tors, high mountains, low valleys, bogs, plains, being neither in any hazard of fear of danger, without wetting your foot in the many meers, or fouling your shoes in the many mires. Now I suppose you hope and expect more delightsome objects, pleasant ways, and comfortable travel (after these uneven, rocky, stumbling, tiring, melancholy paths), but I cannot promise you presently: I see a spacious, coarse, barren, and wild object, yielding little comfort by his rough, cold, and rigorous complexion. I doubt you will say with the poet,

> In shunning of Charibdes' paws
> He falleth into Scylla's jaws.

Have a little patience, your stay shall not be long; I will shorten the way by directing you by a straight line without any turning or needless ambages; you shall not have a bough of a tree to strike off your hat, or drop in your neck; it is the other forest I have formerly told you of, part of which lies in this county, and is called Exmoor Forest. The greatest part belongeth to Somersetshire, and yieldeth no metal as yet found, only good pastures and summering, for sheep and cattle, in quantity and quality.

243   Here Lyeth a Lady

*The wife of Thomas Heale Knight and Baronet of Flete who dyed the 14 day
of Martch Ana Doni 1645*

Here lyeth a lady of this life bereft
Whose husband dear and children sweet hath left
If goodness beauty modesty or will
might have prevaild she had been living still
She sinned but just enough to let us see
That gods word must be true all sinners bee.
'Tis now in heaven part of spirituall mirth
to see how well the good act her on earth
Spirituall treason atheism is to saye
That any can thy summons disobaye
Wherefore to thee this is my earnest suite
The tree being dead I pray thee spare ye fruit.

244   Plain Western Men

Thus their valour and fortitude hath been misconstrued, and termed by
some, audaciousness, and the actors, boisterous: but the action that procured
them this harsh epithet I will offer to your censure, and will transcribe
verbatim in Speed's own words,

"There presented themselves" (saith he) "unto him" (intending King
Henry IV) "a boisterous troop of plain western men, who brought unto his
view three lords and twenty knights of note, their prisoners, and whom the
country people near Dartmouth in Devon had gotten in plain fight. The
king by them was given to understand that the Lord Castle, the Briton
(who had formerly burnt Plymouth), thinking to do the like at Dartmouth,
came on shore with his forces, where these and the like people fiercely
encountered them; at which their women, like Amazons, by hurling flints
and pebbles, and other such like artillery, did greatly advance their husbands'
and kinsfolks' victory. The lord of Castle himself was slain, and many other
together with him. These other were saved; as many more of them might
have been, but the ignorance of language confounded alike the cries of
indignation and pity. They therefore, in reward of this hazard and service,
do pray they may reap some commodity by their captives. It was but reason:
wherefore the king, who took great pleasure to talk with these lusty Denshire-
men, himself caused their purses to be stuffed with golden coin; reserving
the prisoners to pay himself with advantage out of their ransoms."

Here it plainly appeareth that every hearer and author hath his private
opinion, and every opinionist his peculiar judgment and censure; not
always according to his true apprehension, but often agreeable to his

melancholic (I will not say envious, but asper) nature, by which he censureth other men and their actions, as here. But we neither hunt nor travel after men's opinions; but when we shall see others perform the like actions, we do (and still will) entitle them valiant, famous, illustrious, heroical. But not a word of this more, nor of them; only a verse of the poet Pindar, which he wrote to Lacedemonia, comes to my mind, in regard it may be fitly applied to this country:

> Their grave advice is found in aged brains;
> Their gallant youths are lusty lads indeed,
> Which can both sing and dance in courtly trains,
> And daunt their foes with many a doughty deed.

245   Go Range

Who seeks the way to win renown,
Or flies with wings of high desire;
Who seeks to wear the laurel crown,
Or hath the mind that would aspire:
Tell him his native soil eschew,
Tell him go range and seek anew.

246   Sea Dogs

In 1584 Sr ffrancys Drake toke shipping at Plymmouthe and sayled to hispaniola; where most valyantly toke the Townes of St Domingo and of Carthegene and the countrie there about, and returned with greate spoyles and ryches and honor, which inflamed the whole countrie with a desyre to adventure unto the seas, yn hope of the lyke good successe, that a greate nomber prepared shipps maryners and soylders and travelled every place at the seas where any proffite might be had. Some yn to Indians, some to syndganne de Coye, some seeking a waye to China by the northe pole, and some to fynde that which was not loste, whereby many were undonne and theym selffs yn the end nevere the better.

247   Great Drake

Sir Drake, whome well the world's ends knewe
  Which thou didst compasse rounde:
And whome both poles of Heaven ons saw,

Which North and South do bound:
The starrs above will make thee known,
  If men here silent were:
The Sunn himself cannot forgett
  His fellow Traveller.

Great Drake, whose shippe aboute the world's wide wast
  In three years did a golden girdle cast.
Who with fresh streames refresht this Towne that first,
  Though kist with waters, yet did pire for thirst.
Who both a Pilott and a Magistrate
  Steer'd in his turne the Shippe of Plymouth's state;
This little table shews his face whose worth
  The world's wide table hardly can sett forth.

248   A Day in Early Summer

A day in early summer
The first year of the war,
Davy Jones and I sat down
By the North Sea-shore.

The sun was bright, warm was the sand,
The sky was hot and blue.
How long we sat there
I never knew:

Rigged in brand-new uniforms,
Two naval sprogs
Dozing in the dancing sun,
Tired as dogs.

Suddenly a child's voice spoke
Across the silent shore:
'Look at those two sailors!
I wonder who they are?'

I sat up and looked about
The yellow and the blue
For the sailors on the shore.
I wondered, too.

Not a seaman could I see
As far as sight could reach:
Only the locked-up pier, the rolls
Of barbed-wire on the beach;

Only the tank-traps on the prom
By the shallow bay;
A woman and a little child
Wandering away;

Only Davy Jones and I
Wearing tiddley suits,
Lanyards, caps with 'HMS',
Shiny pussers' boots.

God help England, then I thought,
Gazing out to sea,
If all between it and the foe
Is Davy Jones and me.

249   Buildings on the Dock

The mouth of the river just at the town is a very good harbour [Devonport] for ships; the dockyards are about two miles from the town—by boat you go to it the nearest way—it is one of the best in England. A great many good ships built there, and the great depth of water which comes up to it though it runs for two miles between the land, which also shelters the ships. There is a great deal of buildings on the Dock, a very good house for the masters and several lesser ones, and house for their cordage and making ropes and all sorts of things required in building or refitting ships. It looks like a little town. The buildings are so many, and all of marble with fine slate on the roofs, and at a little distance it makes all the houses show as if they were covered with snow and glisters in the sun, which adds to their beauty.

250   Pot de Chambre d'Angleterre

In a mood like this, with the hemisphere wrapt in cloudy darkness, and the barometer rapidly sinking, you will not be surprised that I formed the resolution of curtailing my intended tour, of leaving Cornwall and the Scilly islands to longer days and clearer skies, and passing by its eastern skirts into the southern parts of Devon. I recollected with dread the appropriate name which had been imposed by a wicked French wit on the country of tin (*Pot de Chambre d'Angleterre*), and concluding that if it only drizzled in Devonshire, it must pour in Cornwall, I determined to turn my back at once upon its torrents, floods, and fogs.

251   *A Dangerous Journey*

From Plymouth I went one mile to Cribly Ferry, which is a very hazardous passage by reason of three tides meeting. Had I known the danger before, I should not have been very willing to have gone it, not but this is the constant way all people go, and saved miles' riding. I was at least an hour going over; it was about a mile, but indeed in some places, notwithstanding there were five men rowed and I set my own men to row also, I do believe we made not a step of way for almost a quarter of an hour, but, blessed be God, I came safely over; but those ferry boats are so wet and then the sea and wind are always cold to be upon, that I never fail to catch cold in a ferry boat, as I did this day, having two more ferries to cross, though not so bad or half so long as this.

Thence to Milbrooke two miles and went all along by the water, and had the full view of the dockyards. Here I entered into Cornwall, and so passed over many very steep, stony hills, though here I had some two or three miles of exceeding good way on the downs, and then I came to the steep precipices—great rocky hills. Ever and anon I came down to the sea and rode by its side on the sand, then mounted up again on the hills, which carried me mostly in sight of the South Sea. Sometimes I was in lanes full of rows of trees, and then I came down a very steep, stony hill to Lonn [Looe] 13 miles, and here I crossed a little arm of the sea on a bridge of 14 arches. This is a pretty big seaport, a great many little houses all of stone, and steep hill much worse and three times as long as Dean Clapper hill, and so I continued up and down hill. Here, indeed, I met with more enclosed ground, and so had more lanes and a deeper clay road, which by the rain the night before had made it very dirty and full of water in many places; in the road there are many holes and sloughs wherever there is clay ground, and when by rains they are filled with water, it is difficult to shun danger. Here my horse was quite down in one of these holes full of water, but by the good hand of God's providence which has always been with me ever a present help in time of need, for giving him a good strap he flounced up again, though he had gotten quite down his head and all, yet did retrieve his feet and got clear off the place with me on his back.

252   *West Country Play*

The play of Cornwall and Devonshire is the same, with a difference. The wrestlers step into the ring in the same way, they wear the same clothing and jacket, and they play for a hitch in the same fashion. Sticklers are appointed, who keep the ring, and the public are present in crowds. In Cornwall, however, the man steps into the ring in his stockings or socks. In Devonshire he wears his shoes, made for the express purpose. He is bound by rule not to have any iron or other metal whatever, in his shoe, but he has the soles so hardened by baking that they are very formidable weapons.

The difference in the play has been called the in-and-out play, the off-and-on play, the toe-and-heel play. Or the Cornish play—the hugging and heaving; the Devonshire play—the kicking and tripping. It might be thus defined: in Cornwall the shoulders and arms are chiefly relied on, in Devonshire the legs.

In Cornwall the Cornish game is always played, in Devonshire the Devonshire game is played; but on the borders of the counties, in Plymouth especially, where a great deal of play used to be seen, Cornwall and Devonshire met one another, and sometimes each would play his own game.

It is not difficult to understand the difference in the play, bearing in mind broadly the Cornish hug and the Devonshire kick. If an unlucky victim had to choose as a fate between one and the other, he might not be able to make up his mind in a hurry. But as the resort to kicking, instead of the true play, fell away sometimes into a kicking match, the Devonshire play got into disrepute, and the kicking was very properly held in scorn, especially in Cornwall.

The style of the two counties being the same, as explained, it cannot be said that in Cornwall the leg-play was not known, or in Devonshire the shoulder-play was not known, but it came to pass that in the one the shoulder play was chiefly followed, and in the other the leg-play. The shoulder-play and the leg-play are here used shortly to refer to a great many different ways of throwing a man a back fall.

In Cornwall a player having got his hitch would proceed to very close quarters, the in-play or on-play, and taking his man round the body, not lower than the waist, throw him over his shoulder, giving him the flying mare (which is poetical enough, considering that Pegasus was a flying horse), and, turning him over on his back while falling, get the back fall. The flying mare might be an affair of some danger. There was a little man at Truro some years ago who could throw the biggest of men by the flying mare. He did not take more than a few minutes about it, and if he failed at first he failed altogether. Big men stood off from him. He was so short that before they could get a hitch of him he was under them, and the flying mare was their due.

In West Country wrestling it would appear that small men can enter the ring with big men, and that would be especially the case in the Devonshire play. At Penzance in the year 1839 I saw a great wrestling at fair time. It was given out that the St Just men would play the world—the Cornish world of course, though they were ready for all the world, no doubt. A very fine young St Just man stepped into the ring with great confidence, and was followed, to my great surprise, but not to the surprise of the company in general, by a very small man. The small man gave himself up to the big young man without playing for a hitch, and was taken into the arms of the big one to be dealt with. Suddenly I saw the big one on his back, a fair back fall. It was done by the inside lock, leg-play.

In shoulder-play, a little man could have but small chance with a big one, except in the case of the Truro man described, but in the leg-play he might trip up the giant.

Besides the flying mare, there is the cross-buttock fall in shoulder-play, the back heave, and others. In the leg-play, there are the fore-lock, the back-lock, heaving toe, the back-heel, and others. Cornish players know them all, and Devonshire players know them all. Some are not readily played without the shoe, hence the lapse into kicking.

On the borders of the Tamar, at Plymouth, for example, famous wrestlings have taken place, and the best players of both counties have met there. In making the standards usually Cornwall would play Cornwall, and Devonshire Devonshire. And in the double play the sticklers would match them in like fashion, but in the end Cornwall must meet Devonshire, nothing loth on either side. The Cornish player would play for his hitch to draw his man in, the Devonshire man would play for his hitch to keep his man off. As long as the Devonshire player could keep his man off, he could play with his toe. The Cornish player did not seem to fear the kick, the stop to which is the knee. The kick, supposing the toe-play to be played without the savage kicking which was discountenanced for good-fellowship sake, is directed against the inside of the knee just under the joint. The stop is bending the knee to meet the kick, stopping the toe by receiving the shin against the knee, a most effective and punishing stop. In kicking, the player must of necessity have but one leg on the ground, and having an off-hitch might be thrown by a quick player with a trip or a lock. The Devonshire play is a lively play: the kick and the leg-play in general must be very quick, and it is undoubtedly fine play when properly played. If the Cornish player were not thrown in the Devonshire out-play, he would get his man too close to him for a kick, and try his own Cornish play on him. The Devonshire player would still play his leg-play, and a couple of hours might pass before one or the other got his back fall. The play would be well understood and be intensely interesting to a large company, the rivalry between the two counties always being at fever heat.

I well remember Johnny Jordan, an enormous Devonshire player, who used to walk about Plymouth in his old age. I also remember James Cann, a brother of Abraham Cann, and himself a well-known wrestler, who in his later years was an under-gamekeeper, respected for his fearlessness when poachers were to the fore.

Has football taken the place of wrestling, even in Cornwall where kicking is despised? In football there are symptoms of a degeneration into kicking matches. Is the fine manly game of wrestling to be one of the victims of this nineteenth century, civilized off the face of the earth? I have even

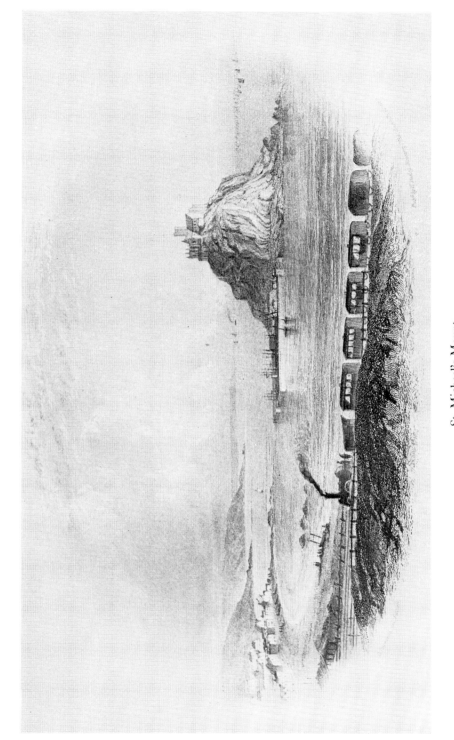

St. Michael's Mount

Botallack Mine

heard that the police constable has taken upon himself to put a stop to young men playing to 'wrastling' in their own fields. Have we come to this? Is Bumbledom to reign over us? And is the law really 'a hass?' I appeal to Cornwall to re-establish wrestling as a famous and manly West Country play.

253 *How Dick Stephens Fought the Bear*

There in the lane was Dick, the farmer of Trevissick, before me, his arms shrunken, neck shrivelled, and a good bit bent; but still standing over six feet in his socks and his eye bright though a little sunken. The bell at Penrice sounded mellow and clear out over the rock-laden woods and the deer-park. I thought he might be willing to tell me, but I had no idea what a performance it would be—one in a thousand. To make sure, I told him father had always told me to get him to tell me the story, but had never told me himself.

"Well,—it must 'a been fifty-one or fifty-two year ago. I was a young chap, twenty-two, I remember—I mind as if it was yesterday. 'Twas one evenin' after work, and I walked into town in nothin' but me shirt-sleeves and old clothes—I thought nothin' of walkin' in to town. There was a fair down to Fair Park, an' crowds of people. An' there was a wrastlin' saloon with a notice op an' two chaps—Guest they was called, from South Wales: ' 'Oo would wrastle the bear?' 'Ee was proper trained for it you knaw. They 'ad a leather aapern, a g'eat blacksmith's aapern for 'ee to put on to protect 'ee from the bear's claws: rolled up 'ee was. An' twas, ' 'Oo wud fight the bear? 'Oo wud wrastle the bear?' Nobody wud come forward. I went down with y'r uncle Bill—reglar sportin' man 'ee was: anythin' for a bit o' sport. An' 'ee said, 'Damn 'ee, Dick, go in and fight the beggar'—that was 'ow 'ee used to talk. Well—I was a bit bashful and never one for pushin' meself forward. An' when they said ' 'Oo'll fight the bear?' your uncle said, ' 'Ere, mister, I've got a man that'll wrastle your bear.' So after that I 'ad to, like. So I said to'n, 'Darn 'ee, then, I will.' An' 'ee op an' 'eaved out the aapern—'ee was all rolled up—out over th'eads of the crowd. When they 'eard somebody was goin' to wrastle the bear, they come in in 'underds.

"You knaw that a boxin' saloon is like. Well—'twas like that. But aw—I forgot—before I took on there was a chap called Bob Saunders—lives in town now, 'ee was a maason's labourer or else a maason, g'eat big fellow 'ee was—aw fine fellow, g'eat arms on'n: 'ee was goin' to fight the bear first. So we went in, and all the people come pushin' in—the plaace was crammed: I never saw nothin' like et. An' they 'ad a few roun's of boxin' and wrastlin', you knaw, like they do; and then Bob Saunders' turn come.

" 'Ee was the sort of chap that drink a lot, went round to pubs and anybody that was drunk 'ee'd op an giv'n a blaw an' knock'n out. That was the sort of chap 'ee was. Mind you a fine-built fella—aw—g'eat arms on'n. Well—'ee

12

took his plaace in one corner and the bear in th' other. G'eat brown bear 'ee was, four 'underd poun' weight. When they said 'Time', 'ee rawse up from 'is corner on 'is 'ind legs and come forward—'ee was trained to et. My God, Bob Saunders didn' stop to meet'n 'alf way: 'ee no sooner seed'n rise op on 'is 'ind legs th'n 'ee give one lep and lepped right out over the rope in among the people.

"You should 'ave seed the people laugh. Laugh? Bob Saunders never 'eard th'end of it for months and months. People'd ask'n, ' 'Ow did 'ee fight the bear then, Bob? Deffer'nt thing to knockin' out drunk men in pubs, wudn't it?'

"Well, that put the wind up me a bit, I can tell 'ee. But I didn' say nothin'. They 'ad a few more roun's of boxin', you knaw like they do, and then my turn come. They put up the leather aapern on me, an' then before we begin, the man said, 'There's two things I want for 'ee to understand, young man. This 'ere bear is muzzled. If you touch the muzzle 'ee'll bite your 'ead off. And the second thing is, you take'n on at your own risk; we wun't be responsible fur anythin' that 'appens.'

"Well—they said that to put 'ee off a bit. 'N I was a braave bit frightened, but I didn' say nothin'. Well, they said 'Time', and the bear got op from his corner, roase op on 'is 'ind legs and come forward. Mind you, I thought 'underds o' things. 'Ee come for to meet me and put out his g'eat arms an' we met. An' 'ee 'oogged me and I 'oogged 'ee. I cudn' shif'n. I tried to lift'n off his feet. But 'twas impossible. He was that weight, four 'underd pound. 'Ee was that firm—'

"Firm as a rock," I put in.

"Ess, as a rock," he repeated with emphasis and a sense of rightness. "I tried'n this way, and I tried'n that way, and I cudn' move'n. I tried to give'n a cant, an' tilt'n over. I kicked at his leg, but 'ee wudn' let go. What was I to do with'n? I thought an' I thought: I 'ad 'old ov'm an' I didn' let'n go, An' 'ee was clever, trained to et. I noticed that 'ee was always trying to keep me op nuzzlin' me chin and pushin' me op. An' once 'ee got one of 'is g'eat long arms right over me shoulder, and th'other under th'other. I thought me back was goin' to crack. But 'ee didn'.

"Then I thought that's 'is game, to keep me op. After that I kep'n down there, like that. I noticed 'ee was doin' all 'is work with his forearms; an' I thought if I can get 'old of 'is arms an' pinch they, 'ee wun't be able to do so much. So I got a 'old of 'is arms, and I pinched 'em an' pinched 'em, an' I didn't let go. I was sweatin' like a bull, and I could feel 'ee pantin' an' strugglin'. An' I thought, Now, mister, I've got 'ee. An' sure 'nough I 'ad. I 'eld on and went on pinchin' like this—"

Here it was necessary to give me a demonstration. Farmer Dick threw down his raincoat on the grass by the roadside under the bush of honeysuckle, threw down his fairings and his stick; I threw my walking-stick down and had my arms clinched together.

"Tha's 'ow I held'n. I cud feel 'is breath comin' an' goin'. When the people saw I'ad'n', they was shoutin' out, 'Give it to'n, Dick. You've got'n. 'Old on, oleman. You'll do'n.' And then I 'eaved'n op sideways and give'n a twist, and thrawd'n right over on 'is back.

"You should 'ave 'eard the cheerin'. You knaw what tes like—some kick-op. They said you cud 'ear the cheerin' op town.

"The fellow that run the shaw—'ee was a decent sort of chap, 'ee said, 'Well, th's the first time that I've been served that trick, young man. 'Underds of people 'ave tried to thraw'n, but nobody yet 'ave been aable to do et.' Then 'ee said, 'Would 'ee tackle'n again?'

"Well, now me blood was op, an' I felt confident like I cud thraw'n; 'n I said, 'Ess, I'll tackle'n and thraw'n again.'

"An' all the people cheered, an' said, 'Good ole Dick, you'll thraw'n. Try'n again.' An' I did. There 'ee was back in 'is corner pantin', an' I was sweatin' like wan thing.

"Well, w'en they said 'Time', 'ee come for me. 'Ee was angry, min' you: never been thraw'd like that before. 'Ee come at me, and got 'is fore-paw roun' the back of me 'ead: 'ee give me a blaw, drawd blood, made me smart, I can tell 'ee. I got the mark, a little mark, there now."

We stopped to inspect the place, which I must confess, after half a century, in the fading light was indecipherable.

"But this time I knew 'ow to thraw'n, an' it didn' take me long. But before I thraw'd'n, he op with 'is 'ind leg, and give me such a blaw in the guts— my God, it made me feel sick, fit to spew, for a minute. But I got 'is arms pinched and it didn't taake me long this time, I give'd'n a cant and 'eave'n right over, a'most out into where the people was.

"You shud 'ave 'eard the cheerin'. Aw, my dear life, there was some kick-op. I can mind it now, and all the people comin' op town was tellin' 'bout it, 'ow Dick Stephens thraw'd the bear. I didn' knaw et at the time, but et seems between the first an' secon' roun' father was in town, and people said to 'n, 'Your boy is down there goin' to wrastle the bear', and 'ee come in and saw the second roun'. I didn' knaw then. But afterwards—

"Aw, I forgot to tell 'ee. I 'ad me shirt-sleeves op; and w'en we was swayin' to and fro, the bear got 'is nawse op and through his muzzle with a twick, 'ee twicked me sleeve right off be the 'em. So in th' interval, 'ee falled down on me 'and, an' I put'n in me pocket.

"W'en I got 'ome that 'evenin', mother was in the kitchen—I can mind et as if 'twas yesterday; good mother she was to me an' a mother to everybody —I come in an' sit down in the chair. An' I said, ' 'Ere, Mother, 'ere's me sleeve for 'ee to mend.'

"She said, 'All right, boy. Ow did 'ee come to tear'n like that?'

"So I said, ' 'Aw, I've been in town fightin' the bear.'

"With that father come in and 'ee op and told the story. An' all she said was, 'You ought to 'ave a box on the side of your ear.' Wonderful mother she was to we. An' tha's about all was said about it."

The story had come to an end. It had been told with a wealth of action: the old man had put himself into it for me: he was re-living the experience that was the high-water mark of his life. His fine dark eyes flashed; strength came back into the shrunken arms. Once we had to scuttle into the hedge for a passing car; still the story went on. Now it was finished.

Farmer Dick has a splendid, broad-shouldered son, as strong as his father, in the Metropolitan Police. As a postscript, he added: "W'en I was op to London with George an' we went to the Zoo, we saw a big brown bear. An' I said to'n, 'There's a bear, George, like the one I fought in town that time.' People d'knaw that story from Penzance to Plymouth."

The sun was going down behind the woods of Penrice, as the sun was going down, gently, evenly, hardly perceptibly, for him. The mellow notes of the bell struck ten. It was time to part and go home our respective ways.

"Yes," he said, "it must 'ave been fifty-one or fifty-two year ago." And a dark shadow, the shadow of time, came into his eyes.

254 Hospitality and Nationality

Thus is hospitality practised in Cornwall—a county where, it must be remembered, a stranger is doubly a stranger, in relation to provincial sympathies; where the national feeling is almost entirely merged in the local feeling; where a man speaks of himself as Cornish in much the same spirit as a Welshman speaks of himself as Welsh.

255 The Merry Ballad of the Cornish Pasty

When that I view my Country o'er:
Of goodly things the plenteous store:
The Sea and Fish that swim therein,
And underground the Copper and Tin;
Let all the World say what it can,
Still I hold by the Cornishman,
And that one more especially
That first found out the Cornish Pastie.

When the Tinner to Bal takes a touchpipe for crowse
He cannot have Hot-meat sent from his house;
Yet hath no stomach for victuals cold,
So a Pasty he takes in a Napkin rolled:
And though he leave it for half the day,
Within his Hogan Bag warm 'twill stay.
So I wish him joy whoever he be
That first found out the Cornish Pastie.

And when the Fisher a-fishing goes,
Though rough winds redden his ears and nose,
Little he careth how hard it blow,
So his Pasty lie safe in the locker below.
For though the lugger should ship a sea
Within its crust still dry 'twould be.
So I wish him joy whoever he be
That first found out the Cornish Pastie.

When lasses and lads to Country go
To bring in the May with a halantow:
The men choose the field-path (longer by miles)
To help the maidens over the stiles.
Belike then a Basket may fall to the ground:
Yet if it hold Pasties they still are sound.
So I wish him joy whoever he be
That first found out the Cornish Pastie.

When of dancing the Maidens have had their fill:
Although their swains would be dancing still:
Is not Mick's Pasty the sweeter yet
For being shared with his sweetheart Bet?
And does not Jan's the better taste,
For that his Jenifer made the paste?
So I wish him joy whoever he be
That first found out the Cornish Pastie.

For a Hearty Man's dinner 'tis ample fare,
With naught too little nor none to spare;
And here again it deserveth praise
That when it has vanished its virtue stays:
For it gives sweet ease to the scullery quean,
Who hath nor platters nor knives to clean.
So I wish him joy whoever he be
That first found out the Cornish Pastie.

Now in the World since it first began,
What other dish has been made by man,
Both Knife and Fork: both Plate and Table,
Meat and Bread and Vegetable?
So one and all come drink to his health:
May he live merry in peace and wealth!
And give him a cheer with three times three
That first found out the Cornish Pastie!

256   *Sir Henry Irving's Childhood*

Then there is another anecdote already recorded by Mr Hatton, and of which I reminded Sir Henry [Irving], "It is quite right and I recall it well," was his response. "I told it to Hatton to show how these two strong natures, one strong and cheerfully stern—if I can use the expression—and the other strong and passionate, could yet live together in perfect concord. Nothing could disturb my aunt's appreciation of the sterling qualities of her husband. She was away from home one afternoon when he strode into the house and surprised us youngsters playing in the kitchen by starting to smash up the furniture. He was in a great rage about something, I forget what, and he broke the chairs across his knees as if they were matchwood, threw over the tables, and made havoc generally. We had scuttled into shelter like startled rabbits and trembled at the destruction, wondering if our turn would come next. But having smashed up everything portable he went out again, and we could see his big figure striding along the road to the mine, with arms waving.

"It was not in the scope of our youthful minds," Sir Henry continued, smiling introspectively, "to guess what my aunt's attitude would be to this extraordinary outbreak. We wondered and waited, fearing trouble. But none came. When the time arrived to meet him in the evening, my aunt gathered her brood together and out we set. There was no difference in our greeting, and we all returned in the best of humours. At the threshold of the kitchen—it was our living-room, by the way, and looked cosy enough with its ingle-nook and old oak beams embellished with rows of hams—my uncle stopped to laugh. You might have heard it for miles. It was the hearty guffaw of a giant. You know what the laughter was about? Aunt Penberthy had gathered together the wreckage of the furniture and hung it on the walls as if it composed a collection of precious works of art. A woman of less character would have found ample justification for angry recriminations; my aunt was strong enough to treat the affair as a joke. I shall not easily forget our childish wonderment and subsequent admiration at this turning of the tables, or the table legs. We were a very happy family that night."

257   *Holiday Land*

Then in the matter of train service from London there is much to be desired. Eight and a half hours from Paddington to Penzance is considered a somewhat formidable journey. It is eighty miles further to Edinburgh, and the journey is accomplished in six and a half hours. Of course the Northern lines have not the same difficulties of gradient and curve to contend with as the Great Western Company, who are spending vast sums in doubling the line and in rebuilding bridges and stations with a view to improving and increasing the facilities for travel. It is said that when the link lines from

Devizes to Westbury, and from Castle Cary to Langport are completed, the Cornish trains will run over the new route from Reading to Taunton, avoiding the longer journey via Bristol, and, by running from Paddington to Exeter without a stop, save about forty minutes in time, which, with a more rapid service through Cornwall, will probably shorten the journey from Paddington to Penzance to not exceeding seven hours. The Great Western directors are evidently alive to the possibilities of Cornwall as a holiday resort.

In order to attract people of wealth and position who do not mind any cost so long as their requirements are provided for in an adequate manner, hotel accommodation of absolutely the highest class is necessary, and in this direction much is being done by local capital and enterprise in many parts of the county.

In my next and concluding suggestion for the development of Cornwall as a holiday resort I shall probably tread upon more debatable ground. I frequently hear from people who have travelled extensively in all parts of the world remarks to the following effect:

"Yes, we admit to the full the beauty of your coast scenery, which has a certain charm of its own scarcely equalled elsewhere, and we acknowledge the many advantages of the Cornish climate, but one cannot live on scenery alone, and, to be perfectly candid, we find after the first few days that it becomes exceedingly dull. Why cannot you do something to enliven your towns? At the Continental holiday resorts people are never at a loss—the fashionable promenade to the strains of the fine military bands, the open-air cafés and concerts lend animation to the scene, which is wanting in Cornwall, and until you do something of the kind you will never attract the class of people you want."

I fear that from the visitors' point of view there is much truth in this contention. The gifted authoress of 'An Unsentimental Journey through Cornwall' was evidently influenced by the dullness of many of the places she visited. I should gather from her remarks that she reached St Ives some time after dark and left it before daylight next morning, putting up at a second-rate hotel. The shops were closed, and there were no public lamps alight, because the almanac said there was, or ought to have been, a moon, and her only source of information was a talkative old gentleman who regretted he could not spare any more of his time as he was "on his way to chapel."

258 At Risk

The chief peril is in the intrusion of the summer holiday and the 'weekend'. Irreparable damage is sometimes prompted by the desire to attract visitors. . . . In moments of pessimism one may fear that the very capacity of peaceful enjoyment is being killed, and that ceaseless grinding work destroys the power of resting. When the ordinary tourist visits places of peaceful solitariness he usually does so in crowds that rifle and ravish the sacredness of this solitude; he ruthlessly desecrates that which he does not understand; he never learns its secrets; the most commonplace of public parks would have responded fully to his needs and their gratification. But the West has long been a resort of that wiser, certainly better endowed, minority that seeks for direct personal contact with Nature, face to face, and not merely as seen through the glass windows of huge pavilions or from the seats of fashion-haunted promenades. Therefore the majority of Western watering-places are not yet spoiled; their physical features have often assisted to preserve them. They have not lost the quaint simplicity of their parochialism, to become national if not cosmopolitan. Constant intercourse with even the most sober of visitors must take something from the provincialism, the cherished traditions and local customs, the personal peculiarities and dialect. But there is still a good deal left; there is still the possibility of reaching Nature in her inmost sanctuaries, and at the same time winning some of those elusive and shy confidences that are the charm of locality.

259   A Way Out?

On the other hand I see Cornwall impoverished by the evil days on which mining and (to a less degree) argiculture have fallen. I see her population diminishing and her able-bodied sons forced to emigrate by the thousand. The ruined engine-house, the roofless cottage, the cold hearthstone are not cheerful sights to one who would fain see a race so passionately attached to home as ours is still drawing its vigour from its own soil. In the presence of destitution and actual famine (for in the mining district it came even to this, a little while ago) one is bound, if he care for his countrymen, to consider any cure thoughtfully suggested. . . . Were it within human capacity to decide between a revival of our ancient industries, fishery and mining, and the development of this new business, our decision would be prompt enough. But it is not. Well then, since we must cater for the stranger, let us do it well and honestly. Let us respect him and our native land as well.

260   Brave Spirits of the West

O generous hearts, brave spirits of the West,
   Clear-sighted, open brow and open hand,
   Wise, wistful, laughter-loving, fearless band,
So swift to clasp the stranger to your breast,   .
   So faithful to remember; ye are blest,

Who 'twixt the bleak moor and the blowing sand,
  Live hardly, love your frugal mother-land,
Can toil, and, rarer gift of Heaven, can rest!

So ordered He, who made you shrewd and brave,
  And bade your myriad streamlets blithely run,
    And knit the marble promontories, and nursed
    A sacred race, and bade them know the first
Kiss of the stately landward-marching wave,
  And latest flash of the ocean-dipping sun.

261 Her'd Shrump Up

About five miles on one side of this highway [the Launceston–Bodmin road], but whether to the north or to the south I will not say; near, however, to the steep flank of the granite mass where it heaves itself out of the altered slate and volcanic beds that engirdle it; lived Roger Kerneu, a stonecutter, along with his aged mother. Their cottage, called 'Nankivel', or 'Nancivale', was built against a steep bank, and was constructed of rude blocks of granite, quite unshaped, but neatly set together, and the joints filled in with turf. It was thatched with reeds from the bog, and was of one storey alone. It possessed but a single chimney, and comprised but one room, which served every purpose. The window was exceedingly small, and such panes of glass as remained in the casement were so dirty as to admit hardly any light. But the door was usually kept open, partly to afford light, mainly to assist the smoke from the open hearth in getting out of the cottage.

Roger Kerneu roved over the moorside for a mile or two and took stone wherever he listed. Not an errant block was spared, and when a node of granite showed through the moss, he attacked it and sliced out of it gate-posts or window-sills. The entire district was marked by his chisels, and not a piece of native rock remained that did not bear tokens of having been split by his 'jumper'. As to the precious relics of prehistoric populations within reach, he effaced them all.

Roger Kerneu possessed a rough moor cob, and this brute he fastened by chains to a strong 'truckamuck' he had, on which he bound the pieces of stone he had shaped or at least cut, and he made the cob drag the load down the steep and rugged track from the moor to the lowlands, and deposited the stones beside the way, where that way began to be practicable for wheeled conveyances, and thence farmers or builders fetched them at their convenience.

No one who has not seen a moor stonecutter at work has any conception of the facility with which he manipulates prodigious masses of granite. Any block, so long as he can succeed with a lever in moving it sufficiently to slip a marble under one corner, is at his mercy. Masses of rock that to the eye of the inexperienced would seem impossible of being turned about and moved from place to place, yielded to the unaided labours of this one man, helped indeed occasionally by Sparrow, his horse.

I have said that Roger's house door was usually open, but after a certain period this ceased to be true. Thenceforth it was not only shut but locked. This was what produced this change: Roger's mother died.

Now it was some time after that the rumour got about that the old woman was dead; but Roger had made no movement towards burying her.

At length the report gained consistency and force, so that the police and the registrar deemed it expedient to mount to the moor to inquire into the matter.

They found the house open, but no Roger there; he was away 'nogging out' gate-posts. They made free to enter, and, to their horror, discovered the body of the old woman lying in a sort of bed dug out of the bank in the rear, littered with heather and bracken, and the rats had gnawed and horribly defaced the corpse. The man was at once sought out, and an explanation demanded.

Now Roger was a fellow of few words, morose, shy, uncivilised. All the explanation he could give was that "it warn't convaynient to bury her. He had an order for a lot of stone quoins for a new bridge as was bein' built; and he thought there wor' no hurry—her wouldn't run away, and the longer her wor keeped, sure the more her'd shrump up."

262 Dozmary

Two miles from this place is a large standing water called Dosenmere [Dozmary] Pool in a black moorish ground, and is fed by no rivers except the little rivulets from some high hills, yet seems always full without diminution and flows with the wind and is stored with good fish, and people living near it take the pleasure in a boat to go about it. There is also good wild-fowl about it; it seems to be such a water as the mere at Whitlesome in Huntingtonshire by Stilton; it is fresh water and what supply it has must be the rivulets that must come from the South Sea, being that wayward towards Plymouth. As I travelled I came in sight of a great mountain [Brown Willy] esteemed the second highest hill in England, supposing they account Black Combe in Cumberland the first, but really I have seen so many great and high hills I cannot attribute preeminence to either of these, though this did look very great and tall, but I think it is better said the highest hill in each county.

263   A Midsummer Eve Rhyme from Cornwall

I place my shoes like a letter T
In hopes my true love I shall see
   In his apparel and in his array
In the clothes he wears every day
Let him come to me!

264   Piran Round

When you leave this dreary scene, you only leave it for the wild flat heath,
the open naked country once more. You follow your long road, visible miles
on before you, winding white and serpent-like over the dark ground, until
you suddenly observe in the distance an object which rises strangely above
the level prospect. You approach nearer, and behold a circular turf embankment; a wide, lonesome, desolate enclosure, looking like a witches' dancing-
ring that has sprung up in the midst of the open moor. This is Piran Round.
Here, the old inhabitants of Cornwall assembled to form the audience of
the drama of former days.
   A level area of grassy ground, one hundred and thirty feet in diameter,
is enclosed by the embankment. There are two entrances to this area cut
through the boundary circle of turf and earth, which rises to a height of
nine or ten feet, and narrows towards the top, where it is seven feet wide.
All round the inside of the embankment steps were formerly cut; but their
traces are now almost obliterated by the growth of the grass. They were
originally seven in number; the spectators stood on them in rows, one above
another—a closely packed multitude, all looking down at the dramatic
performances taking place on the wide circumference of the plain. When it
was well filled, the amphitheatre must have contained upwards of two
thousand people.

265   Ancient Mysteries

And the play!—to see the play must have been a sight indeed! Conceive
the commencement of it; the theatrical sky which was to open awfully
whenever Heaven was named; the mock clouds coolly set up by the 'property-
man' on an open-air stage, where the genuine clouds appeared above them
to expose the counterfeit; the hard fighting of the angels with swords and
staves; the descent of the lost spirits along cords running into the plain;
the thump with which they must have come down; the rolling off of the
whole troop over the grass, to the infernal regions, amid shouts of applause
from the audience as they rolled! Then the appearance of Adam and Eve,

packed in white leather, like our modern dolls—the serpent with the virgin's face and the yellow hair, climbing into a tree, and singing in the branches— Cain falling out of the bush when he was struck by the arrow of Lamech, and his blood appearing, according to the stage directions, when he fell— the making of the Ark, the filling it with livestock, the scenery of the Deluge, in the fifth act! What a combination of theatrical prodigies the whole performance must have presented.

266   The End of the Play

The end of the play, too—how picturesque, how striking all the circumstances attending it must have been! Oh that we could hear again the merry old English tune piped by the minstrels, and see the merry old English dancing of the audience to the music! Then, think of the separation and the return home of the populace, at sunset; the fishing people strolling off towards the seashore; the miners walking away farther inland; the agricultural labourers spreading in all directions, wherever cottages and farmhouses were visible in the far distance over the moor. And then the darkness coming on, and the moon rising over the amphitheatre, so silent and empty, save at one corner, where the poor worn-out actors are bivouacking gipsy-like in their tents, cooking supper over the fire that flames up red in the moonlight, and talking languidly over the fatigues and the triumphs of the play. What a moral and what a beauty in the quiet night-view of the old amphitheatre, after the sight that it must have presented during the noise, the bustle, and the magnificence of the day!

267   Alien Corn

And then there was the man I knew, who was a munition-worker in London during the last war. Overworked day in and day out, and too tired for any strenuous breach with routine when the holiday came, on Sundays he used to make his way up from the East End to Paddington to watch the trains come in from the West. He was a Cornishman, and the one thing that refreshed him in homesickness, in all that waste and at such a time, was to hear the soft western speech of his own people that always gives Paddington a certain homeliness to the Westerner.

Such are cases of the instinctive turning of the exile's thoughts to his home. But it is possible to make it a conscious part of your mental life, to rely upon calling up what you most would remember, when there is the need for some release from the too great oppression of the present, for some refreshment and inner peace. The great strength of being so able to control your mind is that it makes you less dependent upon outside circumstances. It has been said, by Dean Inge I think, that the true sign of the intellectual is that he is never bored; and it is for this reason, that he who knows how to explore the resources of the mind has illimitable reserves at his disposal, and is less at the mercy of outside circumstances than most people.

268 Launceston and Weather

Here I met with some showers which by fits or storms held me—to Lanston [Launceston] 4 miles more; these 12 miles from Cambleford [Camelford] were not little ones, and what with the wet and dirty lanes in many places I made it a tedious journey. I could see none of the town till just as I was, as you may say, ready to tumble into it, there being a vast steep to descend to, when the town seemed in a bottom, yet I was forced to ascend a pretty good hill into the place. Lanston is a chief town in Cornwall where the assizes are kept. I should have remarked at the Land's End that Pensands [Penzance] was the last corporation in England, so this is one of the last great towns, though no city, for Cornwall is in the diocese of Devonshire, which is Exeter. There is a great ascent up into the Castle, which looks very great, and in good repair the walls and towers round it. It is true there is but a part of it remains, the round tower or fort being still standing and makes a good appearance. The town is encompassed with walls and gates. It is pretty large, though you cannot discover the whole town, being up and down in so many hills. The streets themselves are very steep unless it be at the market place, where is a long and handsome space set on stone pillars with the town hall on the top, which has a large lantern or cupola in the middle, where hangs a bell for a clock, with a dial to the street. There are in this place two or three good houses built after the London form by some lawyers, else the whole town is old houses of timber work.

At a little distance from the town, on a high hill I looked back and had the full prospect of the whole town, which was of pretty large extent. A mile beyond I crossed on a stone bridge over a river and entered into Devonshire again, and passed through mostly lanes which were stony and dirty by reason of the rains that fell the night before, and this day, which was the wettest day I had in all my summer's travels, hitherto having had no more than a shower in a day, and that not above three times in all, except when I came to Exeter. As I came down from Taunton there was small rain most of the afternoon, but this day was much worse, so that by that time I came through lanes and some commons to Oakingham [Okehampton] which was 15 miles, I was very wet.

This was a little market town, and I met with a very good inn and accommodation, very good chamber and bed, and came in by 5 of the clock, so had good time to take off my wet clothes and be all dried and warm to eat my supper, and rested very well without sustaining the least damage by the wet. I should have remarked that these roads were much up and down hill through enclosed lands and woods in the same manner the other part of Cornwall and Devonshire was, gaining by degrees the upper grounds by one hill to another, and so descending them in like manner. These rains fully convinced me of the need of so many great stone bridges, whose arches were so high that I have wondered at it, because the waters seemed shallow streams, but they were so swelled by one night and day's rain that they came up pretty near the arches, and ran in most places with such rapidity and looked so thick and troubled as if they would clear all before them. This causes great floods, and the lower grounds are overwhelmed for a season after such rains, so that had I not put on and gotten beyond Lanston [Launceston] that day there would have been no moving for me till the floods, which hourly increased, were run off.

269   The End of an Era

The dream of many country-lovers is that one day they might retire to some quiet little village and find a modestly priced cottage where they can grow their own fruit and vegetables, perhaps keep a few hens, even a pony. They might well be interested in these particulars,
"A freehold detached stonebuilt and slated cottage with stable, linhay, piggeries, gardens, paddock and orchard, in all about 1½ acres."
Or in these:
"A freehold stone-built and slated dwelling-house with out-buildings, garden and pasture land, in all about two acres."
And the prices of these desirable properties? Very reasonable. For the first, £200, and for the second, £225.
"Where is the catch?" the country-lovers will ask. Sadly, they are fifty-three years too late. These cottages and many others, together with 31 farms, an inn, water-mills, a blacksmith's shop, a wheelwright and carpenter's shop, and a Post Office are all described in a fascinating document, dated August 1919, which sets out the particulars and the conditions of sale of almost a whole parish, that of Quethiock, in East Cornwall.
The Corytons of Pentillie Castle, in St Mellion, were the squires of the parish, the heavy burden of death duties the reason for the sale. Thus was a tie broken between squire and tenant which had lasted for many centuries.
The Corytons were descended by marriage from the Kyngdons of Trehunsey, in Quethiock. A splendid brass memorial to Roger Kyngdon (1395–1471) is set in the chancel floor of the parish church.
Four of Quethiock's six medieval manors, Trehunsey, Penpoll, Hammett and Trecorme, had thus belonged to the ancestors of the Corytons since the Middle Ages. The other two manors, Hollough Wood and Leigh, were added to the estate later.

By 1919, with the exception of the church, churchyard, and school, and of the Methodist Church and the almshouses, (a trust set up by the Corytons in 1633 for needy spinsters) the entire parish came up for sale—4,200 acres of land in all.

In my copy of the sale brochure someone has written, in pencil, the price fetched by each property, and the name of the purchaser. Cottages were sold for £30 upward, a good small-holding for £170, a sound 170-acre farm for £3,500.

One cottage had special conditions of sale which are of particular interest in these post-Rachman days:

"Rose Cottage. Very attractive Freehold Property. Detached stone and slated cottage residence, 3 bedrooms, parlour, kitchen with range, scullery, and a good fruit and vegetable garden. This Property is in the occupation of Mr. J. H. Heddon (who is in his 85th year) and is to be sold subject to Mr. Heddon being allowed to reside there for the remainder of his life free of rent and all outgoings. The property to be maintained in tenantable order for him by the Purchaser."

After reading this one can well believe that the squire's rents were "in almost every case extremely low" as claimed.

But the conditions of sale and the prices the properties fetched are by no means the only points of interest. As one studies the brochure one is forced to realise that this is a document of great social importance.

Here, exactly described, is a community and a way of life that had continued basically unchanged for centuries. Not only had the Corytons owned land in Quethiock since the Middle Ages, many of their tenants and cottagers had lived in the parish just as long.

They formed a close-knit and ecologically stable society, extraordinarily self-sufficient and making small demands upon the environment.

The particulars of the farmhouses show them to have been the scene of busy activity. Here is a typical set of domestic offices: "Kitchen, Pantry, Back Kitchen with Open Fireplace, Baking Oven, Furnace and Boiler, Dairy and Stone and Slated Pump House with Pump."

Others mention three-pan copper scalding stoves, cider cellars and apple lofts, salting houses and separator houses. Clearly home baking and butter-making were taken for granted.

Nothing was wasted. Skim milk and edible kitchen and garden waste fed pigs and poultry. The rest went on the rubbish heap, now more grandly termed the compost heap, and was either dug into the garden, or drawn out with the dung.

Horses provided agricultural power, and also were the means of getting to market and back. There was no electricity, only paraffin lamps. Everyone burned wood in their open fireplaces or kitchen ranges, for Quethiock was a well-wooded parish.

There was no mains water, so great attention was paid to water rights, for the smallest cottages as well as for the farms and mills.

Hammett possessed a mill and a threshing machine, driven by water power. "The occupier of Hammett Farm is entitled to use the water flowing through the farm for the purpose of driving the water-wheel as fixed, and for irrigation, but only when this can be done without detriment to the working of Trecorme Mill."

So all the parish was sold. The squires of Quethiock who, over the centuries, had carefully conserved the soil, the woods and the streams were its squires no longer. Probably at first there was little change, for many tenants bought their farms and cottages, the publican bought his inn, and the village carpenter his cottage and shop.

Yet now, 53 years later, we realise that this was just before the coming of the internal combustion engine which was to set the agricultural revolution in motion.

Now every single farming operation is utterly dependent upon fuel oil or electricity. Tractors and combine harvesters have replaced horses. A whole range of powered equipment has displaced the farm workers, whose former homes are occupied by commuters or the retired.

Where 50 years ago there was cheap land in plenty, with four acres of allotment gardens in the village and other garden plots to let for a few shillings a year, now each one is a potential building site. The water mills are dismantled; the dusty roads along which the horses clip-clopped are now metalled and busy with traffic.

Quethiock is self-sufficient no longer. August 1919, was the end of an era.

270   Smuggling Money

The following observations of an old man who had known Cawsand in the days referred to will form a fitting conclusion to this sketch: 'It was a very good thing for the place that smuggling was put down, for it was the ruin of a lot of people, especially young fellows who served in the Navy. For, you see, in those days men only shipped for a commission, and when they came home again they wouldn't be over and above flush of money; and, finding smuggling going on briskly, they would take a trip across to France. If the goods were landed safe there would be grog going all night afterwards, aye, and all next day, too, for those who liked it. So it was difficult for a young fellow of spirit to keep out of the business, whether he intended to go smuggling or not. I can tell you this, though, none of the smugglers bettered themselves by it. There was an old saying that "Smuggling money never did good to anyone." One moment there would be money and to spare, but it would all be lost later on; and every smuggler that I remember died poor.'

A Tin Mine, between Camborne and Redruth

Tol-Peden-Penwith—near the Land's End

271   In Cawsand Bay Lying

In Cawsand Bay lying, with the Blue Peter flying,
  And all hands on deck for the anchor to weigh,
We spied a young lady, as fresh as a daisy,
  And modestly hailing, this damsel did say—

'Ship ahoy! bear a hand there! I wants a young man there,
  So heave us a man-rope, or send him to me:
His name's Henry Grady, and I am a lady
  Arrived to prevent him from going to sea.'

Now the Captain, his Honour, when he looked upon her,
  He ran down the side for to hand her on board.
Cried he with emotion, 'What Son of the Ocean
  Can thus be looked arter by Elinor Ford?'

Then the lady made answer, 'That there is a man, sir,
  I'll make him as free as a Duke or a Lord.'
'Oh no!' says the Cap'en; 'that can't very well happen;
  I've got sailing orders—you, sir, stop on board.'

But up spoke the lady, 'Don't you heed him, Hal Grady;
  He once was your Cap'en, but now you're at large:
You sha'n't stop on board her, for all that chap's order!'—
  And out of her bosom she drew his discharge.

Said the Captain, 'I'm hanged now, you're cool, and I'm banged now!'
  Said Hal, 'Here, old Weatherface, take all my clothes!'
And ashore he then steered her: the lads they all cheered her:
  But the Captain was jealous, and looked down his nose.

Then she got a shore tailor for to rig up her sailor
  In white nankeen trowsers and long blue-tailed coat;
And he looked like a squire, for all to admire,
  With a dimity handkercher tied round his throat.

They'd a house that was greater than any first-rater,
  With footmen in livery handing the drink,
And a garden to go in, with flowers all a blowing—
  The daisy and buttercup, lily and pink.

And he got eddication befitting his station,
  For we all of us know we're not too old to larn;
And his messmates they found him, his little ones round him,
  All chips of the old block from the stem to the starn.
13

272   Tregeagle on the Run

It is said that the terrible Cornish giant, or ogre, Tregeagle, was trudging homewards one day, carrying a huge sack of sand on his back, which—being a giant of neat and cleanly habits—he designed should serve him for sprinkling his parlour floor. As he was passing along the top of the hills which now overlooked Loo Pool, he heard a sound of scampering footsteps behind him; and, turning round, saw that he was hotly pursued by no less a person than the devil himself. Big as he was, Tregeagle lost heart and ignominiously took to his heels: but the devil ran nimbly, ran steadily, ran without losing breath—ran, in short, like the devil. Tregeagle was fat, short-winded, had a load on his back, and lost ground at every step. At last, just as he reached the seaward extremity of the hills, he determined in despair to lighten himself of his burden, and thus to seize the only chance of escaping his enemy by superior fleetness of foot. Accordingly, he opened his huge sack in a great hurry, shook out all his sand over the precipice, between the sea and the river which then ran into it, and so formed in a moment the Bar of Loo Pool.

273   Tristan—Iseult—Mark

Consideration of the topographical problems raised by the Tristan-Iseult-Mark stories is illuminating. The Tristan romance seems originally to have been told about a member of the Pictish royal family, and in Welsh literature Tristan is always known as Tristan ap Talorc, who is certainly Pictish. In south-west Scotland we find Trusty's Hill and Mote of Mark. How far we can talk about Picts in Galloway is itself a matter of dispute, but at best we can say, on archæological grounds, that Mote of Mark was occupied at broadly the right time for Tristan, and Trusty's Hill has a secondary fortification which could be contemporary. In the developed versions of the romance, however, the setting is in Cornwall or Brittany. Relevant here is a memorial stone just north of Fowey to *Drustanus filius Cunomori*: 'Tristan son of Cynfawr'. Already by the ninth century Cunomorus was being equated with Mark, and by the twelfth century the area north of Fowey—St Sampson in Golant—was made the setting for the romance. As part of the same process, the nearby Iron-Age hill-fort of Castle Dore has come to be identified as King Mark's Palace, despite the fact that the most likely candidates for the historical Mark are Welsh or Breton. We can at least affirm that the Cornish Tristan was historical—indeed the Tristan memorial stone is the only strictly contemporary evidence for any Tristan. His father Cynfawr was historical too; and excavation at Castle Dore has revealed a large timber building which may well have been his feasting hall.

274 *West Country Tarts*

Well, to Pass on, I went over some little heath ground but mostly lanes, and those stony and dirty, three miles and half to Parr; here I ferried over again, not but when the tide is out you may ford it. Thence I went over the heath to St Austins [St Austell] which is a little market town where I lay, but their houses are like barns up to the top of the house. Here was a pretty good dining-room and chamber within it, and very neat country women. My landlady brought me one of the West Country tarts; this was the first I met with, though I had asked for them in many places in Somerset and Devonshire. It is an apple pie with a custard all on the top. It is the most acceptable entertainment that could be made me. They scald their cream and milk in most parts of those countries, and so it is a sort of clotted cream as we call it, with a little sugar, and so put on the top of the apple pie. I was much pleased with my supper, though not with the custom of the country, which is a universal smoking, men, women, and children have all their pipes of tobacco in their mouths and so sit round the fire smoking, which was not delightful to me when I went down to talk with my landlady for information of any matter and customs among them. I must say they are as comely sort of women as I have seen anywhere, though in ordinary dress—good black eyes and crafty enough and very neat.

275 *Old Prospects, Old Manners, Old Names*

And no less frail, unhappily, is the actual appearance of the town and its villages as we grew to know them. Changes must come, roads be made and houses built, we all know. But are we doing all we can do to ensure that the work of this generation is in keeping with the spirit of the old? The place as we knew it was a place of original and individual aspect. Strangers came and admired its quaintness. The tendency of much recent addition has been to flatten St Austell to the dull level of any other place. We gain little but lose a great deal by suburbanising our villages and changing the names of our places and streets. What we gain is to be one degree more like Surbiton; what we lose is the infinite variety of old prospects, old manners, and old names.

Everything depends in this matter on the growth of an informed local opinion. We should learn to be ashamed when vulgar and tactless and showy houses, complete with cheap wood verandahs and coloured panes of glass in the windows, appear along the country lanes and spoil our views. As for building in prominent positions on the cliffs, the pride and glory of Cornwall, the thing should be placed beyond the pale by public opinion. And with names, too, we can do much to preserve our distinctive characteristics from being overwhelmed in the flood of ignorance and semi-education. What is better than the simple homespun names with their roots in the past and with their meanings, though hidden in our forgotten language: names like Polketh (spelt as it was pronounced), Treleaven's Cross, Watering Hill, Menacuddle Street? There is poetry in names; when we are touched by the names of flowers, it is the flowers of Shakespeare's England, as he tells them over in the Plays.

> The fairest flowers o' the season
> Are our carnations and streaked gillyvors . . .
> Here's flowers for you;
> Hot lavender, mints, savory marjoram . . .

The moral of it all is there. There is not so much beauty about us that we can afford to destroy it. And if we have been fortunate in our birth-place, and in a heritage of a distinctive character, we ought to do our duty in preserving it from despoilment. The responsibility is not only to ourselves and to later generations who may come to love our common home as we love it, but to the men and women in all parts of the world who have gone forth from home, yet who retain a living image of their native place and would not have it much changed.

276   In Truro

From Redruth I went to Truro, 8 miles, which is a pretty little town and seaport, and formerly was esteemed the best town in Cornwall; now is the second, next Lanstone [Launceston]. It is just by the copper and tin mines, and lies down in a bottom, pretty steep ascent as most of the towns in these countries, that you would be afraid of tumbling with nose and head foremost. The town is built of stone—a good pretty church built all stone and carved on the outside; it stands in the middle of the town, and just by there is a market house on stone pillars and hall on the top; there is also a pretty good quay. This was formerly a great trading town and flourished in all things, but now as there is in all places their rise and period, so this, which is become a ruinated disregarded place. Here is a very good meeting, but I was hindered by the rain the Lord's Day, else should have come to hearing, and so was forced to stay where I could hear but one sermon at the church, but by it saw the fashion of the country, being obliged to go a mile to the parish church over some grounds which are divided by such stiles and bridges uncommon, and I never saw any such before; they are several stones fixed across, and so are like a grate or large steps over a ditch that is full of mud or water, and over this just in the middle is a great stone fixed sideways, which is the stile to be clambered over. These I find are the fences and guards of their grounds one from another, and indeed they are very troublesome and dangerous for strangers and children. I heard a pretty good sermon,

but that which was my greatest pleasure was the good landlady I had—
she was but an ordinary plain woman, but she was understanding in the
best things as most—the experience of real religion and her quiet submission
and self-resignation to the will of God in all things, and especially in the
placing her in a remoteness to the best advantages of hearing, and being
in such a public employment which she desired and aimed at the discharging
so as to adorn the Gospel of her Lord and Saviour, and the care of her
children.

277 A New Cathedral

The site of the new cathedral was determined mainly by the fact that
St Mary's Church was named as the cathedral church in the Act of Parliament
constituting the See. By some an entirely new building on some lofty spot
in the outskirts of the city, visible far and wide, was suggested. Against
this, among other difficulties, was objected the creation of a new ecclesiastical
centre in addition to the already numerous parish churches of Truro. It was
indeed, thought inexpedient by many to plant a splendid architectural pile
low down in the city, with little space round it, with houses and clustering
shops to it. But, on the other hand, the desirability of identifying the cathedral
with the old ecclesiastical centre of Truro, of linking it with the many
associations and historic memories of a most ancient municipality and
parish, prevailed. On the whole, this cannot be regretted. The narrow
streets and lanes by which the cathedral is approached remind those who
visit it of many an old French town with its ancient minster hemmed in by
humble dwellings in the heart of the population, close by its market, town
hall, and other daily resorts of the inhabitants. What was wanted was not
a show-place for visitors with a pleasant, trim environment, but a mother-
church and working ecclesiastical centre. The agreeable 'amenities' (as a
Scotch gardener would say) of a cathedral close with the peaceful retirement
of a deanery and its garden, quiet canonical residences and the like, are
necessarily wanting under existing circumstances, or at least indefinitely
postponed. But, on the other hand, it is a real advantage that Truro Cathedral
is not altogether new. It has incorporated into itself a substantial portion
of the old parish church, and retains much of the ancient associations of
the past; it stands in the old 'High Cross', and is reached through the old
'Church Lane'. Underneath its crypt and nave lie the buried remains of
many a citizen and worthy of olden times: their monuments are preserved
and their history not altogether forgotten. Those who worship in the old
parish aisle, and even in the new cathedral, are kneeling on the ground
consecrated by at least six centuries of prayer and praise.

278   *A Cornish Dream*

A word about the grim substance of a dream. A friend who has been looking
up Hancock's *Selworthy* writes to remind me that this book contains an
interesting reference to a subject with which I was dealing last week—the
assassination of Prime Minister Spencer Perceval. . . . Preb. Fred Hancock,
touching on dreams, wrote this: 'The number of instances in which relations
of dying people have been apparently warned by the passing spirit are
certainly most curious, and some very well authenticated. . . . Perhaps the
most striking, as it is certainly one of the best authenticated of modern
dreams of this nature, is the well known vision of a Mr Williams, a landowner
and magistrate, at that time living near Truro, of the approaching murder
in 1812 of the Rt. Hon. S. Perceval, then Prime Minister.'

Preb. Hancock relates that Mr Williams dreamt three times during the
same night, very vividly, that he was standing in the lobby of the House of
Commons, and that he saw a man enter whose dress he accurately noted;
and then another man, whose appearance was just as clearly impressed upon
his mind, step forward and shoot the first man. Unable to sleep, Williams
rode into Truro and told his tale. Some of his friends, who knew Mr Perceval
by sight, at once identified the man murdered in the dream as the Prime
Minister. So strongly impressed was Mr Williams with his vision that he
wished to ride at once to London to warn the Prime Minister of possible
danger, but he was persuaded that he would be looked upon as a madman
for his pains. Shortly afterwards, the news that the Prime Minister had been
assassinated by John Bellingham reached Cornwall. Mr Williams hurried
to London and recognised in Bellingham the murderer he had seen in his
dream, and found that every detail of the scene in the dream, even down to
the particulars of the dress of the assassin and his victim, corresponded
exactly with those of the actual occurrence.

279   *Kilvert in Cornwall*

He [Kilvert] came down in July 1870, the summer that the Franco-German
War broke out; never was the English countryside more peaceful or more
prosperous. It was but a few years before the agricultural depression of
the later seventies involved landowner, farmer, and labourer in common
trouble. His impression of the first few miles of Cornwall was that the country
was "bleak, barren, and uninteresting, the most striking feature being the
innumerable mine works of lead, tin, and copper crowning the hills with
their tall chimney shafts and ugly, white, dreary buildings or nestling in a
deep, narrow valley, defiling and poisoning the streams with the white tin
washing." That takes us back to the years when the mines were still at their
height; but a short time and they were to close down and the great emigration
from the county begin. Those later seventies must have been a hard time
for Cornwall! A little further down the line Kilvert notes that the country

soon grew prettier. He was much impressed by the great timber viaducts crossing the ravines "at a ghastly height in the air"—the spider-bridges which were such a feature of Cornwall and such a decoration to our landscape. Many people must remember them: they have only recently vanished from their last hold, the line from Truro to Falmouth.

Kilvert calls his arrival at Tullimaar "the fulfilment of two years' dream", so that he must have known his friends, the Hockins, for at least that time. He was on intimate, indeed affectionate terms with them, and it would be interesting to know if any of the family remembers the young, attractive clergyman with the full beard and lively fine eyes that observed everything, who has enshrined them so charmingly in his diary. He was evidently fond of them; and a very good time they gave him in that hospitable house. Nor were they hospitable only to fellow human beings. Mrs Hockin, he writes, "has two pet toads, which live together in a deep hole in the bottom of a stump of an old tree. She feeds them with bread crumbs when they are at home, and they make a funny little plaintive squeaking noise when she calls them. Sometimes they are from home, especially in the evenings. In the kitchen live a pair of doves in a large cage, and the house is filled with their soft, sweet, deep cooing." Tullimaar is an attractive spot, looking across the woods of Carclew and down Restronguet Creek; and Kilvert gives us an enchanting picture of the place in its best summer colours, "the rich mingling of the purple beech tints with the bright green of the other trees about the lawns and shrubberies."

Next day they went into Truro and down the river to Falmouth. It was market day at Truro; a market day in the seventies, before ever the Cathedral was built. What a pleasant picture of the old market he conjures up! He notes that the road was lively with market folk and evidently we made a good impression on him: "The Cornish people seem fine tall folk, especially the women, much taller, larger people than the Welsh, and most of them appear to be dark-haired". He and Mrs Hockin went marketing together, and, of course, they bought some pasties for lunch. While waiting on the quay they watched an old invalid man from the infirmary being very tenderly helped by two or three men into the stern of a boat. Dear Mrs Hockin told Kilvert that "the Cornish are very kind and neighbourly to each other, especially when they are in trouble".

280   Vaccination in Lizard Town

The man who first distinguished the little group of cottages that we now looked on, by the denomination of Lizard Town, must have possessed magnificent ideas indeed on the subject of nomenclature. If the place looked like anything in the world, it looked like a large collection of farm out-buildings without a farmhouse. Muddy little lanes intersecting each other at every possible angle; rickety cottages turned about to all the points of the compass; ducks, geese, cocks, hens, pigs, cows, horses, dunghills, puddles, sheds, peat-stacks, timber, nets, seemed to be all indiscriminately huddled together where there was little or no room for them. To find the inn amid this confusion of animate and inanimate objects, was no easy matter; and when we at length discovered it, pushed our way through the live stock in the garden, and opened the kitchen door, this was the scene which burst instantaneously on our view:

We beheld a small room literally full of babies, and babies' mothers. Interesting infants of the tenderest possible age, draped in long clothes and short clothes, and shawls and blankets, met the eye wherever it turned. We saw babies propped up uncomfortably on the dresser, babies rocking snugly in wicker cradles, babies stretched out flat on their backs on women's knees, babies prone on the floor toasting before a slow fire. Every one of these Cornish cherubs was crying in every variety of vocal key. Every one of their affectionate parents was talking at the top of her voice. Every one of their little elder brothers was screaming, squabbling, and tumbling down in the passage with prodigious energy and spirit. The mothers of England—and they only—can imagine the deafening and composite character of the noise which this large family party produced. To describe it is impossible.

Ere long, while we looked on it, the domestic scene began to change. Even as porters, policemen, and workmen of all sorts, gathered together on the line of rails at a station, move aside quickly and with one accord out of the way of the heavy engine slowly starting on its journey—so did the congregated mothers in the inn kitchen now move back on either hand with their babies, and clear a path for the great bulk of the hostess leisurely advancing from the fireside, to greet us at the door. From this most corpulent and complaisant of women, we received a hearty welcome, and a full explanation of the family orgies that were taking place under her roof. The great public meeting of all the babies in Lizard Town and the neighbouring villages, on which we had intruded, had been convened by the local doctor, who had got down from London, what the landlady termed a "lot of fine fresh matter," and was now about to strike a decisive blow at the small-pox, by vaccinating all the babies he could lay his hands on, at 'one fell swoop'. The surgical ceremonies were expected to begin in a few minutes.

This last piece of information sent us out of the house without a moment's delay. The sunlight had brightened gloriously since we had last beheld it—the rain was over—the mist was gone. But a short distance before us, rose the cliffs at the Lizard Head—the southernmost land in England—and to this point we now hastened, as the fittest spot from which to start on our rambles along the coast.

281 Lizard Coast

Daw's Hugo and the Lion's Den may be fairly taken as characteristic types of the whole coast scenery about the Lizard Head, in its general aspects. Great caves and greater landslips are to be seen both eastward and westward. In calm weather you may behold the long prospects of riven rock, in their finest combination, from a boat. At such times, you may row into vast caverns, always filled by the sea, and only to be approached when the waves ripple as calmly as the waters of a lake. Then, you may see the naturally arched roof high above you, adorned in the loveliest manner by marine plants waving to and fro gently in the wind. Rocky walls are at each side of you, variegated in dark red and dark green colours—now advancing, now receding, now winding in and out, now rising straight and lofty, until their termination is hid in a pitch dark obscurity which no man has ever ventured to fathom to its end. Beneath, is the emerald green sea, so still and clear that you can behold the white sand far below, and can watch the fish gliding swiftly and stealthily out and in: while, all around, thin drops of moisture are dripping from above, like rain, into the deep quiet water below, with a monotonous echoing sound which half oppresses and half soothes the ear, at the same time.

On stormy days your course is different. Then, you wander along the summits of the cliffs; and looking down, through the hedges of tamarisk and myrtle that skirt the ends of the fields, see the rocks suddenly broken away beneath you into an immense shelving amphitheatre, on the floor of which the sea boils in fury, rushing through natural archways and narrow rifts. Beyond them, at intervals as the waves fall, you catch glimpses of the brilliant blue main ocean, and the outer reefs stretching into it. Often, such wild views as these are relieved from monotony by the prospect of smooth cornfields and pasturelands, or by pretty little fishing villages perched among the rocks—each with its small group of boats drawn up on a slip of sandy beach, and its modest, tiny gardens rising one above another, wherever the slope is gentle, and the cliff beyond rises high to shelter them from the winter winds.

But the place at which the coast scenery of the Lizard district arrives at its climax of grandeur is Kynance Cove. Here, such gigantic specimens are to be seen of the most beautiful of all varieties of rock—the 'serpentine'— as are unrivalled in Cornwall; perhaps, unrivalled anywhere. A walk of two miles along the westward cliffs from Lizard Town, brought us to the top of a precipice of three hundred feet. Looking forward from this, we saw the white sand of Kynance Cove stretching out in a half circle into the sea.

282   The Furry

In short, the town [Helston] has nothing to offer to attract the stranger, but a public festival—a sort of barbarous carnival—held there annually on the 8th of May. This festival is said to be of very ancient origin, and is called

'The Furry'—an old Cornish word, signifying a gathering; and, at Helston particularly, a gathering in celebration of the return of spring. The Furry begins early in the morning with singing, to an accompaniment of drums and kettles. All the people in the town immediately leave off work and scamper into the country; having reached which, they scamper back again, garlanded with leaves and flowers, and caper about hand-in-hand through the streets, and in and out of all the houses, without let or hindrance. Even the 'genteel' resident families allow themselves to be infected with the general madness, and wind up the day's capering consistently enough by a night's capering at a grand ball. A full account of these extraordinary absurdities may be found in Polwhele's *History of Cornwall*.

283   The King of Prussia

John Carter, the great 'King' of Prussia Cove, himself set the high example. On one occasion, during his absence from home, the excise officers from Penzance came round in their boats and took a cargo which had lately arrived from France to Penzance, where it was secured with other captured goods in the Custom House store. In due course, John Carter returned to the Cove and learned the news. What was he to do? He explained to his comrades that he had agreed to deliver that cargo to his customers by a certain day, and his reputation as an honest man was at stake. He must keep his word. That night a number of armed men broke open the Custom House store at Penzance, and the 'King of Prussia' took his own again. In the morning the officers found that the place had been broken open during the night. They examined the contents, and when they noted what particular things were gone they said to one another that "John Carter had been there, and they knew it, because he was an honest man, who would not take anything that did not belong to him."

284   Audacious Thieves

All these tales which we hear along the coast are the smugglers' version of affairs, and we are naturally led to deduct some discount before giving them credit as authentic history; but the official records of the Custom House are not open to the same criticism, and they bear overwhelming testimony to the daring and the success of the smugglers. One report from the Collector at Penzance to his superior in London, out of many, will give some idea of how things appeared to him. Writing on June 29, 1775, he refers to the 'great audacity of the smugglers on this coast', and goes on: "Last Saturday two Irish wherries full of men and guns (one about 130 tons, and the other less) came to anchor within the limits of this port, and within half a mile of the shore, and lay there three days, in open defiance discharging their contraband goods. We are totally destitute of any force to attack them by sea, and, as the whole coast is principally inhabited by a lot of smugglers under the denomination of fishermen, it is next to an impossibility for the officers of the revenue to intercept any of these goods after they are landed, unless by chance a trifling matter. The smugglers escort their goods in large parties when on shore. A few nights ago, while the above-mentioned wherries were on the coast, the officers, being on the look-out, saw a boat come off from one of them and come ashore near where the officers had secreted themselves, and the crew began to land the goods. The officers interfered, and attempted to make a seizure of said boat and goods; but a blunderbuss was immediately presented to one of their breasts, and the smugglers, with great imprecations, threatened their lives. The officers, not being in sufficient force, were glad to get off, and the boat reshipped the goods and went off again. We humbly beg leave to remark the smugglers were never on this coast more rife than at present, nor less goods taken in proportion to the quantity supposed to be smuggled."

285　S. Michel Mont

The Cumpace of the Roote of the Mont of S. Michael is not dim. Myle abowt. The Sowth Sowth-Est Part of the Mont is pasturable and breedeth Conys. The Resydue [is] hy and rokky. To the North North-West is a Peere for Bootes and Shyppes. In the North North-Est ys a Garden with certen Howses with Shoppes for Fyschermen. The way to the Chyrche enteryth at the North Syd fro half Heb to half Fludde to the Foote of the Mont, and so assendeth by Steppes and Greces Westward, and thens returneth Estward to the utterward of the Chyrch. Withyn the sayd Ward is a Cowrt stronly walled, wher yn on the South Syde is the Chapel of S. Michael, and yn the Est Syde a Chapel of our Lady. The Capytayne and Prestes Lodginges be yn the Sowth Syde and [to] the West of S. Mich. Chapel. Comes Moritaniæ & Cornubiæ made a Celle of Monkes in S. Michel Mont; this Celle was ons gyven to a College in Cambridge, [and it was] syns given to Syon. [There is] a fair Spring in the Mount. The Mont is enclosed with the Se fro dim. Flud to dim. Ebbe, otherwise Men may cum to the Mont a foote.

In the Bay betwyxt the Mont and Pensants be fownd neere the lowe Water Marke Rootes of Trees yn dyvers Places, as a Token of the Grownde wasted.

286　The Figure-Head of the Caledonia

We laid them in their lowly rest,
　The strangers of a distant shore;

We smoothed the green turf on their breast,
  'Mid baffled Ocean's angry roar;
And there, the relique of the storm,
We fixed fair Scotland's figured form.

She watches by her bold, her brave,
  Her shield towards the fatal sea:
Their cherished lady of the wave,
  Is guardian of their memory.
Stern is her look, but calm, for there
No gale can rend or billow bear.

Stand, silent image! stately stand,
  Where sighs shall breathe and tears be shed,
And many a heart of Cornish land,
  Will soften for the stranger dead.
They came in paths of storm—they found,
This quiet home in Christian ground.

287   Unfortunate Land

We returned into the turnpike road north of Kilkhampton by a long path across the moor-grounds, which gave me an opportunity of remarking the miserable and destructive husbandry of these parts. The extensive tracts of land, called the moor-grounds, are of two descriptions, the high and low lands; the former chiefly prepared for grain, the latter for hay and grass. Nothing can evince the viciousness of the agriculture here more than the low rent at which much of this ground is let, namely, from 7s. down to 3s. per acre. The land, it is true, in this predicament, is not of superior quality, being light and poor, a thin staple upon a basis of argillaceous slate; but a great quantity of it is such, as with fair treatment and good manuring might easily be increased to the value of from 13s. to 18s. per acre. This will be allowed, perhaps, when the system of agriculture is understood, by which the farmer is at present able to pay his rent for it. Intending to take a course of crops from his arable land, he first pares off its surface to the depth of two inches. The turfs thus cut are piled into heaps, and burned on the ground. A quantity of ashes is by these means procured, called in this country *Beat*. This is ploughed in, and wheat sown on the land. Unrecompensed for its efforts by any dung or manure, the ground is next year compelled to bear a scanty crop of oats; and on the third year, the pernicious routine is closed by another compulsory produce of clover. Compleatly exhausted by these unmerciful requisitions the farmer gives it up in despair for fifteen or sixteen years; at the conclusion of which it recovers another surface, which is again pared off, burned, and ploughed in, and the un-

fortunate land forced to the same rotation as before. The low-lands are
equally maltreated, or entirely neglected; so that where heavy burthens of
hay might be expected, if draining and irrigation were practised, little else
is now to be seen than rushes and moss, swamps and bog.

288   Kilkhampton Belfry

Amongst the remarkables, however, I must not omit to mention the mode in
which the bells (five in number) are rung. The management of this parish
musick is a matter of pride and consequence in every country village;
at Kilkhampton, some profit being attached to it also, the command of the
belfry is still more desirable. A self-constituted Directory of five laymen
had taken charge of these bells, and pocketed all the money allowed by the
parish for the peals rung on particular festivals. This obtrusion on the
rights of the church was deeply resented by its servants, the clerk and
sexton; but being unable to manage the whole peal themselves, they were
obliged to endeavour to compromise the matter, by offering to accept a
proportion of the money arising from the belfry. With this proposition,
however, the ringers very unreasonably refused to comply, under the
pretence that as Moses and his brother did not partake the labour, they
should not touch any part of the profit. What was to be done? The brothers
in office could indeed prevent the ringers from going into the belfry, but
then the parish must have lost its accustomed peals, and their own hands
were insufficient for all the bells. A woman's wit cut at length the Gordian
knot, and brought them off triumphant in the dispute. My guide, the sexton's
wife, provided with a hammer and nails, took her husband and the clerk into
the belfry, and making them strain the five ropes, and bring them all to one
point in the centre of the floor, she fixed them firmly there. Thus tightened,
the least pressure of the rope of each bell produced a pulsation of its clapper;
and introducing herself between the five, by the nimble motion of her arms,
knees, and head, dame Partlet chimed a peal with such skill and ease as
delighted and astonished the two gaping spectators, who found themselves,
by these means, able to undertake the business of the belfry without the
assistance of the insubordinate ringers. The ingenious contriver of the plan
was so good as to exhibit her abilities to me, and went through all the varieties
of double-bobs and triple-bobs, majors and minuses, with great exactness
and facility.

289   He Went on his Journey

Of all the women who stayed at home and wept in Cornwall during those
great days, there was none who had set more happiness on the cast of

battle than Grace Grenvile; nor was there any to whom the terrors of war came home more nearly. For having watched the muster of the tenantry at Stowe all armed, having seen them ride away, headed not only by Sir Beville, but by their son John—he who afterwards held out in Scilly for the King—and followed by the burly giant, Anthony Payne, whose towering height and vast strength were worth ten men in a melee, she had but a few months to wait before a great army of Parliament troops marched near Stowe, and took up their position on Stamford Hill, some eight miles west. She knew that the Cornish army, headed by Hopton and her husband, were marching from Launceston to attack this strong position; and on the next day from early morning till dusk she must have heard the sound of battle rolling along the coast, till at last when night fell her long agony was turned to joy by the news of a total victory won by the Cornish against amazing odds. It is said that Sir Beville himself rode home that night—the meeting of husband and wife must have been a scene comparable only to that drawn by the tenderest of Latin poets, who tells us how another husband came home suddenly from the wars, and found his wife Lucretia spinning among her maidens, and watched her weeping out of love and fear for him, and sprang forward to let her see that he was safe. Such must have been the meeting of Grace Grenvile with Sir Beville; followed quickly by what was probably their last parting, for it was in May that Stamford's horse was driven headlong out of Cornwall; and ere July was out Sir Beville lay stark and dead on the slope of Lansdown Hill, while his own troops, gasping, bleeding, and sore laboured, gained the top and held it.

"Maddam," wrote Sir John Trelawney, "hee is gone on his journey but a little before us; wee must march after when it shall please God." It was four years before Grace Grenvile heard and answered to the marching bugle—years of anxiety as well as sorrow; for the cause of the King began to fail in Cornwall, and there were evil days for those who would fain have held it up. But in June 1647 the signal came for release; the true wife marched after her husband, and we may well believe he lingered on his way until she caught him up.

290 Last Will and Testament

While the body is physically well and strong, and the mind within is un-hampered by its weakness, it enjoys fuller reasoning powers than an infirm body (which) when it is weighed down by divers weaknesses, cannot ponder carefully upon what it is bound to. Wherefore, the determination of a man's last will in which the exercise of the reasoning power of a tranquil mind is required, is more healthfully and prudently seen at that time. On which accounts, I, Ranulph de Albo Monasterio, knight, [lord of the manor of Stratton] being sound in mind and body on Saturday next after the Feast of the Ascension of the Lord, A.D. 1348 make and ordain my testament after this manner.

291 *Featherstone's Doom*

Twist thou and twine! in light and gloom
  A spell is on thine hand;
The wind shall be thy changeful loom,
  Thy web, the shifting sand.

Twine from this hour, in ceaseless toil,
  On Blackrock's sullen shore;
Till cordage of the sand shall coil
  Where crested surges roar.

'Tis for that hour, when, from the wave,
  Near voices wildly cried;
When thy stern hand no succour gave,
  The cable at thy side.

Twist thou and twine! in light and gloom
  The spell is on thine hand;
The wind shall be thy changeful loom,
  Thy web, the shifting sand.

Note

The Blackrock is a bold, dark, pillared mass of schist, which rises midway on the shore of Widemouth Bay, near Bude, and is held to be the lair of the troubled spirit of Featherstone the wrecker, imprisoned therein until he shall have accomplished his doom.

292 *Beeny Cliff (March 1870–March 1913)*

O the opal and the sapphire of that wandering western sea,
And the woman riding high above with bright hair flapping free—
The woman whom I loved so, and who loyally loved me.

The pale mews plained below us, and the waves seemed far away
In a nether sky, engrossed in saying their ceaseless babbling say,
As we laughed lightheartedly aloft on that clear-sunned March day.

A little cloud then cloaked us, and there flew an irised rain,
And the Atlantic dyed its levels with a dull mis-featured stain,
And then the sun burst out again, and purples prinked the main.

—Still in all its chasmal beauty bulks old Beeny to the sky,
And shall she and I not go there once again now March is nigh,
And the sweet things said in that March say anew there by and by?

What if still in chasmal beauty looms that wild weird western shore?
The woman now is—elsewhere—whom the ambling pony bore,
And nor knows nor cares for Beeny, and will laugh there nevermore.

293 Tintagel

From Bossinny to Tintagel Castle on the Shore is a Mile. This Castelle hath bene a marvelus strong and notable forteres, and almost *situ loci inexpugnabile*, especially for the Dungeon that is on a great and high terrible cragge environid with the Se, but having a Draw Bridge from the Residew of the Castelle onto it. The Residew of the Buildinges of the Castel be sore wether beten and yn Ruine, but it hath bene a large thinge. The Castel had be likehod iii. Wardes, wherof ii. be woren away with gulfyng yn of the Se, yn so much that yt hathe made ther almost an Isle, and no way ys to enter ynto hyt now but by long Elme Trees layde for a Bryge. So that now withowte the Isle renneth alonly a Gate Howse, a Welle, and a fals Braye dyged and walled. In the Isle remayne old Walles, and yn the Est Part of the same, the Ground beyng lower, remayneth a Walle embateled, and Men alyve saw theryn a Postern Dore of Yren. Ther is yn the Isle a prety Chapel of S. Ulette alias Uliane, with a Tumbe on the left side. There ys also yn the Isle a Welle, and ny by the same ys a Place hewen owt of the Stony Grownd to the Length and Brede of a Man. Also ther remayneth yn the Isle a Grownd quadrant walled as yt were a Garden Plot; and by this Walle appere the Ruines of a Vault. The Grownd of this Isle now nuryshyth Shepe and Conys.

294 The Huers and the Silver Shoals

With the discovery of the first shoal, the active duties of the 'look-out' on the cliffs begin. Each fishing-village places one or more of these men on the watch all round the coast. They are called 'huers', a word said to be derived from the old French verb, *huer*, to call out, to give an alarm. On the vigilance and skill of the 'huer' much depends. He is, therefore, not only paid his guinea a week while he is on the watch, but receives, besides, a perquisite in the shape of a percentage on the produce of all the fish taken under his auspices. He is placed at his post, where he can command an uninterrupted view of the sea, some days before the pilchards are expected to appear; and, at the same time, boats, nets, and men are all ready for action at a moment's notice.

The principal boat used is at least fifteen tons in burden, and carries a large net called the 'seine', which measures a hundred and ninety fathoms in length, and costs a hundred and seventy pounds—sometimes more. It is simply one long strip, from eleven to thirteen fathoms in breadth, composed of very small meshes, and furnished, all along its length, with lead at one side and corks at the other. The men who cast this net are called the 'shooters', and receive eleven shillings and sixpence a week, and a perquisite of one basket of fish each out of every haul.

As soon as the 'huer' discerns the first appearance of a shoal, he waves his bush. The signal is conveyed to the beach immediately by men and boys watching near him. The 'seine' boat (accompanied by another small boat, to assist in casting the net) is rowed out where he can see it. Then there is a pause, a hush of great expectation on all sides. Meanwhile, the devoted pilchards press on—a compact mass of thousands on thousands of fish, swimming to meet their doom. All eyes are fixed on the 'huer', he stands, watchful and still, until the shoal is thoroughly embayed in water which he knows to be within the depth of the 'seine' net. Then, as the fish begin to pause in their progress, and gradually crowd closer and closer together, he gives the signal; the boats come up, and the 'seine' net is cast, or, in the technical phrase 'shot', overboard.

The grand object is now to enclose the entire shoal. The leads sink one end of the net perpendicularly to the ground; the corks buoy up the other to the surface of the water. When it has been taken all round the fish, the two extremities are made fast, and the shoal is then imprisoned within an oblong barrier of network surrounding it on all sides. The great art is to let as few of the pilchards escape as possible, while this process is being completed. Whenever the 'huer' observes from above that they are startled, and are separating at any particular point, to that point he waves his bush, thither the boats are steered, and there the net is 'shot' at once. In whatever direction the fish attempt to get out to sea again, they are thus immediately met and thwarted with extraordinary readiness and skill. This labour completed, the silence of intense expectation that has hitherto prevailed among the spectators on the cliff, is broken. There is a great shout of joy on all sides—the shoal is secured!

295 Pilchard Trade

Having now inspected the progress of the pilchard fishery, from the catching

14

to the curing, we have seen all that we can personally observe of its different processes, at one opportunity. What more remains to be done, will not be completed until after an interval of several weeks. We must be content to hear about this from information given to us by others. Yonder, sitting against the outside wall of the salting-house, is an intelligent old man, too infirm now to do more than take care of the baby that he holds in his arms, while the baby's mother is earning her threepence an hour inside. To this ancient we will address all our inquiries; and he is well qualified to answer us, for the poor old fellow has worked away all the pith and marrow of his life in the pilchard fishery.

The fish—as we learn from our old friend, who is mightily pleased to be asked for information—will remain in salt, or, as the technical expression is, 'in bulk', for five or six weeks. During this period, a quantity of oil, salt, and water drips from them into wells cut in the centre of the stone floor on which they are placed. After the oil has been collected and clarified, it will sell for enough to pay off the whole expense of the wages, food, and drink given to the 'seiners'—perhaps defraying other incidental charges besides. The salt and water left behind, and offal of all sorts found with it, furnish a valuable manure. Nothing in the pilchard itself, or in connection with the pilchard, runs to waste—the precious little fish is a treasure in every part of him.

After the pilchards have been taken out of 'bulk', they are washed clean in salt water, and packed in hogheads, which are then sent for exportation to some large sea-port—Penzance for instance—in coast traders. The fish reserved for use in Cornwall are generally cured by those who purchase them. The export trade is confined to the shores of the Mediterranean—Italy and Spain providing the two great foreign markets for pilchards. The home consumption, as regards Great Britain, is nothing, or next to nothing. Some variation takes place in the prices realized by the foreign trade—their average, wholesale, is stated to be about fifty shillings per hogshead.

As an investment for money, on a small scale, the pilchard fishery offers the first great advantage of security. The only outlay necessary is that for providing boats and nets, and for building salting-houses—an outlay which, it is calculated, may be covered by a thousand pounds. The profits resulting from the speculation are immediate and large. Transactions are managed on the ready money principle, and the markets of Italy and Spain (where pilchards are considered a great delicacy) are always open to any supply. The fluctuation between a good season's fishing and a bad season's fishing is rarely, if ever, seriously great. Accidents happen but seldom; the casualty most dreaded, being the enclosure of a large fish along with a shoal of pilchards. A ling, for instance, if unfortunately imprisoned in the seine, often bursts through its thin meshes, after luxuriously gorging himself with prey, and is of course at once followed out of the breach by all the pilchards. Then, not only is the shoal lost, but the net is seriously damaged, and must be tediously and expensively repaired. Such an accident as this, however, very seldom happens; and when it does, the loss occasioned falls on those best able to bear it, the merchant speculators. The work and wages of the fishermen go on as usual.

Some idea of the almost incalculable multitude of pilchards caught on the shores of Cornwall, may be formed from the following data. At the small fishing cove of Trereen, 600 hogsheads were taken in a little more than one week, during August, 1850. Allowing 2,400 fish only to each hogshead—3,000 would be the highest calculation—we have a result of 1,440,000 pilchards, caught by the inhabitants of one little village alone, on the Cornish coast, at the commencement of the season's fishing.

At considerable seaport towns, where there is an unusually large supply of men, boats, and nets, such figures as those quoted above, are far below the mark. At St. Ives, for example, 1,000 hogsheads were taken in the first three seine nets cast into the water. The number of hogsheads exported annually, averages 22,000. In 1850, 27,000 were secured for the foreign markets. Incredible as these numbers may appear to some readers, they may nevertheless be relied on; for they are derived from trustworthy sources—partly from local returns furnished to me; partly from the very men who filled the baskets from the boat-side, and who afterwards verified their calculations by frequent visits to the salting-houses.

Such is the pilchard fishery of Cornwall—a small unit, indeed, in the vast aggregate of England's internal sources of wealth: but yet neither unimportant nor uninteresting, if it be regarded as giving active employment to a hardy and honest race who would starve without it; as impartially extending the advantages of commerce to one of the remotest corners of our island; and, more than all, as displaying a wise and beautiful provision of Nature, by which the rich tribute of the great deep is most generously lavished on the land most in need of a compensation for its own sterility.

296   John Opie and Harmony Cot

Some years ago when I was on the north coast of Cornwall at Perranporth, recovering from illness, I made a pilgrimage to Harmony Cot where John Opie was born. He was, I think, the one Cornish painter of undisputed genius, and one of the more distinguished of English painters. His career was a romance of successful achievement. Starting from nothing, born in poverty, with no one to teach him, with nothing but his own gifts and that "energy of mind which men call genius", as Bernard Shaw puts it, with great determination and willpower and hard work, Opie made himself a great artist, one of the best painters of his day, and was buried in state in St. Paul's Cathedral, beside that other great West Country painter, Sir Joshua Reynolds.

Getting to Harmony Cot was quite an adventure, for I was not yet steady on my legs, and it was a two-mile walk up one of those valleys that run down to the sea and meet at Perranporth. This one is called Perran

Combe; and in the quiet of the summer evening, taking my time, I followed the lane up through it: an entrancing valley, very Cornish in character, with traces of tin-streaming and little old tin-works all overgrown with greenery now; with close groups of Cornish elm, very decorative and plume-like, and ash and young sycamore growing, not much honeysuckle left—there had been a lot—but plenty of earth-nut, cow-parsley, and innumerable wild flowers I didn't know the names of. Then at the end of the valley, uphill towards St. Agnes, there is the hamlet of Trevellas, with Harmony Cot a little way up on the right.

Opie was born in the middle one of a row of three whitewashed and thatched cottages, now all one house, with a fine screen of tall elms and a well-kept grass border before it. I stopped at the garden gate and leaned over: there was, very appropriately, a laurel bush growing over it, I noticed. Within, it was a typical Cornish cottage garden with fine ferns growing in profusion, honeysuckle, fuchsia, and rambler-roses growing over the doors. I felt as if I were the first person to have tracked down the house, all was so perfect and what one might have hoped—though there must have been many people who had been here before.

Presently an old gentleman came out and talked to me about the Opies. He was the last representative of the family, himself a bachelor, descended, I think, from Opie's brother; for the painter had no children. He told me a number of things about the family; that Opie's father came down from the parish of Egloshayle. "They were carpenters, and mine-carpenters at that," he said. "They got well-to-do, and then afterwards they got poor"—all this he told me with extraordinary melancholy, his voice going downhill as the Cornish voice does when referring to poverty.

I could see the whole picture in his words: the great growth of mining activity in this district nearly two hundred years ago brought them down here, provided work for a time, and when it slackened off there was nothing for them to do. Hence the poverty which surrounded Opie's childhood and hardened his fibre, his whole outlook. There was a certain pessimism which underlay his temperament; in that he was not unrepresentative of the Cornish, though his mental energy burned with a fierce ardour from the first.

He was for ever drawing in crayons and chalks when a boy, in face of the active discouragement of his father, who wanted to make him a good carpenter. "The boy was good for nothin'," he said. "He was always gazin' upon cats, and starin' volks in the faace." Nothing, of course, could have been more suitable training for the lad's vocation; and it is worth noting that his great strength as a painter later on was his realism, his absolute fidelity to what he was in nature, when the more fashionable painters of the time were engaged in dressing up their subjects and making them more romantic and poetical. Opie in this matter was, I like to think, more akin to the French school of painters.

His father was always putting difficulties and obstacles in his way, to discourage him from his passion for drawing; and many are the stories that are told of him as a lad: how as a boy of ten he began with the boast, "I think I can draa a buttervlee as well as Mark Oates"—and did. And how, when a little later he was paid 5s. for copying a picture at Mithian farm, he ran about the house shouting, "I'm set up for life! I'm set up for life!" His father said, "That boy'll come to hangin', sure as a gun."

But Opie had one great stroke of luck. The lad was noticed by Dr. Wolcot, himself a man of parts—he became celebrated afterwards as 'Peter Pindar', a satirist and writer of poetical verse. Wolcot took Opie to Truro to live with him for some time, taught him all he could about painting, sent him round the county to execute commissions for portraits and to paint subjects from the life, and at length, when he thought the raw, uncouth young man was ready, took him to London and launched him on the precarious career of a portrait painter.

297　Tin-Blowers

Half a mile from thence they blow their tin, which I went to see. They take the ore and pound it in a stamping mill which resembles the paper mills, and when it is as fine as the finest sand—some of which I saw and took—this they fling into a furnace and with it coal to make the fire. So it burns together and makes a violent heat and fierce flame; the metal, by the fire being separated from the coal and its own dross, being very heavy falls down to a trench made to receive it at the furnace hole below. This liquid metal I saw them shovel up with an iron shovel, and so pour it into moulds, in which it cools, and so they take it thence in sort of wedges, or pigs I think they call them. It is a fine metal in its first melting—looks like silver; I had a piece poured out and made cold for to take with me. The ore as it is just dug looks like the thunderstones, a greenish hue full of pendust—this seems to contain its full description—the shining part is white.

I went a mile farther on the hills, and so came where they were digging in the tin mines. There were at least 20 mines all in sight, which employ a great many people at work almost night and day, but constantly all and every day, including the Lord's Day, which they are forced to prevent their mines being overflowed with water. More than 1,000 men are taken up about them; few mines but had then almost 20 men and boys attending it, either down in the mines digging and carrying the ore to the little bucket which conveys it up, or else others are draining the water and looking to the engines that are draining it, and those above are attending the drawing up the ore in a sort of windlass as it is to a well. Two men keep turning, bringing up one and letting down another. They are much like the leather buckets they use in London to put out fire, which hang up in churches and great men's halls. They have a great labour and great expense to drain the mines of the water with mills that horses turn, and now they have the mills or water engines that are turned by the water which is conveyed on frames of timber and trunks to hold the water, which falls down on the wheels as an overshot mill, and these are the sort that turns the water into the several towns I have seen about, London, Darby, and Exeter, and many places more. They do five times more good than the mills they use to turn with horses, but then they are much more chargeable. Those mines do require a great deal of timber to support them and to make all those engines and mills, which makes fuel very scarce here. They burn mostly turves, which is an unpleasant smell; it makes one smell as if smoked like bacon. This ore, as said, is made fine powder in a stamping mill which is like the paper mills, only these are pounded dry and no water let into them as it is to the rags, to work them into a paste. The mills are all turned with a little stream or channel of water you may step over; indeed they have no other mills but such in all the country. I saw not a windmill all over Cornwall or Devonshire, though they have wind and hills enough, and it may be it is too bleak for them. In the tin mines there is stone dug out and a sort of spar something like what I have seen in the lead mines at Darbyshire, but it seemed more solid and hard; it shines and looks like mother of pearl. They also dig out stones as clear as crystal, which are called Cornish diamonds. I saw one as big as my two fists, very clear and like some pieces of crystal my father brought from the Alps in Italy. I got one of those pieces of their Cornish diamonds as long as half my finger, which had three or four flat sides with edges; the top was sharp and so hard as it would cut a letter on glass.

298   *Botallack Visited*

Our friend the miner saw my difficulty, and extricated me from it at once, with a promptitude and skill which deserve record. Descending halfway by the beams, he clutched with one hand that hinder part of my too voluminous nether garments, which presented the broadest superficies of canvas to his grasp (I hope the delicate reader appreciates my ingenious indirectness of expression, when I touch on the unmentionable subject of trousers!). Grappling me thus, and supporting himself by his freehand, he lifted me up as easily as if I had been a small parcel; then carried me horizontally along the loose boards, like a refractory little boy borne off by the usher to the master's birch; or—considering the candle burning on my hat, and the necessity of elevating my position by as lofty a comparison as I can make—like a flying Mercury with a star on his head; and finally deposited me safely upon my legs again, on the firm rock pathway beyond. "You are but a light and a little man, my son," says this excellent fellow, snuffing my candle for me before we go on; "only let me lift you about as I like, and you shan't come to any harm while I am with you!"

Speaking thus, the miner leads us forward again. After we have walked a little farther in a crouching position, he calls a halt, makes a seat for us by sticking a piece of old board between the rocky walls of the gallery, and then proceeds to explain the exact subterranean position which we actually occupy.

We are now four hundred yards out, under the bottom of the sea; and twenty fathoms or a hundred and twenty feet below the sea level. Coast-trade vessels are sailing over our heads. Two hundred and forty feet beneath us men are at work, and there are galleries deeper yet, even below that! The extraordinary position down the face of the cliff, of the engines and other works on the surface, at Botallack, is now explained. The mine is not excavated like other mines under the land, but under the sea!

Having communicated these particulars, the miner next tells us to keep strict silence and listen. We obey him, sitting speechless and motionless. If the reader could only have beheld us now, dressed in our copper-coloured garments, huddled close together in a mere cleft of subterranean rock, with flame burning on our heads and darkness enveloping our limbs—he must certainly have imagined, without any violent stretch of fancy, that he was looking down upon a conclave of gnomes.

After listening for a few moments, a distant, unearthly noise becomes faintly audible—a long, low, mysterious moaning, which never changes, which is felt on the ear as well as heard by it—a sound that might proceed from some incalculable distance, from some far invisible height—a sound so unlike anything that is heard on the upper ground, in the free air of heaven; so sublimely mournful and still; so ghostly and impressive when listened to in the subterranean recesses of the earth, that we continue instinctively to hold our peace, as if enchanted by it, and think not of communicating to each other the awe and astonishment which it has inspired in us from the very first.

At last, the miner speaks again, and tells us that what we hear is the sound of the surf, lashing the rocks a hundred and twenty feet above us, and of the waves that are breaking on the beach beyond. The tide is now at the flow, and the sea is in no extraordinary state of agitation: so the sound is low and distant just at this period. But, when storms are at their height, when the ocean hurls mountain after mountain of water on the cliffs, then the noise is terrific; the roaring heard down here in the mine is so inexpressibly fierce and awful, that the boldest men at work are afraid to continue their labour. All ascend to the surface, to breathe the upper air and stand on the firm earth: dreading, though no such catastrophe has ever happened yet, that the sea will break in on them if they remain in the caverns below.

299 *We Don't Complain*

Upon the whole, setting his successful and his disastrous speculations fairly against each other, the Cornish miner's average gains, year by year, may be fairly estimated at about ten shillings a week. "It's hard work we have to do, sir," said my informant, summing up, when we parted, the proportions of good and evil in the social positions of his brethren and himself—"harder work than people think, down in the heat and darkness underground. We may get a good deal at one time, but we get little enough at another; sometimes mines are shut up, and then we are thrown out altogether—but, good work or bad work, or no work at all, what with our bits of ground for potatoes and greens, and what with cheap living, somehow we and our families make it do. We contrive to keep our good cloth coat for Sundays, and go to chapel in the morning—for we're most of us Wesleyans —and then to church in the afternoon; so as to give 'em both their turn like! We never go near the mine on Sundays, except to look after the steam-pump: our rest, and our walk in the evening once a week, is a good deal to us. That's how we live, sir; whatever happens, we manage to work through, and don't complain!"

300 Cornish Miners

It was not the least interesting part of my visit to the cottage where he [a miner's son] lay ill, to observe the anxious affection displayed towards him by both his parents. His mother left her work in the kitchen to hold him in her arms, while the old dressings were being taken off and the new ones applied—sighing bitterly, poor creature, every time he winced or cried out under the pain of the operation. The father put several questions to the doctor, which were always perfectly to the point; and did the honours of his little abode to his stranger visitor, with a natural politeness and a simple cordiality of manner which showed that he really meant the welcome that he spoke. Nor was he any exception to the rest of his brother workmen with whom I met. As a body of men, they are industrious and intelligent; sober and orderly; neither soured by hard work, nor easily depressed by harder privations. No description of personal experiences in the Cornish mines can be fairly concluded, without a collateral testimony to the merits of the Cornish miners—a testimony which I am happy to accord here; and to which my readers would cheerfully add their voices, if they ever felt inclined to test its impartiality by their own experience.

301 Education and Notions

My opportunities of correctly estimating the state of education among the people, were not sufficiently numerous to justify me in offering to the reader more than a mere opinion on the subject. Such few observations as I was able to make, inclined me to think that, in education, the mass of the population was certainly below the average in England, with one exception —that of the classes employed in the mines. All of these men with whom I held any communication, would not have been considered badly informed persons in a higher condition of life. They possessed much more than a common mechanical knowledge of their own calling, and even showed a very fair share of information on the subject of the history and antiquities of their native county. As usual, the agricultural inhabitants appeared to rank lowest in the scale of education and general intelligence. Among this class, and among the fishermen, the strong superstitious feelings of the ancient days of Cornwall still survive, and promise long to remain, handed down from father to son as heirlooms of tradition, gathered together in a remote period, and venerable in virtue of their antiquity. The notion, for instance, that no wound will fester as long as the instrument by which it was inflicted is kept bright and clean, still prevails extensively among them. But a short time since, a boy in Cornwall was placed under the care of a medical man (who related the anecdote to me) for a wound in the back from a pitchfork; his relatives—cottagers of respectability—firmly believe that his cure was accelerated by the pains they took to keep the prongs of the pitchfork in a state of the highest polish, night and day, throughout the whole period of his illness, and down to the last hour of his complete restoration to health.

302 Rock and Roll

In the year 1824, a certain lieutenant in the Royal Navy, then in command of a cutter stationed off the southern coast of Cornwall, was told of an ancient Cornish prophecy, that no human power should ever succeed in overturning the Loggan Stone. No sooner was the prediction communicated to him, than he conceived a mischievous ambition to falsify practically an assertion which the commonest common sense might have informed him had sprung from nothing but popular error and popular superstition. Accompanied by a body of picked men from his crew, he ascended to the Loggan Stone, ordered several levers to be placed under it at one point, gave the word to 'heave'—and the next moment had the miserable satisfaction of seeing one of the most remarkable natural curiosities in the world utterly destroyed, for aught he could foresee to the contrary, under his own directions!

But fortune befriended the Loggan Stone. One edge of it, as it rolled over, became fixed by a lucky chance in a crevice in the rocks immediately below the granite slab from which it had been started. Had this not happened, it must have fallen over a sheer precipice, and been lost in the sea. By another accident, equally fortunate, two labouring men at work in the neighbourhood were led by curiosity secretly to follow the lieutenant and his myrmidons up to the Stone. Having witnessed, from a secure hiding-place, all that occurred, the two workmen, with great propriety, immediately hurried off to inform the lord of the manor of the wanton act of destruction which they had seen perpetrated.

The news was soon communicated throughout the district, and thence, throughout all Cornwall. The indignation of the whole county was aroused. Antiquaries, who believed the Loggan Stone to have been balanced by the Druids; philosophers who held that it was produced by an eccentricity of natural formation; ignorant people, who cared nothing about Druids, or natural formations, but who liked to climb up and rock the stone whenever they passed near it; tribes of guides who lived by showing it; innkeepers in the neighbourhood, to whom it had brought customers by hundreds; tourists of every degree who were on their way to see it—all joined in one general clamour of execration against the overthrower of the rock. A full report of the affair was forwarded to the Admiralty; and the Admiralty, for once, acted vigorously for the public advantage, and mercifully spared the public purse.

The lieutenant was officially informed that his commission was in danger, unless he set up the Loggan Stone again in its proper place. The materials for compassing this achievement were offered to him gratis, from the dockyards; but he was left to his own resources to defray the expense of employing workmen to help him. Being by this time awakened to a proper sense of the mischief he had done, and to a tolerably strong conviction of the disagreeable position in which he was placed with the Admiralty, he addressed himself vigorously to the task of repairing his fault. Strong beams were planted about the Loggan Stone, chains were passed round it, pulleys were rigged, and capstans were manned. After a week's hard work and brave perseverance on the part of everyone employed in the labour, the rock was pulled back into its former position, but not into its former perfection of balance: it has never moved since as freely as it moved before.

It is only fair to the lieutenant to add to this narrative of his mischievous frolic the fact, that he defrayed, though a poor man, all the heavy expenses of replacing the rock. Just before his death, he paid the last remaining debt, and paid it with interest.

303   *A Frightful Ghost*

A small farmer living in one of the most western districts of the county, died some years back of what was supposed at the time to be 'English Cholera'. A few weeks after his decease, his wife married again. This circumstance excited some attention in the neighbourhood. It was remembered that the woman had lived on very bad terms with her late husband, that she had on many occasions exhibited strong symptoms of possessing a very vindictive temper, and that during the farmer's life-time she had openly manifested rather more than a Platonic preference for the man whom she subsequently married. Suspicion was generally excited: people began to doubt whether the first husband had died fairly. At length the proper order was applied for, and his body was disinterred. On examination, enough arsenic to have poisoned three men was found in his stomach. The wife was accused of murdering him, was tried, convicted on the clearest evidence, and hanged. Very shortly after she had suffered capital punishment, horrible stories of a ghost were widely circulated. Certain people declared that they had seen a ghastly resemblance of the murderess, robed in her winding-sheet, with the black mark of the rope round her swollen neck, standing on stormy nights upon her husband's grave, and digging there with a spade in hideous imitation of the actions of the men who had disinterred the corpse for medical examination.

304 Knights and Ladies

The Land's End terminates in a point of great rocks which runs a good way into the sea. I clambered over them as far as safety permitted me. There are abundance of rocks, and shoals of stones stand up in the sea a mile off, some here and there, some quite to the shore, which they name by several names of Knights and Ladies rolled up in mantles from some old tradition or fiction.

The poets advance description of the amours of some great persons; but these many rocks and stones, which look like the Needles in the Isle of Wight, make it hazardous for ships to double the point, especially in stormy weather. Here at the Land's End they are but a little way off France; two days' sail at farthest convey them to Hauve de Grace in France, but the peace being but newly entered into with the French, I was not willing to venture, at least by myself, into a foreign kingdom, and being then at the end of the land, my horse's legs could not carry me through the deep, and so returned again to Pensands [Penzance] ten miles more, and so came in view of both the seas and saw the Lizard Point and Pensands and the Mount in Cornwall, which looked very fine in the broad day, the sun shining on the rock in the sea.

305 Have You Been to the Land's End?

Something like what Jerusalem was to the pilgrim in the Holy Land, the Land's End is—comparing great things with small—to the tourist in Cornwall. It is the *Ultima Thule* where his progress stops—the shrine towards which his face has been set, from the first day when he started on his travels—the main vent, through which all the pent-up enthusiasm accumulated along the line of route is to burst its way out, in one long flow of admiration and delight.

The Land's End! There is something in the very words that stirs us all. It was the name that struck us most, and was best remembered by us, as children, when we learnt our geography. It fills the minds of imaginative people with visions of barrenness and solitude, with dreams of some lonely promontory, far away by itself out in the sea—the sort of place where the last man in England would be most likely to be found waiting for death, at the end of the world! It suggests even to the most prosaically constituted people, ideas of tremendous storms, of flakes of foam flying over the land before the wind, of billows in convulsion, of rocks shaken to their centre, of caves where smugglers lurk in ambush, of wrecks and hurricanes, desolation, danger, and death. It awakens curiosity in the most careless—once hear of it, and you long to see it—tell your friends that you have travelled in Cornwall, and ten thousand chances to one, the first question they ask is:—"Have you been to the Land's End?"

306   Pedn an Laaz

From Lanant [Lelant] by the North Se to S. Just, alias Justini, beyng the very West Poynt of al Cornewayle, and wher ys no thing but a Paroch Chyrch of divers sparkeled Howses, the North Part ys Montaynes and Baren Growne, but plenteful of Tynne. The very West Poynt, as yt ys cawled now yn Cornysch, ys Penwolase, id est, *infinum caput*, Pedn an Laaz, i.e. Land's End.

Index of Authors

SOURCES AND DATES OF THE EXTRACTS

The references are to the numbers of the extracts
* indicates that the extract is here published in a book for the first time